ONE AT A TIME ALL AT ONCE

ONE AT A TIME ALL AT ONCE: The Creative Teacher's Guide To Individualized Instruction Without Anarchy.

Jack E. Blackburn, Auburn University
W. Conrad Powell, University of South Carolina

Goodyear Publishing Company, Inc.
Santa Monica, California

Library of Congress Cataloging in Publication Data
Blackburn, Jack E.
One at a time all at once.
(Goodyear education series)
Bibliography: p.
1. Individualized instruction. 2. Classroom
management. 3. Teaching—Aids and devices.
I. Powell, William Conrad, joint author.
II. Title.
LB1031.B6   371.39'4   75-21174
ISBN 0-87620-637-2

Library of Congress Catalog Card Number: 75-21174
ISBN: 0-87620-637-2
Y-6372-0
Current Printing (last number):

10   9   8   7   6   5   4   3

Interior and cover design: John Isely
Project editor: Sherri Butterfield
Illustration: Joyce Kitchell
Art production and graphics: Louie Neiheisel
                              Kitty Anderson

Printed in the United States of America

Contents

Worksheets

Indicated by a broken cutting line, these pages are intended to be reproduced by the teacher as examples or actual worksheets for students.

Preface

Students in our society typically spend 12 to 13 years, 2,160 days, or 15,120 hours in precollege schooling. During this time, their lives are strongly influenced by the choices they make, and by the choices teachers and other educational personnel make for them, regarding curriculum and instruction.

A part of the American educational dream is to provide, through curriculum and instructional practices, schooling opportunities that allow the individual student to move ever closer to the realization of his or her full potential. This value is reaffirmed in contemporary society as more recognition is accorded to cultural diversity, individual life-styles, and humanistic schooling.

Over the years curriculum and instruction decision making has come to reflect this desire to facilitate individual growth and to enhance human potential. Yet, with all the progress educators have made toward individualization, much remains to be done to make schooling as worthwhile as educators—and society in general—would wish it to be.

One of the perennial concerns of educators about individualization is that few guidelines for integrating theory and practice are available. This book is our attempt to accept the challenge of providing a theoretical framework for individualizing and for illustrating the theory in practical and concrete terms. It focuses on alternative procedures for individualizing, and provides a wide variety of field-tested examples of each procedure described. The examples represent a cross section of subjects and grade levels, and most can be adapted to other subjects and/or levels.

The theory presented in this book is our own. The practices and ideas related to it were developed with our students. The ideas have been field tested and critiqued by university colleagues and by classroom teachers at all levels, from kindergarten through the twelfth grade.

A book with so many examples and resources, and with so much field testing over a period of years, has received more assistance from more people than could possibly be personally acknowledged. Appreciation goes to our graduate students who examined, implemented, and critiqued many of the ideas found here. Special thanks go to Martha Bryan, David Howell, Debbie Powers, Charles Rives, and Sally Wakefield, who helped compile the resources for the Yellow Pages, and to Ruth McLellan and Jane Fruitt for most of the preliminary artwork; in addition, Jane contributed the designs for most of the learning center examples. Members of the University of South Carolina Model School Project staff and the following University of North Carolina students helped develop many of the procedures and ideas found in the text: Betty Brewer, Ron Carroll, Dicky Corbett, Elizabeth Harper, Ray Hite, Hugh McManus, Janet McNairy, Neill Powers, Becky Shoulders, and Ira Trollinger. Brenda Webster typed and retyped the manuscript, and her patience was infinite.

Jack E. Blackburn
Auburn University

W. Conrad Powell
University of South Carolina

Individualizing–
A
Point Of View

Schools are human inventions which exist to foster human growth and development. Creating alternative educational environments in schools and classrooms to accommodate similarities and differences and to promote human growth and development is the basic mission of schools. Developing and using alternative plans and designs to individualize curriculum and instruction are consistent with this educational mission.

This book is about creating alternative individualized curriculum and instruction environments and practices in schools and classrooms. Because the theme of this book is individualizing curriculum and instruction through alternative means, we feel that it is our responsibility to share with you the basic beliefs and assumptions upon which our ideas are based:

- People learn at different rates, and in different ways.
- Individuals are cherished for their uniqueness, as well as for their similarities to other individual persons.
- Schools are human inventions created to nurture individual differences and similarities and to assist students in their affective, cognitive, and psychomotor growth.
- Curriculum and instruction are the school environment's primary means of providing opportunities for student growth.
- Educators, students, and parents are more than ever willing to individualize curriculum and instruction in the school setting; one means for making individualizing a reality is for teachers to acquire specific and alternative techniques which can be used in a typical classroom.
- A student's school experiences become more individualized and meaningful when the school environment offers a wide variety of curriculum and instruction alternatives.
- Alternatives in curriculum and instruction must be related to the students being served and to the competencies of teachers and other education personnel.
- Individualized curriculum and instruction are dynamic, changing concepts and processes which reflect: (a) the nature of students, (b) the social realities of the times, (c) the nature of knowledge and subject matter, and (d) the values and goals of schools and students.
- Teachers and students should be involved in planning, implementing, and evaluating curriculum and instruction alternatives.
- Individualized curriculum and instruction based upon viable alternatives means that there is no single, best way to individualize.
- Success experiences foster other success experiences; curriculum and instruction should be designed and implemented in such a way that each student has a good chance of being successful each day.

DEFINING INDIVIDUALIZED CURRICULUM AND INSTRUCTION

The practice of individualization cannot be based upon beliefs alone. Characteristics, definitions, and a conceptual framework, or some kind of reasoned approach, are needed to provide direction for our intentions.

One way of beginning to define and conceptualize individualization is to analyze some of the distinctions between programs that are individualized and those that are not.

Probably no school is completely individualized; similarly every school has some characteristics of individualization. Thus the representative generalizations in Table I are meant to serve as definitions and guides for moving toward individualization, not as referents for specific schools. (In reality, all schools probably fall somewhere between the two positions presented.) The lists might provide assistance in determining the type of school or classroom desired.

Curriculum and Instruction Definitions

Individualized curriculum and instruction in this book has broad meaning. It encompasses what is variously called personalized instruction, independent study, Individually Guided Education, diagnostic-prescriptive teaching and learning, self-paced instruction and / or learning, and other such terms.

The curriculum and instruction ideas and practices presented in this book are based upon the following definitions:

Curriculum
consists of all the planned educational activities within the school environment. It is primarily concerned with how the environment is organized, what activities and content are offered to students, and what learning resources are available.

Instruction
occurs in the curriculum environment. It encompasses the interactions and transactions that occur between students and teachers, as well as between students and peers, students and community members, and students and other learning resources.

Curriculum Plan
is a design for a specific area of learning or educational activity within the curriculum environment. The plan lists what students are to learn, proposed ways of learning, and means of assessing learning. The curriculum plan is developed prior to instruction and provides direction and suggested resources for instructional activities. The various curriculum plans within a school, taken together, help to make up the school curriculum.

NONINDIVIDUALIZED SCHOOLS AND CLASSROOMS	INDIVIDUALIZED SCHOOLS AND CLASSROOMS
Require all students to be exposed to the same subject areas	Provide choice and decision making by students in courses and other educational experiences in schools
Assume that all students should be presented materials for learning at the same time	Arrange for students to have encounters with learning materials at times appropriate for them
Have set times when students are to complete learning tasks	Enable students, with teacher assistance, to pace their own learning
Stress a single learning activity at a given time for all students	Offer learning activity alternatives related to differences among students
Require all students to achieve the same objectives	Select and develop objectives for and with students based upon assessment and diagnostic data about students
Schedule student's total time during the school day	Provide more flexibility in scheduling so that students have some choice in the way their time is spent
Have rigid time schedules during the day for organizing instruction, with everyone spending the same amount of time in a given course	Have alternative time arrangements in the forms of block-of-time and modular scheduling
Use singular modes of instruction	Capitalize upon several instructional modes, including learning packages, learning centers, contracts, independent study, group interaction, media
Give all (most) instruction in large group settings	Base group size and individual study and exploration upon instructional purposes to be served
Evaluate student achievement using a single method, with little or no student involvement in evaluation	Utilize several sources for evaluative purposes and involve students in evaluation according to their abilities to participate
Promote little or no teacher involvement in curriculum and instruction decision making	Maximize teacher involvement in and responsibility for curriculum and instruction decision making
Have little student participation in curriculum and instruction matters	Increasingly involve students in curriculum and instruction planning according to their abilities to participate
View the school setting as the learning center	Perceive the community as a learning center with the school being only one component of the learning environment
Use a limited amount of learning resources and media	Collect and use extensive types of learning resources within the school and community, including commercial and teacher- and student-made materials
Base instruction on what is needed by the middle, average part of any given class	Base instruction on specific, individual assessment of achievement, interest, ability in relation to the curriculum plan

Individualized Curriculum
is based upon a curriculum plan. It occurs in one or a combination of the ways that follow:
1. A predetermined curriculum plan is developed (either commercially or by a local staff), and students are matched to the plan based upon their abilities, interests, and learning styles.
2. Teacher(s) and student(s) jointly develop a curriculum plan for an individual student or group of students.
3. Students, with teacher guidance, develop their own educational objectives and activities.

Individualized Instruction
consists of all those activities and processes involved in the actual implementation of the individ-ualized curriculum plan. Specifically, it means providing content and processes at the appropriate times for students, either through teacher prescription or student choice. Individualized instruction does not necessarily mean that students work alone all the time; nor does it mean that the teacher works with only one student at a time.

Individualized instruction can occur when one student works alone or with other students and when a teacher works with one student or a group of students. It usually includes some combination of all of these.

Learning Packages
are designed to allow students to learn particular skills or concepts, or pursue areas of interest, at their own learning paces. Packages are usually in printed form and are organized around a specific content or interest area.

Classroom Learning Centers
are specified areas in the classroom designed by the teacher, by the teacher and the students, or by the students. They contain a variety of materials and activities for individual or small groups of students to enhance the development of concepts, skills, and student interests.

Contracts
are agreements between a student and a teacher (or a small group of students and their teacher) for specified educational activities, or mastery of an objective agreed upon in advance, with a clear understanding of and agreement about the assessment procedures to be used.

CONCEPTUAL MODEL FOR INDIVIDUALIZING CURRICULUM AND INSTRUCTION

Beginning an individualized curriculum and instruction program involves determining the educational activities in which students will engage. These decisions are based upon the overall goals of a school, which are derived from several sources. These sources include staff perceptions of and beliefs about how people learn, the relationship between a school and the society that supports it, social realities of a given time and location, the nature of knowledge, and optimum ways of organizing knowledge for instructional purposes.

School goals should determine the scope and meaning of a school's curriculum and instruction program.

Once school goals have been established, the success of individualizing depends heavily upon the development of suitable curriculum plans, a decision about how the plans can best be individualized, and the implementation of those decisions through instructional activities. A plan, its implementation, and its evaluation are crucial to individualized learning.

The following discussion elaborates upon the component parts of a curriculum plan, the instructional processes needed to implement the plan, and procedures for evaluating curriculum and instruction.

Components of a Curriculum Plan

Selection of Content
Individualization must start with general goals and move toward more specific plans for various curriculum and subject areas, grade levels, and distinct groups of students. As curriculum is planned for specified groups and individual students, certain themes, topics, concepts, skills, interests, problems, and processes will be identified for those students to inquire about, discover, study, learn, and enjoy. This process results in a clear specification of the content of a curriculum area. It occurs before instruction takes place, sometimes far in advance (e.g., a summer curriculum planning workshop for teachers) and sometimes in a classroom, with students, immediately preceding instruction.

Curriculum plans may be derived from numerous sources. Appropriateness of any of these sources depends upon school goals, staff attitudes regarding student involvement in curriculum planning, and the content area to be taught. Generally, when teachers and students have major roles in curriculum planning, there is greater likelihood of implementing a successful individualized program.

Below are listed some examples of sources for curriculum plans:

Outside Sources of Curriculum Plans	*Teacher-Student Derived Curriculum Plans*
Curriculum guides developed by state education agencies, local school districts, individual schools, colleges, or universities.	Teacher-student planning of content and / or instructional experiences, using outside sources (e.g., district curriculum guides) for setting direction, parameters.
Commercially prepared curriculum materials, e.g., *Man: A Course of Study, BSCS Biology, SRA Reading Labs, Distar Reading and Math Programs.*	Teacher-student planning without constraints of any outside source.
Textbooks (historically the primary source of curriculum plans).	Student-designed plan.
Programmed instruction.	Open classroom with multiple choices for students.

Course Sequence

After the desired content is identified, it is necessary in some areas of instruction to arrange the content in the sequential order in which it is to be learned. This is more likely to be true in skill areas, such as reading, mathematics, industrial arts, typing, home economics, physical education, and certain parts of science courses, than in humanities, language arts, and social studies. In the latter category, students might determine their own individual sequence, but in a science course, for example, a student probably should demonstrate proficiency in measurement before conducting laboratory experiments with chemicals.

Instructional Objectives

Instructional objectives are based on the selected content and are a part of the curriculum plan. They are the specific statements of intent that give direction to both long-range and day-to-day instructional planning. The familiar unit plan is an example of long-range planning. A unit includes instructional objectives and suggested activities for students and teachers to engage in for accomplishing the objectives. Units might be planned with objectives and activities which could require one week, six weeks, or a semester to complete.

In day-to-day planning, instructional objectives specify the nature of what is to be accomplished in a given period, set of modules, lesson, problem-solving task, inquiry session, contract, learning center, or other educational activities.

The use of instructional objectives in an individualized program requires matching the objectives to the abilities and interests of students.

Learning Alternatives and Resources

Learning alternatives and resources are the proposed educational activities and materials from which students and teachers choose in order to achieve instructional objectives or accomplish eduational plans. Learning alternatives can be based upon constructing, experimenting, listening, reading, dramatizing, and film making. Learning resource examples are films, people, books, magazines, field trips, and animals. The proposed learning alternatives and resources are a part of the curriculum plan and are implemented in the on-going instructional activities of the classroom. The curriculum plan should include many proposed alternatives to maximize opportunity for individualization. Teachers and students should be encouraged to create additional learning alternatives as they implement the curriculum plan in actual classroom environments.

Pre and Post Assessment

The curriculum plan should include proposed means for pre and post assessment. Preassessment includes those processes that help determine (1) what a student already knows in relation to the objectives of the curriculum plan, and (2) which learning alternatives are most appropriate for students, based on preferred learning modes, interests, and other background information.

Postassessment follows selecting and engaging in learning alternatives and provides information regarding how well a student or students have done in achieving instructional objectives or other desired outcomes. Such information is used in determining whether a student needs to engage in further learning alternatives or move on to new areas of study. Postassessment should also be concerned with student perceptions of the instructional processes.

What Can Be Individualized?

The development of a curriculum plan does not ensure individualization nor does it tell how the plan can be individualized. Questions relating to time and rate of learning, selection of content, objectives and learning alternatives, and scope of learning need to be considered in translating the plan into individualized instruction. The essential question seems to be: *What* is to be individualized? Table 2 provides criteria for deciding what can be individualized.

Implementing Curriculum Plans Through Instructional Processes

Instructional processes are the educational activities involved in implementing the curriculum plan in actual classroom environments. These processes and educational activities encompass the interactions and transactions that occur between and among the students and the teacher(s), students and peers, students and community persons, students and other educational personnel, and students and media and materials. Instructional processes include activities related to preassessment, prescription, learning alternatives, and postassessment.

The primary mechanism for going from the curriculum plan (intent) to instructional processes (student experiences) is known as prescription, the process of choosing, selecting, or assigning objectives and learning alternatives to students. In an individualized program, prescription is based upon the preassessment of students.

Prescription activities include:
(1) Prescribing appropriate objectives from the curriculum plan on which individual students will work;
(2) Selection, or guiding student selection, of learning alternatives and resources appropriate for individual students in order for them to accomplish objectives.

The act of prescribing involves choosing and creating appropriate activities from learning alternatives for students. The teacher prescribes for individual students, and for groups of students

Table 2
Criteria for Deciding What Can Be Individualized

WHAT IS INDIVIDUALIZED?	DEFINITION	PURPOSE
1. Rate	Individualization occurs in the rate at which students progress through a sequence of work. Objectives and learning alternatives are essentially the same for all students, but are prescribed only when a student is ready for them.	To allow students to proceed through a skills sequence at their own rate; assures mastery of one part of sequence before moving to another.
2. Learning Alternatives	Individualization occurs as students choose from various learning alternatives; students usually choose the type and number of activities they will engage in, in order to meet objectives, which are essentially the same for all students.	(a) To involve students as much as possible in *means* for achieving objectives. (b) Seeks to have students help identify and capitalize on their own best learning style(s). (c) Allows for as few or as many activities as necessary to achieve objective.
3. Schedule	Based on the assumptions that (1) some courses require more time than others, and (2) some students require more time to master one course, others another. Usually involves some type of flexible schedule where student can sign back into a course for as much time as he wishes until the level of mastery required and / or chosen is achieved.	To allow students the amount of time they need to master content / skills. Students might finish one course in a few months, while another course might take more than a year.
4. Content	Students have choices about both the objectives and the learning alternatives they will pursue. Often students must contract with the teacher for what they plan to do, and by when.	To provide maximum choice for students, in both content and method.
5. Depth of Exploration	Students might study the same concept, skill, topic, or theme at essentially the same time; but, based on teacher assessment, some will do more work and gain deeper understanding.	To allow students to go into as much detail and depth as they are able; to allow students of varying abilities to work together productively on the same objectives.

when there is a common need. Some individualized approaches provide for student self-prescription. Prescription can occur during individual or small group conferences. It might also be done through the use of classroom management activities such as prescription sheets and records, student folders, assignment boards, and students' classroom study and activity schedules.

The prescribing of learning alternatives is the heart of the process of individualization. Students have either assessed themselves or have been assessed, instructional objectives to be accomplished have been identified, and selections have been made from learning alternatives. Now the student begins the pursuit of learning, understanding, and appreciating a concept, theme, topic, skill, or other area of interest. Students will read, draw, write, discuss, construct, report, inter-

view, figure, experiment, plan, dramatize, and listen. They will also use contracts, learning packages, media, peer teaching, learning centers, independent study, textbooks, self-paced materials, role playing, group work, trips, projects, and simulations. The success of any individualized program is directly dependent upon the appropriateness of the prescriptions for individual students.

Postassessment activities as a part of instruction provide information for reporting student progress and for making decisions about subsequent student prescriptions and/or curriculum plans.

APPROPRIATE SUBJECT AREA(S)	ROLE OF TEACHER	ROLE OF STUDENT
Any skill courses or skill areas within courses; mathematics and beginning reading are especially conducive to this type individualization; especially appropriate when mastery of one skill is dependent upon understanding of a prior one.	Prepares or selects sequence (including objectives); assesses individual students in relation to sequence; prescribes materials, activities, based on assessment; evaluates; recycle or move on to next skill.	Relatively passive acceptance and completion of prescription.
Any.	Establishes course sequence (including objectives); develops alternative means for accomplishing objectives and makes available to students; assesses progress, determines mastery.	Chooses types and number of learning alternatives; completes as many as necessary for mastery.
Any.	Specifies total course sequence, with knowledge and skills necessary to complete the course; develops learning alternatives for students to pursue individually; guides students through alternatives; assesses for mastery level.	Determines level of mastery (usually in terms of a grade) desired for course; chooses time to be spent on course (when, how much); completes necessary work for desired grade.
Areas of preferred exploration (any area identified by the student which goes beyond required curriculum); portions of many humanities and social science courses.	Helps students define areas of need / interest; provides resources; helps students set realistic goals and completion dates and establishes evaluative criteria; assesses work in conjunction with student.	Determines areas of interest / need for study. With teacher decides on appropriate materials, learning alternatives (this might involve a student-teacher contract), and assessment criteria; completes work, evaluates.
Courses with few skills and where maximum personal interaction is desired (e.g., American history).	Preassesses; prescribes (often with students) learning alternatives appropriate for each student, all based on the same objective(s). Designs some alternatives and ensures interaction across ability levels. Helps design independent study project when appropriate.	Helps (with teacher) prescribe learning experiences appropriate for given background and previous experiences, speed, and ability and interest. Completes learning alternatives, including interacting with peers.

Evaluation of the Curriculum Plan and Instructional Processes

Evaluation is distinguished from assessment in that it focuses on the curriculum and instruction program, while assessment focuses on student needs and/or performance. Evaluation procedures should be designed to determine the overall effectiveness of curriculum plans and their implementation through instructional activities. More specifically, curriculum evaluation is concerned with such questions as:

1. Is there congruence between curriculum plans and school goals?
2. Do curriculum plans communicate intent? Are they specific? Do they have necessary components?
3. Are they internally consistent (i.e., do objectives flow from goals; do resources and planned activities relate to objectives)?
4. Do curriculum plans (either commercial or staff-developed) conform to design specifications, that is, do they do what is expected / needed?

Evaluation of instruction focuses on areas such as:

1. Congruence between instructional activities and the curriculum plan;
2. Appropriateness of instructional activities and resources for specified students and teachers;
3. Conformity to design specification, that is, does instruction accomplish objectives?
4. Feasibility of implementation, for example, are specified resources readily available?

The following chart depicts the component parts of the conceptual model presented above and the relationship of those parts to each other.

EDUCATIONAL GOALS OF THE SCHOOL

I. CURRICULUM PLAN
(provides direction for planned educational activities)

—Selection of content (concepts, themes, topics, skills)
—Instructional objectives
—Proposed learning alternatives and resources
—Assessment activities

II. INSTRUCTIONAL PROCESSES
(processes and educational activities for implementing curriculum plan)

Preassessment (diagnosis)
Determines
—what student knows in relation to objectives
—student interests, background, experience
—student learning styles

Prescription
—Selection and choice of learning alternatives for students to engage in, based upon informal / formal assessment

Learning Alternatives
Student engages in alternative instructional modes, e.g.,
—contracts
—learning packages
—learning centers
—independent study, which contain specific activities, using
—self-paced materials
—role playing
—group work
—lectures, speeches
—trips
—projects
—simulations
—peer teaching
—textbooks

Postassessment (student evaluation)
Determines
—student achievement in relation to objectives
—student reactions to and attitudes toward the instructional processes

III. PROGRAM EVALUATION

A. Curriculum Plan
1. Is there congruence between the curriculum plan and school goals?
2. Does the curriculum plan communicate intent? Is it specific? Does it have necessary components?
3. Is it internally consistent (i.e., do objectives flow from goals; do resources and planned activities relate to objectives)?
4. Does the curriculum plan (either commercial or staff developed) conform to design specifications, that is, does it do what is expected / needed?

B. Instruction
1. Congruence between instructional activities and the curriculum plan.
2. Appropriateness of instructional activities and resources for specified students and teachers.
3. Conformity to design specifications, that is, does instruction accomplish objectives?
4. Feasibility of implementation, e.g., are specified resources readily available?

This chart suggests that:

1. The curriculum plan encompasses notions about the educational activities in which students will engage, including what is to be learned, ways of learning, pre and post assessment of learning, and evaluation of the plan and its implementation.

2. Instructional processes follow the development of the curriculum plan and are the actual processes involved in implementing the curriculum plan.

3. Evaluation procedures are used to evaluate curriculum plans in relation to the goals of the school and the overall effectiveness and consistency of the curriculum plan. The procedures also provide information regarding the effectiveness and appropriateness of the instructional activities in implementing the curriculum plan.

PLAN OF THE BOOK

The remainder of this book elaborates upon certain components of the model presented in this chapter and suggests alternative individualized approaches based upon the design. Chapter 2 further describes assessment and evaluation and gives specific examples of assessment procedures. The nature and role of instructional objectives in individualization, and examples of these objectives, are expanded upon in Chapter 3. Chapter 4 presents a viewpoint about learning alternatives and illustrates, by examples, how learning alternatives can be developed for themes, concepts, topics, and skills.

The second section of the book deals with individualization alternatives. Chapters 5 through 10 are respectively related to the following alternatives and processes of individualizing: learning centers, learning packages, contracts, other individualized approaches, classroom management, and educational games.

The last part of the book is a Yellow Page section. The Yellow Pages contain bibliographies, resources for information and data collection, and guides to materials, people, and places related to individualizing curriculum and instruction.

2

The Role Of Assessment And Evaluation In An Individualized Program

The authors are indebted to Michael DeNoia, a doctoral student at the University of South Carolina, for his assistance in preparing the manuscript for this chapter.

ach element of the instructional process is important in the act of individualizing, but three crucial steps in the process are pre-assessment, postassessment, and evaluation. These elements provide a basis for individual student activities and prescriptions, tell how well the student is doing, and provide feedback to teachers and other school personnel about the overall quality and consistency of the individualized program.

Pre and post assessment are processes that focus upon student knowledge, skills, needs, interests, values, learning styles, progress, achieve-

Table 3

PROCESS	PURPOSES	SUGGESTED PROCEDURES	WHEN IMPLEMENTED
Preassessment	—To determine a student's overall knowledge of and attitude toward a subject area —To assess student interests, goals, learning styles —To determine student proficiency in any prerequisite skills needed for successful completion of an area of study, e.g., reading level, safety rules for laboratory or shop work —To determine what a student already knows in relation to the objectives of a curriculum plan —To select and/or develop objectives and learning alternatives from curriculum plans for individual students or groups of students —To facilitate learning by informing the student of his progress —To inform the teacher about a student's success and problems and to enable the teacher to guide the student's activities and learning	The following suggested means can be used in both pre and post assessment activities. Determination of how to use the means will depend upon teacher/ student purposes. For example, standardized test results can be used to determine what a student already knows (preassessment) or to determine what a student has achieved following instruction; role playing can provide information about student attitudes and knowledge which can be either for prescription (preassessment) or for determining progress (postassessment). —Standardized tests —Teacher-made diagnostic test (pre and post) —Observation of student behavior —Anecdotal records —Sociograms —Role playing —Model building —Construction activities —Demonstration of skill or performance —Individual and group physical education activities —Value clarification activities —Dramatizations and puppet shows —Group work assessment forms	At the beginning of the school year or semester Prior to the beginning of an individualized mode (e.g., learning center, learning package, contract) or curriculum plan During the process of engaging in a curriculum plan
Post-assessment	—To determine the student's achievement of an objective or set of objectives —To enable the student and teacher to select other learning alternatives to help the student achieve objectives not yet attained —To inform interested parties of a student's growth and progress	—Nonverbal activities —Essays and creative writing —Translation activities —Conducting experiments —Cooking and sewing activities —Personal journals	Upon completion of an objective, a set of related objectives, or a student's curriculum plan

ment, and performance. Preassessment facilitates the development and revision of individualized plans for students, and postassessment enables a student and teacher to determine progress and whether or not objectives have been attained.

Evaluation is designed to provide information regarding the individualized curriculum and instruc-

tion program. Procedures are developed to determine the overall effectiveness of curriculum plans and their implementation through instruction. Table 3 shows the three processes, their major purposes, procedural examples, and suggested times for implementation.

Evaluation	—To determine if school goals are consistent with the educational beliefs of parents, students, and staff	—Questionnaire to each group for rank-ordering sets of beliefs	Yearly
		—Meetings of representatives of each group to analyze and revise school goals —Accreditation and self-study reports	Self-study period for accreditation
	—To determine if school goals, curriculum plans, and school organization (e.g., scheduling, grouping) are consistent	—Principal and faculty curriculum committee analyze program, recommend needed changes, and work with staff on implementation	On-going
	—To determine if curriculum plans meet needs/expectations	—Examine achievement test scores	Yearly
		—Develop system, including target dates and persons responsible, for monitoring implementation steps (e.g., Are materials ordered on time? Has necessary staff training occurred? Are facilities ready?)	Continual monitoring
		—Follow-up studies of students (e.g., Do they have job skills? Do they succeed in college? Do they participate in democratic processes?)	On-going
		—Examine records (e.g., Are there fewer dropouts? Is there a reduction in vandalism? Is there a reduction in absenteeism?)	On-going
	—To determine if instruction is appropriate and accomplishes objectives	—Examine learning alternatives to determine if they are (1) clear, (2) varied, (3) consistent with intent of objective(s)	As developed
		—Observe students to determine which alternatives are chosen, which are of no interest	On-going
		—Administer questionnaire (oral or written) to students to determine feelings about instructional processes, materials, and learning alternatives	At the end of units of work
		—Record percent of students able to accomplish objectives	On-going

Assessment And Evaluation Ideas

Cognitive assessment is widely practiced by teachers, usually taking the form of teacher-made tests, commercially prepared diagnostic tests, and standardized achievement tests. Several publishing companies have produced criterion-referenced standardized tests (as opposed to norm-referenced) which provide information about how well an individual student has done on a given objective. This information provides the basis for prescriptions for the student.

The assessment and evaluation instruments that follow are primarily related to the affective domain because teachers often express the need for assistance in this area. Some of these instruments suggest ideas for assessing student reactions to the school and to individual classes. Such information is often vital in making curriculum and instruction decisions/changes. The examples provided are designed to be illustrative only; all can and probably should be modified for specific schools or classes.

School Goals Preference Sheet

Directions: Arrange the goals listed in Column One in the order of their importance to you in Column Two.

COLUMN ONE	COLUMN TWO
School should	*School should*
• prepare me to get a job.	
• help me think critically, solve problems.	
• help me enjoy life.	
• develop my basic skills (e.g., reading, computing, writing).	
• prepare me to live with all types of people.	
• help me feel good about myself.	
• prepare me to participate in a democracy.	
• teach me to develop and maintain a healthy body.	
• teach me ways to enjoy leisure time.	

Name _____ Date _____

My Feelings about School

The best thing about school last year was _____

_____

I hope this class (or room) will _____

_____

The most important thing to me in school this year is _____

_____

I think I accomplish more in school when _____

_____

If I had my choice, I would prefer to learn by _____

_____

The statements listed above might be given to students to complete at the beginning of the school year. Students might be asked to respond to the items that follow, or variations, periodically during the year to determine their feelings about the class.

School is _____ .

This class is _____ .

My classmates are _____ .

My main asset is _____ .

My biggest concern is _____ .

The problems people my age face are _____

_____

The big problems the world faces are _____

_____

_____

_____

_____ .

_____   _____
Name   Date

My Three Wishes Triangle

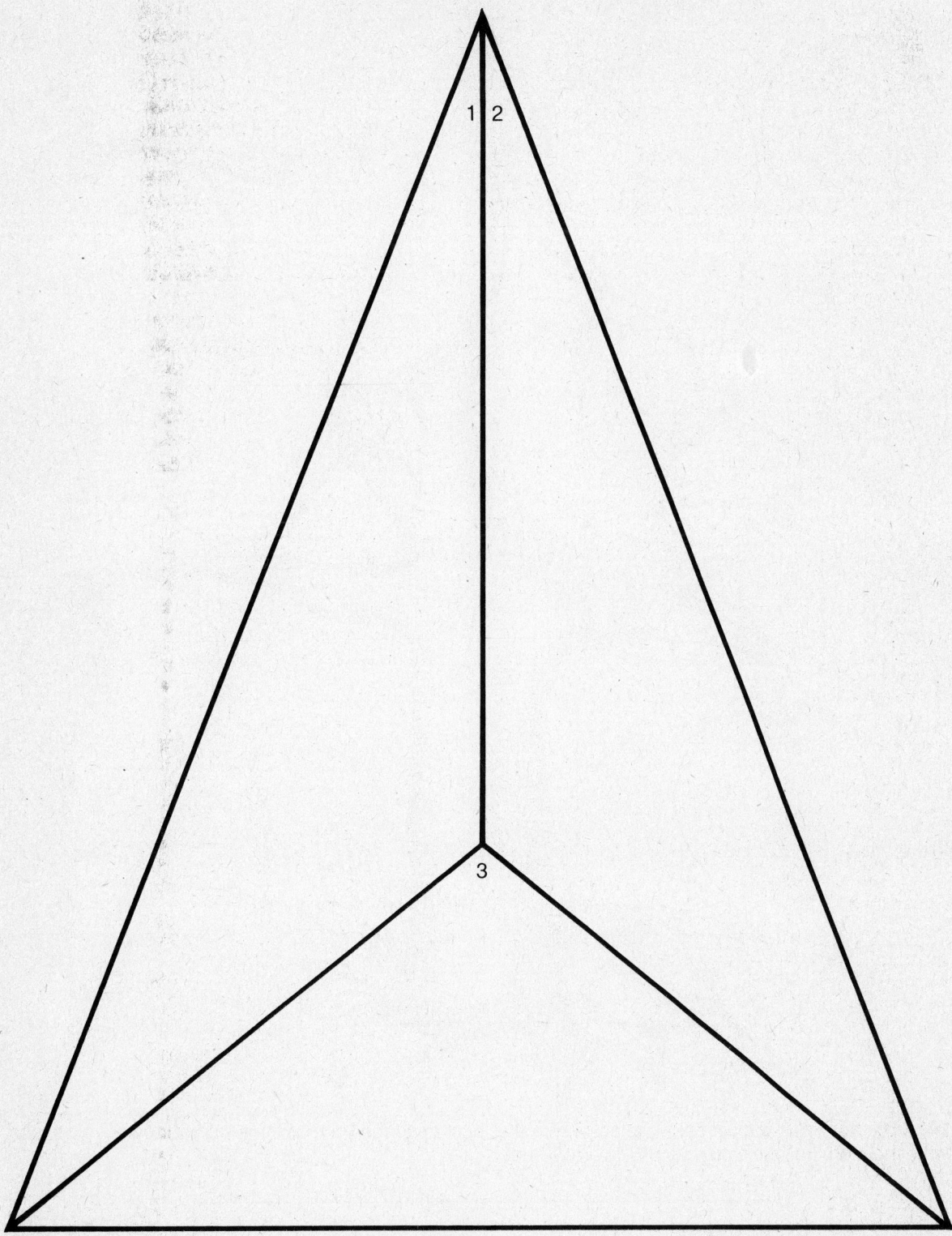

Directions: Draw a symbol or something that stands for your 3 most important wishes in the numbered spaces in the triangle.

Name _____ Date _____

My "Who Am I?" Tree

Directions: From the list below select words that best describe you, or think up your own words, and write them on the labels on your "Who am I?" tree.

HAPPY	RELIABLE	KIND	COOL
FRIENDLY	HANDSOME	SMART	LOVING
BRAVE	PRETTY	DEPENDABLE	BIG
HELPFUL	NEAT	LIKEABLE	LITTLE

Name _____   Date _____

My Self-Assessment

MY ASSESSMENT
TEACHER'S ASSESSMENT OF ME

1. Working for the good of the class, I

   a. respect each individual and his ideas.

   b. accept responsibilities without being urged to do so.

   c. share ideas about problems being studied.

2. In group discussions, I

   a. give my whole attention.

   b. contribute worthwhile ideas to the discussion.

   c. prepare myself for discussions by reading, listening, finding out.

3. Planning and doing my class activities, I

   a. carry out my plans on time.

   b. help plan work in the groups of which I am a member.

   c. turn in assignments on time.

   d. use many sources of information.

   e. take good notes.

4. When I make a presentation or develop a product from an activity, I

   a. strive for better grammar.

   b. present work in an interesting manner.

   c. select important notes.

Name _____   Date _____

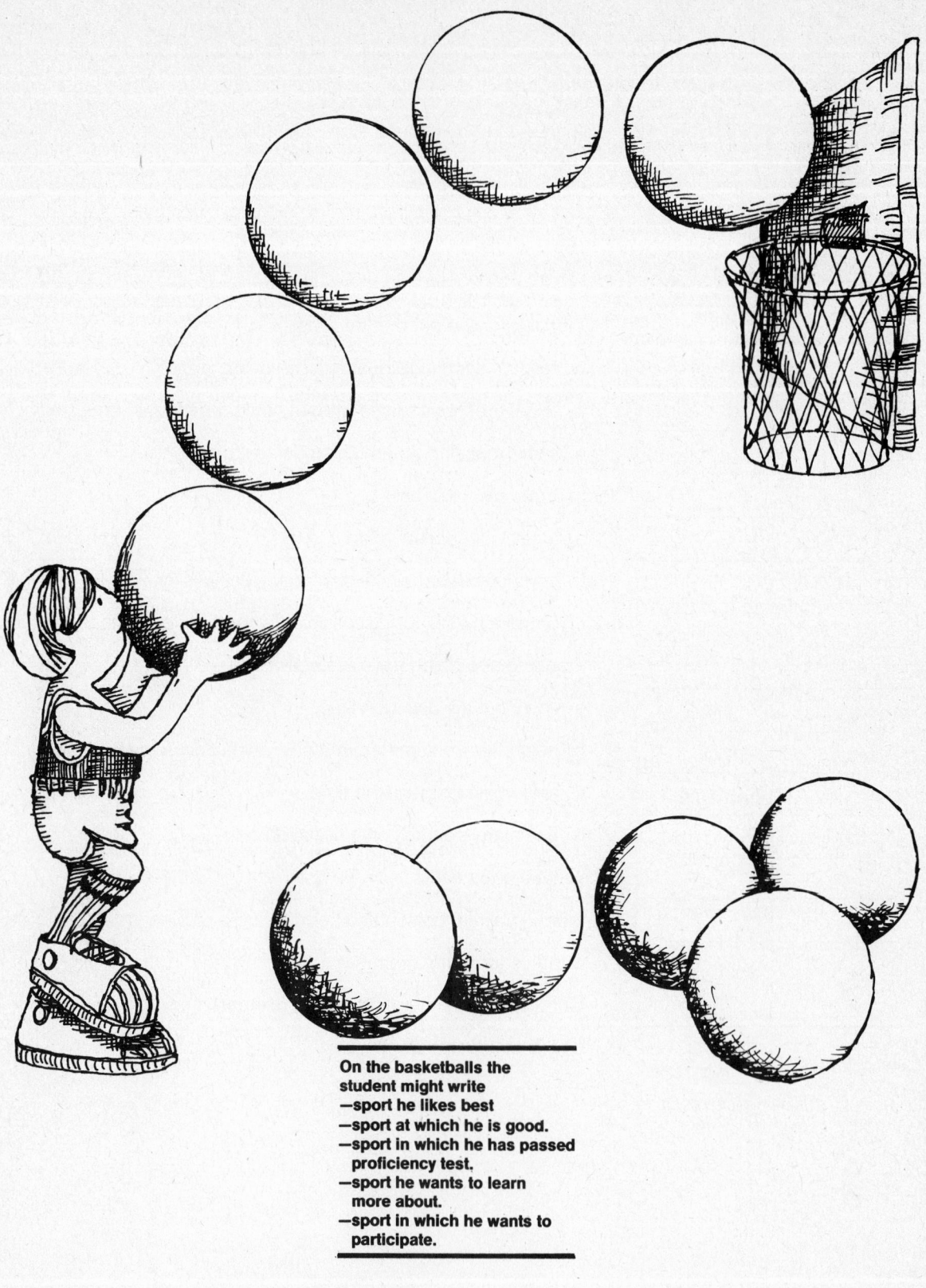

On the basketballs the
student might write
—sport he likes best
—sport at which he is good.
—sport in which he has passed
  proficiency test.
—sport he wants to learn
  more about.
—sport in which he wants to
  participate.

Name

Date

Interest Inventory

1. The things I like best at school are _____ .

2. The things I like least at school are _____ .

3. The things I would like to learn more about at school are _____

_____ .

4. The things I like to do best when I get home are _____

_____ .

5. The things I like to do least when I get home are _____

_____ .

6. I like to read about _____ .

7. I like to see movies and TV programs about _____

_____ .

8. I like to take trips to _____ .

9. When I grow up I want to be _____ .

10. I like to collect _____ .

11. My favorite science activity is _____ .

12. My favorite arithmetic activity is _____ .

13. My favorite music activity is _____ .

14. My favorite art activity is _____ .

15. My favorite social studies activity is _____ .

_____   _____
Name   Date

Things I Do at School

HOW OFTEN DO YOU DO THESE THINGS?

	OFTEN	SOME	NOT MUCH	NEVER
1. Listen to a record or tape recorder at school?				
2. Get to choose and learn something you really need to learn?				
3. Look at a film or filmstrip?				
4. Talk to a teacher about what you really want to study in school?				
5. Tell your family about something good that happened at school?				
6. Do more than you really have to in a class?				
7. Really understand the work you do in class?				
8. Study something in class besides a textbook or workbook?				
9. Enjoy the work you do in a class?				
10. Make up work when you are absent or get behind?				
11. Go to the school library?				
12. Have to stay in or get sent to the office?				

If there is anything else you would like to say about school, please use these lines:

_____

_____

_____

_____

_____

_____

Name _____   Date _____

Things We Do in This Class

Directions: Please think about what you did in this class yesterday. Read each question then check *one* answer. If a question doesn't fit the class, leave it blank.

1. How many students did the same written work in this class yesterday?
   (a) _____ probably nobody
   (b) _____ a few students
   (c) _____ most of us
   (d) _____ everybody
2. If *you* did some written work in class, whose idea was it?
   (a) _____ mine
   (b) _____ a group's
   (c) _____ the teacher's
3. How many students in class yesterday read the same pages in the textbook?
   (a) _____ probably nobody
   (b) _____ a few students
   (c) _____ most of us
   (d) _____ everybody
4. If *you* read some pages in a textbook, whose idea was it?
   (a) _____ mine
   (b) _____ a group's
   (c) _____ the teacher's
5. How many students did the same project or activity in class yesterday?
   (a) _____ probably nobody
   (b) _____ a few students
   (c) _____ most of us
   (d) _____ everybody
6. If *you* did a project or activity in the class, whose idea was it?
   (a) _____ mine
   (b) _____ a group's
   (c) _____ the teacher's
7. How many students got the same homework assignment in class yesterday?
   (a) _____ probably nobody
   (b) _____ a few students
   (c) _____ most of us
   (d) _____ everybody
8. If *you* did some work at home for the teacher in the class, whose idea was it?
   (a) _____ mine
   (b) _____ a group's
   (c) _____ the teacher's

Name _____   Date _____

My Vocabulary Storybook

October

My friends and I went for a boat ride on a small, shiny pond. We went frog gigging. The boat was creaky. It was made from the top of an automobile. One friend paddled the boat while the other friend and I looked for frogs. The dark, shiny water was scary. We found several frogs that made a croaking sound. We rode a farm tractor from the pond to our home. We carried the frogs in a coal scuttle.

by Jackie Purdue

Know Your Tools

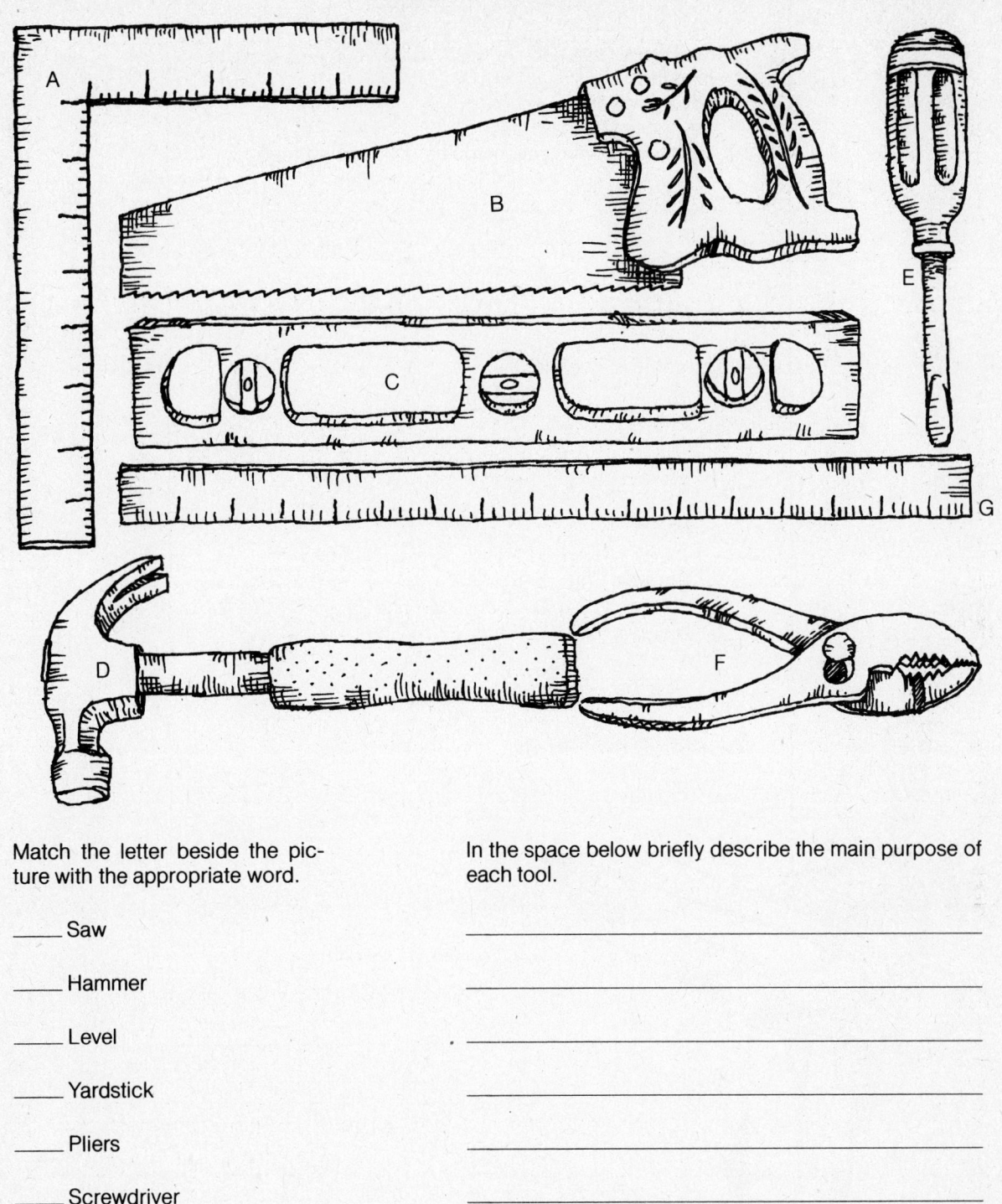

Match the letter beside the picture with the appropriate word.

_____ Saw

_____ Hammer

_____ Level

_____ Yardstick

_____ Pliers

_____ Screwdriver

_____ Square

In the space below briefly describe the main purpose of each tool.

_____

_____

_____

_____

_____

_____

_____

_____ Name

_____ Date

This type of assessment form can be used to help determine knowledge of any objects or tools students would be expected to use.

My Favorite Subjects

Directions: Give each of the following subjects a grade by marking

A by those you enjoy very much

F by those you least enjoy

C by those toward which you have no strong feelings

_____ Art

_____ English

_____ Health

_____ Home Economics

_____ Industrial Arts

_____ Math

_____ Music

_____ Physical Education

_____ Reading

_____ Science

_____ Social Studies

_____ Typing

Name _____   Date _____

School Attitude Survey

Directions: This is your chance to grade the school and suggest some things you might like to see changed. For each statement circle the letter grade that best tells how you feel about the statement. A grade of A + indicates you very much agree. An F means you strongly disagree.

1. Most teachers at this school listen when a student wants to ask a question in class.

   A+   A   B   C   D   F

2. The rules in this school about what you can wear are fair.

   A+   A   B   C   D   F

3. Students usually get to use the school library any time they need to.

   A+   A   B   C   D   F

4. This is a good school and most kids are proud to be students here.

   A+   A   B   C   D   F

5. The food we get at lunch is usually good.

   A+   A   B   C   D   F

6. We have enough time between classes to go places and do things.

   A+   A   B   C   D   F

7. Students of different races are usually friendly to each other at this school.

   A+   A   B   C   D   F

8. The people in the office try to be as fair and reasonable with students as they can.

   A+   A   B   C   D   F

9. Our teachers experiment a lot and help us learn in different ways.

   A+   A   B   C   D   F

10. We have enough sports for students in this school.

    A+   A   B   C   D   F

11. Students here get a lot of choice in what subjects they take.

    A+   A   B   C   D   F

12. Most teachers in this school are not unfair to students because of their race.

    A+   A   B   C   D   F

13. The restrooms in this school are clean.

    A+   A   B   C   D   F

14. Most students in this school don't fight and push but are considerate of other people.

    A+   A   B   C   D   F

15. Students in this school don't usually get sent to the office unless they deserve it.

    A+   A   B   C   D   F

_____   _____
Name   Date

3

Instructional Objectives And The Individualized Classroom

Objectives are a part of the curriculum plan; more than any other part of the plan, they give direction to educational intentions and instructional activities. As an integral part of an individualized program, objectives provide guidelines for making decisions about the selection of individual student activities; that is, they provide a basis on which to assess students and to suggest appropriate prescriptions, learning alternatives, assignments, or other educational activities.

This chapter illustrates the importance of instructional objectives; discusses purposes, types, and levels of objectives; and provides examples of uses of objectives in an individualized classroom.

Objectives, as a part of curriculum plans in an individualized program,

- reflect the desired intentions and outcomes of a school's faculty and students.
- are based upon the beliefs and values a school faculty holds regarding students, the society and the world in which we live, the nature and sources of subject matter, how human beings learn, and other areas which affect curriculum and instruction decisions.
- can be developed and written by teachers or teachers and students, or they can be secured from objective banks (see Yellow Pages for examples).
- should be based upon a humanistic approach; that is, objectives should reflect what is important for and needed by a particular student or group of students and should be written to include opportunities for growth in the affective, cognitive, and psychomotor areas of learning.
- can be designed and arranged so that students can choose from alternative objectives.
- provide direction for instructional activities. Deciding on appropriate materials, resources, and learning alternatives for students becomes an easier task if the question "Will it help to achieve the objectives?" is asked about each possibility.
- communicate to students what is expected of them, thus eliminating an element of game playing from the instructional process. No longer do students have to decide what to study by guessing what is expected of them, and no longer do they have to wonder what is really important in a subject or instructional sequence.
- help teachers set levels of classroom performance, based on student abilities, ages, and content or subject areas, and then hold themselves accountable for those standards. Specifying instructional objectives provides a basis for a teacher to analyze continually both the curriculum plan and the instructional processes and make revisions accordingly. Without specific intents, it is difficult to determine which instructional processes and

materials are helping students achieve and which are not.
- help teachers to reflect on the worth and feasibility of content to be taught and the appropriateness of instructional processes for teaching that content.
- improve procedures for assessing student growth. In a well-written instructional objective, assessment criteria and form are either stated or clearly implied; thus assessment procedures flow directly from instructional processes.
- provide motivation. Many students work much better when there are clear objectives with an end in sight. The feeling of accomplishment which accompanies the completion of objectives is often enough motivation to cause a student to pursue other objectives or move on to other activities.
- help manage student progress in an individualized classroom. Simple individualized progress charts can be constructed to show quickly the objective on which a given student is working. This is particularly helpful in grouping for instruction because the teacher can readily determine which students are working on the same objectives.

TYPES OF INSTRUCTIONAL OBJECTIVES

Instructional objectives are typically written to represent three domains of learning:

1. The *cognitive*[1] domain consists of behaviors and processes related to intellectual growth. The behaviors range from simple recall of information to more abstract and complex problem solving.
2. The *affective*[2] domain categorizes the more personal dimensions of human growth, such as values, attitudes, feelings, interests, and appreciations. Affective behaviors range from compliance with rules or expectations to the development of a personal value system.
3. The *psychomotor* domain refers to physical behaviors and skills, for example, typing, running, sewing, hitting a baseball, talking, and handwriting. Psychomotor learning might be reflected in improved speed, coordination, strength, and consistency.

Identification of the three learning domains is a convenient way of organizing objectives and learning experiences for planning, analysis, and evaluation. Such classification does not mean that an individual's learning occurs in only one domain at a time; nor does it mean that the domains do not interact with and depend upon each other. Rather, learning almost never occurs in only one domain,

---

[1] Benjamin S. Bloom et al., *Taxonomy of Educational Objectives—The Classification of Educational Goals, Handbook I: Cognitive Domain* (New York: David McKay, 1956).
[2] David R. Krathwohl, Benjamin S. Bloom, and Bertram B. Masia, *Taxonomy of Educational Objectives—The Classification of Educational Goals, Handbook II: Affective Domain* (New York: David McKay, 1964).

even though the primary objective for a learning experience might be either cognitive, affective, or psychomotor.

For example, when engaged in learning experiences based upon objectives related to the Presidency and Impeachment, the student extends intellectual processes and gains cognitive knowledge; clarifies and expresses values, beliefs, and feelings about impeachment; and develops psychomotor skills by writing, talking, illustrating, or dramatizing knowledge and feelings related to the Presidency and Impeachment.

Similarly, when a student is called upon to create a product using an art form, his values and interests are called into play, his knowledge of a subject is needed, and his psychomotor skills are required to create the artistic product.

Even though each of the domains interacts with and depends on the others, there is value in gaining knowledge about each domain and identifying objectives representative of the domains. Such activities facilitate and encourage a conscious effort to include growth in all domains.

PURPOSES OF OBJECTIVES IN THE COGNITIVE, AFFECTIVE, AND PSYCHOMOTOR DOMAINS

Cognitive Domain

The purpose of objectives in the cognitive domain is to provide a basis for the selection of learning alternatives designed to enhance varying levels of intellectual development. There is general agreement among educators that there are six levels of cognitive learning. Objectives can be written for each of these levels.

1. *Knowledge* objectives refer to the *recall* of facts, concepts, or principles. Appropriate verbs used in such objectives might be: define, describe, list, name, match. Examples: (1) Given a map of the United States on which individual states are outlined, the student will write the names of 45 of the states in the appropriate places on the map. (2) The student will write the multiplication table through nine's without the use of learning aids.

2. *Comprehension* objectives refer to the translation (to give in own words, to illustrate, to restate) or interpretation (to draw, to distinguish, to demonstrate, to show, to infer, to predict) of information. Examples: (1) Given a graph of the industries of the United States and their yearly rates of production, the student will write the ten industries which were most important to the Gross National Product in any given year. (2) Given a mixed list of ten proper and common nouns, the student will be able to identify which nouns are proper and which are common according to the rules discussed in class.

3. *Application* objectives require the learner to apply knowledge or understanding previously gained to a new situation. Such objectives might ask the learner to transfer, restructure, generalize,

or relate. Examples: (1) After a lesson on the relationship between bodies of animals and their ways of coping/surviving, students will list the primary type of diet of five out of ten previously unstudied animals when presented with pictures showing physical characteristics of those animals. (2) Following a unit on five communication media, the student will select the medium of his or her choice and mediate a situation assigned by the teacher. The mediation will meet all criteria developed in class during the unit of study.

4. *Analysis* objectives require the learner to identify the component parts of concepts, assumptions, organizations, or principles, and then to demonstrate the relationship between or among those parts. Learners might be asked to deduce, to compare and contrast, or to discriminate. Examples: (1) Given an unknown mixture, the student will examine the mixture and describe in writing the properties in the mixture and the relationship each has to all the others. (2) When given the average annual rainfall and length of growing season for different parts of the country, the student will deduce what crops would grow best in what parts of the country, based on determining the amount of rainfall and length of growing season required by each crop.

5. *Synthesis* objectives require the ability to analyze the parts of structures or ideas and put them together in a way which forms relationships new to the learner; the learner, in effect, creates a new whole from various elements or pieces. The student might combine, compare, create, design, or derive. Examples: (1) Given unsequenced parts of a comic strip with which he is not familiar, the student will arrange the parts in a way which at least three other students say is logical. (2) Given a chart of the size and juice content of oranges grown in different types of soil, the student will determine which soil types produce the biggest, juiciest oranges. (3) Given five mice, each of which has been taught to run a maze through a different procedure, the student will derive three principles about procedures for teaching mice to run mazes; each principle will then be written as a hypothesis and tested in the laboratory.

6. *Evaluation* objectives ask students to make judgments based on evidence. Verbs used in such objectives might be: appraise, contrast, validate, assess. Examples: (1) After using both adding machines and calculators, the student will (a) state three advantages of each, and (b) list 4 or 5 types of work each is best suited for. (2) After instruction about philosophy, leadership, and past and present behaviors of the Democratic and Republican Parties, the student will write a one-page paper describing personal reactions to the two parties in which he lists at least three items that might cause him to favor the Democratic and three that might cause him to favor the Republican Party.

Affective Domain

Affective objectives serve at least two purposes. One purpose is to provide a faculty and students with direction for developing specific attitudes, values, interests, or beliefs. When developing curriculum plans, affective objectives might be written related to obeying safety rules, becoming more tolerant of differences in other people, appreciating classical music, increasing enjoyment of reading, or respecting the rights and property of others. Such objectives have evaluation criteria, are directional, and are *not* particularly open-ended. Examples: (1) After experiencing what it is like to be interrupted constantly when trying to make a class presentation, the student will not interrupt more than once per day when someone else is talking. (2) After a unit on the struggles of young artists to support themselves, at least five members of the class will voluntarily write their Congressman urging federal subsidies for promising young artists.

Affective objectives also enable students and teachers to select learning alternatives and develop a classroom climate conducive to (a) clarifying values; (b) extending interests and providing opportunities for developing new ones; (c) providing an open forum for expressing attitudes and feelings, taking positions or making decisions and being able to support them with data; and (d) facilitating personal and interpersonal growth. It is very difficult and perhaps undesirable to include formal criteria for evaluating objectives written for creating such learning alternatives and classroom climates. The individual and personal nature of experiences which this purpose promotes suggests that the emphasis should be upon providing for such objectives and activities rather than upon the evaluation of the objectives. Examples: (1) After a cheating incident in class, each student will participate in a classroom meeting on cheating and will specify some values that are more important than cheating and some that are less important. (2) Given the opportunity to organize their class in the manner most conducive to personal and intellectual growth, the students will participate in decision making to establish a desirable classroom climate.

Psychomotor Domain

Psychomotor learning objectives reflect the belief that the school program has responsibility for helping students enhance their ability in physical and muscular movement and coordination. The purpose of objectives in this domain is to provide guidelines for selecting worthwhile experiences for students in physical and muscular development.

The emphasis of the objectives may change as a student progresses through school. At the elementary level, both general physical coordination and the skills needed for basic manipulations, such as handwriting and counting, are important.

In later years, physical coordination and the value of physical development are extended through physical education. Psychomotor development becomes more specialized in secondary schools. This specialization is usually represented in programs and courses such as home economics, industrial arts, music, woodworking, business education, auto repair, and lab work in science.

COMPONENT PARTS OF INSTRUCTIONAL OBJECTIVES

Correctly stated objectives that provide direction for instructional processes

- *specify observable behaviors* (e.g., lists, performs, chooses, completes, sings, creates, draws).
- *specify the conditions under which the behavior will be observed* (e.g., in not more than five minutes, in a simulated recital, upon completion of this contract, given mood music and asked to write, when given a graph to plot, after viewing your favorite television show).
- *specify performance level, standards, or evaluation criteria* (e.g., writes a grammatically correct paragraph, chooses classical over popular music at least half the time, answers seven questions correctly, creates a script and makes a movie according to criteria developed in class, identifies all locations given on a map, demonstrates 2 out of 3 swimming strokes, takes apart and puts back together a small engine in the time allotted).

Each of these components is illustrated in the sample objectives listed in Table 4.

Once objectives are written or adopted from other sources, decisions must be made regarding instructional procedures that are likely to help students achieve the objectives. Any number of approaches might be used; the following examples suggest some of those approaches.

USING INSTRUCTIONAL OBJECTIVES IN INDIVIDUALIZED CLASSROOMS

Ms. Grady has worked several years at attempting to develop a system for individualization in her social studies classes. She has decided that using learning packages is compatible with her own teaching style and with many of her students' learning styles. Her efforts at individualizing have resulted in the development of several packages that relate to the same topic, but with each package containing different objectives. The objectives relate to various levels of cognitive development. Currently, Ms. Grady has about five learning packages for each topic. To illustrate, Ms. Grady has developed packages on the topic "The Fight for

Table 4
Examples of Objectives Illustrating Components and Domains

AFFECTIVE	COGNITIVE	PSYCHOMOTOR
1. After completing the unit on prejudice, students, when given a choice (conditions), will sit by a person of another race (behavior) at least 50 percent of the time (standard).	1. Following a trip to the zoo, children, when shown pictures of ten animals they observed (conditions), will correctly identify (behavior) at least eight of the animals (standard).	1. After practice in tracing the letters of the alphabet in sand (conditions), the student will legibly (standard) print the letters of the alphabet (behavior).
2. After a presentation on the dangers of playground accidents (conditions), students in the class will obey (behavior) all playground regulations for the remainder of the year (standard).	2. Upon completion of a learning package on Reconstruction (condition), the student will describe in writing two opposing views regarding the results of Reconstruction, choose the one he/she believes to be the most accurate, and defend the choice (behavior) by citing arguments from at least three historians (standard).	2. After instruction in the typing of business letters (conditions), the student will type (behavior) three letters with no more than one mistake each within thirty minutes (standard).
3. After a series of value clarifying experiences (condition), students will list in priority the ideals they cherish most (behavior) and explain the rationale behind their list to other members of the class (standard).	3. After reading this chapter (conditions), a professional educator will write instructional objectives in the cognitive, affective, and psychomotor domains (behavior); each objective must specify *who* will do *what*, under what conditions, and how well (standard).	3. After instruction and practice on correct techniques for shooting free throws (conditions), the student will improve his/her percentage of successful free throws (behavior) by 10 percent (standard).

Civil Rights." The list of objectives below illustrates the different levels of objectives contained in the five packages.

Package 1. *Objective:* You will be able to arrange in chronological order the major events of the Civil Rights movement.
Package 2. *Objective:* You will be able to list at least five examples of Jim Crow Laws.
Package 3. *Objective:* You will be able to list and cite examples of six forms of political action used by blacks in the Civil Rights movement.
Package 4. *Objective:* You will write a paper discussing the evolution of the black image in literature, television, or motion pictures, comparing the image depicted in that medium in at least two different eras.
Package 5. *Objective:* You will write a paper contrasting the beliefs of three black leaders about the means for achieving equality and then describe your own position on this issue.

Based upon her knowledge of individual students, Ms. Grady either prescribes appropriate packages for students or guides students in the selection of the package(s) containing the appropriate objective(s).

Ms. Braun and Ms. Williams have been team teaching for three years. They decided to team teach mainly because they both had become frustrated with trying to help all their students achieve the same objectives from curriculum plans developed for their grade level. Ms. Williams and Ms.

Braun felt that through teaming they could better assess their students and then write objectives suitable for individuals who needed similar types of instruction.

One of the approaches for individualizing which Ms. Braun and Ms. Williams used was contract teaching. Based upon assessment of students, Ms. Braun and Ms. Williams developed contracts containing objectives appropriate for individuals and small groups of students. One topic used for contracts was jazz. The following objectives were written and prescribed for students based upon assessment information:

1. Given a list of musical terms and a list of definitions related to jazz, match at least 80 percent of the terms with the correct definition.
2. After studying the history and theory of jazz, define "improvisation" and illustrate its centrality to jazz through a medium of your choice, drawing on at least three references to support your position.
3. Make an audio tape of various jazz compositions which depicts at least three major shifts in the emphasis and composition of jazz from 1920 to present.
4. After studying the performing styles of various jazz artists, the student will, when hearing a performance, name the artist of at least five out of ten performances.
5. Describe in an essay or through another appropriate medium of your choice (e.g., a tape, a bulletin board display) the relationship of jazz to at least one myth and one legend and make a hypothesis about the relationship of music to myths and legends.

Mr. Terry teaches middle school mathematics. His math program is based upon a sequence of objectives, beginning with simple basic operations and ending in abstract problem solving. Mr. Terry receives a profile for each of his students which indicates to him the abilities of each student relative to the program objectives.

Typically, Mr. Terry has 25 to 30 students assigned to each of his class groups. He usually has a very few students engaged in beginning objectives, several students in the middle of the math sequence, and a few students near the top of the sequence.

The management system Mr. Terry uses (Figure 1) allows students to know the objectives and learning alternatives they are pursuing each day. When class begins, students secure their individual folders from the classroom instructional file and begin their work. Mr. Terry schedules a conference with each student to help assess progress. If several students are attempting to achieve the same objective and are engaged in group work, Mr. Terry often confers with or offers instruction to the group.

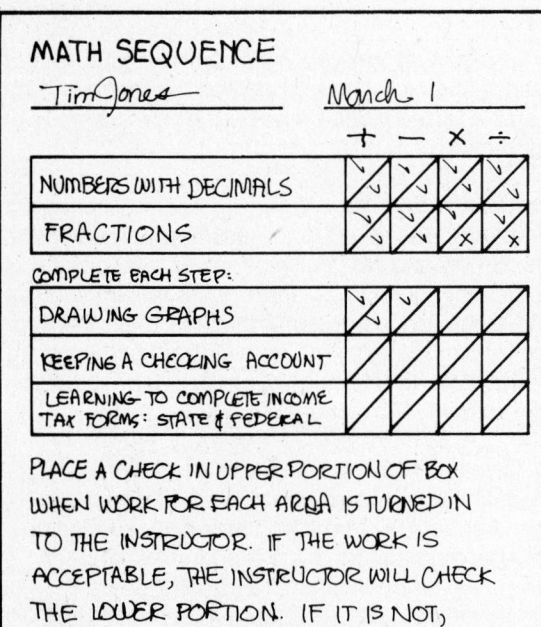

Figure 1. Mr. Terry's math sequence.

Betty Jo Benson enjoys her art course more than any other class. Besides being fond of painting, doing ceramics, and sculpting, she is especially pleased to be in a class where she can write her own instructional objectives and be personally responsible for achieving those objectives. Betty Jo's teacher gave her and the other students a suggested list of topics and projects for class and encouraged the students to propose other projects. The teacher asked each student to select a project to begin. Then each student was required

to develop objectives for the project (see sample contract in Figure 2) and to confer with the teacher on the proposal. When one project is completed, the student designs another.

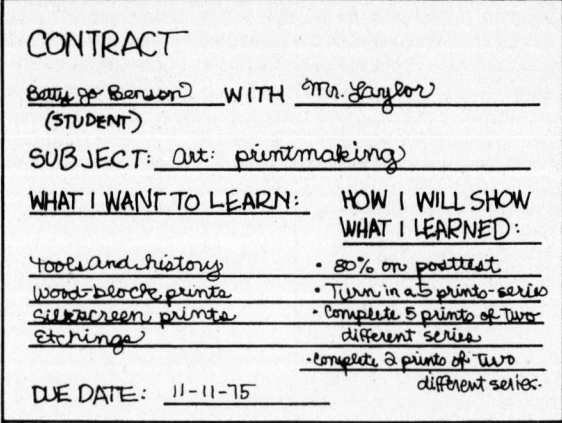

Figure 2. Art project contract.

Mr. Rolls doesn't feel he can fully individualize all activities in his third grade classroom, but he does individualize some parts of the curriculum. Language arts is one area in which he has made real progress in assessing student skills, knowledge, and interests, and in prescribing appropriate learning alternatives for students. Using information about individual student achievement in language from standardized test results and information gained from his own assessment techniques, Mr. Rolls is able to determine
• each student's present interests, learning mode preferences, and home background;
• each student's previous school experiences in language;
• each student's achievement in relation to the language arts objectives in his school.
This information enabled Mr. Rolls to design the management chart in Figure 3. The use of this chart helps to determine
• the progress of each student,
• which students need the same objectives,
• commonalities and differences in interests and learning mode preferences.
Mr. Rolls prescribes learning alternatives for an individual student or for a group of students who may need to achieve the same objective(s). The primary approach to prescribing for the achievement of objectives is through the use of a language arts prescription center (Figure 4). Student names are written on small posters and placed over boxes or trays which contain instructions, activities, and resources for a student or students working toward the same objective. When a student attains an objective, his or her name is moved to another prescription/activity box, or a new box is created.

Student Names	LANGUAGE ARTS OBJECTIVES ATTAINED												MAJOR INTERESTS	LEARNING MODE PREFERENCES
	1	2	3	4	5	6	7	8	9	10	11	12		
Corey	✓	✓		✓			✓						Animals Plants Dolls	Reading Drawing
Laney		✓		✓	✓		✓	✓					Animals Cowboys Girls	Constructing Reading Talking
Dana		✓	✓			✓							Farming Sea Stars	Working in groups Listening Viewing
Ian		✓	✓	✓	✓	✓	✓	✓	✓				Airplanes Encyclopedias Cats	Working alone Reading

Figure 3. Language arts management chart.

Figure 4. Language arts prescription center.

Creating And Prescribing Learning Alternatives

The heart of an individualized program is in the quality of the educational activities students experience. Previous chapters have outlined the planning necessary for creating and identifying curriculum content and objectives as components of an individualized classroom environment. Identification and selection of content and objectives are followed by the creation of resources and activities for students to use to achieve objectives or educational plans.

The resources and activities from which students and teachers choose are referred to as learning alternatives. Alternatives help to promote the learning of concepts, themes, topics, and skills and to clarify values, interests, attitudes, and personal goals. *Learning alternatives* are statements that suggest purposeful educational activity for students. These statements include proposals of what a student is to do, how he is to do it, and what can be done with results or products. Alternatives are usually written prior to instruction, as part of the curriculum plan, and selection of specific activities for students from the alternatives follows, based upon preassessment of particular students and/or student choice.

Curriculum plans must include a variety of learning alternatives to facilitate individualization. They should provide for differences in preferred learning styles, in backgrounds, and in student interests.

Well-defined, varied, and multiple learning alternatives suitable for specific groups of students are major determinants of a successful individualized classroom. Individualized programs where student activities consist only of reading, answering questions, and doing workbook problems—essentially paper-and-pencil activities—are usually no better than more traditional, group-paced classrooms.

In an individualized classroom with a variety of learning alternatives, students and teachers regularly make decisions about which learning alternatives are appropriate for student(s) and what new alternatives are needed to solve spontaneous classroom questions and situations. The teacher in such a classroom spends less time giving students information, and more time prescribing or helping students to select pertinent activities. Well-written alternatives allow the teacher to work with small instructional groups and hold frequent individual conferences; this is true if the alternatives are very specific about student *behavior*. This type of classroom means that the role of the student is primarily one of participant rather than recipient. It requires doing, producing, building, performing, analyzing, demonstrating, and similar kinds of behavior; and it requires behavior that is purposeful, that is, leading toward accomplishment of instructional objectives or leading to a satisfying feeling about an educational activity.

All too often teachers and students create or select alternatives that have not been well planned. It seems important that some general criteria be established for recommending or selecting alternatives. Even though the selection will depend upon the purposes to be served, some general criteria apply to the creation and selection of alternatives, regardless of purposes.

Six criteria are discussed in the following paragraphs. No claim is made that these six are exhaustive or necessarily cover all situations.

Criterion Number One: Are the alternatives designed for individuals with varying interests, learning styles, and levels of ability?

Use of (a) different materials for learning, such as books, manipulatives, and games; (b) different modes of learning, such as viewing, constructing, interviewing, and dramatizing; and (c) different schedules for students help to accommodate this criterion.

Some alternatives can be written for varied levels of abilities and interests; for example, if a class were studying ecological problems within the community, an alternative might be designed for students to interview members of the community to determine their perceptions of problems and their priorities of concern. Other alternatives might be designed for only one student or a small group of students, such as reading and analyzing Rachel Carson's *Silent Spring*.

Criterion Number Two: Are the learning alternatives likely to help students accomplish the objectives for which they were designed?

As a student or a group moves through the implementation of a curriculum plan, with its accompanying objectives, activities will be selected from learning alternatives related to that plan. There must be a logical relationship between the activity chosen and the instructional objective(s) for which it is written. Thus, learning alternatives should be directly related to student and teacher purposes.

Criterion Number Three: Are the alternatives explained fully and concretely enough so that they can be used by students and teachers?

It would probably be undesirable for suggested learning alternatives to be so detailed that they inhibit any planning or creativity on the part of the teacher or pupils; however, at the other extreme, such alternatives as

Take field trips
Read stories
Write reports
Visit historical sites
Invite speakers
Dramatize presentations

are of little value.

These alternatives are typical of what can be found in some commercial and locally developed instructional materials for classroom use. Teachers and students generally express a desire for learning alternative proposals that are more than merely a list. Suggested alternatives need to include information or product needed, ways of obtaining information or developing product, expected outcomes, and ways of sharing information or products.

It is important for individualized activities to be well developed so that individuals and small groups can use them with a minimum of direction from the teacher. This is particularly critical in an individualized classroom where the teacher spends the majority of his or her classroom time in small group instruction and individual conferences, neither of which profits from being interrupted to answer questions about what an activity *really* means.

Criterion Number Four: Are there alternatives available for small group activity as well as individual activity?

The individualized program, in addition to providing for individual student activity and learning, should provide some educational activities that facilitate learning to work with others. Group activities have much potential for providing situations for affective objectives: students participating in them must learn to share, compromise, and relate to others of similar and different backgrounds to solve problems or complete tasks. Learning alternatives that encompass a wide range of student participation are helpful in developing democratic values. To develop understandings and skills necessary for effective living with others in our society and other societies, learning alternatives that provide both individual and group experiences are needed.

Criterion Number Five: Do the alternatives provide for the continuation and reinforcement of desired basic skills?

The school program usually encompasses the development of certain skills, often called "basic." Many learning alternatives and materials are specifically designed to help students develop skills necessary for achieving skill-related objectives. Yet these same skills need to be used, reinforced, and developed in the context of other learning alternatives. It is difficult to say exactly what the "basic skills" are; however, generally the following areas constitute the framework into which the basics most often fall:
1. Reading
2. Writing
3. Speaking
4. Listening
5. Problem solving, inquiry
6. Planning
7. Cooperating in group endeavors
8. Information gathering
9. Computing

Assuming that learning alternatives can provide opportunities for developing skills, what are some possibilities? Suppose a student or a group wants to know more about comparative living standards in the United States and other selected countries. An alternative in which students might engage is: *Select and compare the rate of pay scales of vocations of your choice (e.g., street cleaner, police, mail carrier, physician, lawyer, teacher, professional athlete) in selected United Nations countries. Find your information through the use of classroom learning center and library materials, or through letter writing, interviewing, or other means. Compare your findings with the same vocations in our own country. Select a means of reporting and sharing your findings with other class members and arrange to do so.*

This alternative has potential for introducing, reinforcing, developing, and extending several skills, such as:
1. Reading
   a. to determine pay scales
   b. to determine members of United Nations
   c. to ascertain cost of living in selected countries
   d. to select vocations and determine their nature
2. Writing
   a. to obtain needed data
   b. to report conclusions
   c. to keep records of progress and information concerning the activity
3. Listening
   a. to enjoy and gain information from persons knowledgeable about the topic
   b. to radio, television, films, tape recordings, and interviews to obtain information
4. Planning—the whole educational activity, including stating purposes and objectives, identifying resources, planning steps of the activity, deciding upon product and ways of sharing
5. Speaking
   a. to gather information by asking questions, using the telephone
   b. to communicate plans, ideas, findings

Some learning alternatives written for basic skill development, especially in areas such as reading and computation, must be written in sequential order, with an understanding of the relationship between the alternative and those that precede and follow it.

Criterion Number Six: Does the alternative include all essential information for the student, including:
a. *What he is to do* (read, construct, write, draw, dramatize, listen, view)
b. *Where to find information, and what media to*

use (read three books in the classroom library, construct a model of a stage, write your feelings about ecology, draw a scale model of the United Nations, dramatize scenes from your favorite story or plan, listen to the lecture on atoms on the cassette tape player in the learning center, view the film on how to play basketball)

c. *What to do with any products or results from the alternative* (place your chart on the classroom bulletin board, prepare and present a puppet show to the class depicting your findings, display your model in the school library)

LEARNING ALTERNATIVES SUMMARY STATEMENTS

1. Learning alternatives are created to promote purposeful educational activity for students as they enjoy and learn more about a concept, theme, topic, or skill.
2. Maximizing individualization requires many alternatives from which students and teachers may choose.
3. Both teachers and students can create learning alternatives. Teachers develop alternatives as a part of a curriculum plan and also develop alternatives as needed during instruction. Students create alternatives in planning and learning situations.
4. Alternative statements should be fully developed and should enable the individual student to know the intent of and the procedures for completion of the alternative.
5. Alternatives can be created and developed for all ages and levels of ability. Some ages and ability levels will require careful explanation of the requirements and intent of the alternative.
6. Learning alternatives are designed to accommodate curriculum intentions and will reflect affective, cognitive, and psychomotor areas of learning.

EXAMPLES OF LEARNING ALTERNATIVES

This section presents examples of learning alternatives for selected concepts, themes, topics, and skills. Most of these require some level of proficiency in reading. If a teacher deems an alternative appropriate for a student who cannot read it, some other means must be found for communicating the information. Sometimes teachers read the alternative to the student, sometimes the information is recorded on an audio tape, sometimes the alternative is depicted primarily through pictures, and sometimes another student is asked to read the information to the student.

Concept: Recreation activities vary from country to country and within regions in a country.
Learning Alternatives:

1. Look through books and pictures, watch television and films, and talk to people to find as many human recreational activities as you can. Make a list of these activities. Find pictures to illustrate them, or draw your own illustrations.
2. Sort out the activities you have discovered in alternative 1. For example, list indoor-outdoor activities, individual-group activities, summer-winter activities, and social-physical activities. You might want to make columns for listing the activities that help you see common elements.
3. Divide the activities into categories you design and try to find:
   a. Countries or cultures that engage in the activities
   b. Origins of the activities
   c. Changes that have occurred in an activity over the years since it began
   Keep your findings to share with others and to use for drawing conclusions about recreational activities in various countries.
4. Select an unfamiliar recreational activity that really fascinates you. Find out as much about it as you can. Make arrangements to teach it to your classmates or to some other students.
5. Using all the information you have gained in other learning alternatives about recreational activity, make some hypotheses about how recreation activities vary from country to country and within regions in a country. If you don't have data to substantiate your guesses, find some.

Concept: Careers change as social, economic, and scientific beliefs and inventions change.
Learning Alternatives:

1. Take a poll of the various careers represented by the jobs of your classmates' parents. Determine how often parents have changed jobs and how many parents received some type of education to fulfill their present employment. Develop a chart depicting this information.

2. Visit, write, or interview an official of a factory, store, or some type of commercial firm. Find out how employment opportunities have changed in the place you visit over the past 10 years. Also, determine what new job positions have been added and if any jobs have become obsolete (no longer needed). Add your information to other career information you have collected.
3. Select one or two careers. Choose a way to find how these careers have changed over the past 10 years: some may not have existed 10 years ago! Find out why the changes occurred. Share your findings with the class and add your information to your study of careers. You might begin by (1) reading a pamphlet on your career choice in the *careers* learning center, or (2) listening to a tape on the career of your choice in the audiovisual center.
4. Choose a medium (painting, constructing, filming) to respond to this statement: "Careers change with social, economic, and scientific changes." The medium should be one you haven't used in the last two to three months. Your product should clearly reflect your ideas on and some of the information you collected about the above statement.

Concept: Circles and Squares
Objective: Given a set of geometric figures, the student can identify circles and circular shapes, and squares and square shapes.
Learning Alternatives:
1. Go to our classroom mathematics learning center. Find the packet of geometric cutouts. Study the cutouts and the words that mean the same as the shapes of the cutouts. Practice drawing circles and squares and writing the names of them.
2. Think of foods you know that:
   a. Come in circles or circular containers
   b. Come in squares or square shaped containers
   c. Are cooked in circles or circular shapes
   d. Are cooked in squares or square shapes
   Make a list of the foods under the headings

CIRCLES AND CIRCULAR CONTAINERS	SQUARE & SQUARE-SHAPED CONTAINERS	COOKED IN CIRCLES & CIRCULAR SHAPES	COOKED IN SQUARES & SQUARE SHAPES

Compare your list with the lists of at least two classmates.
3. Cut out pictures from newspapers and magazines of items that are circles or circular and squares or square shaped. Identify the items and their shapes. Paste them on a piece of poster paper and put this in your work folder. Use it for practice and sharing in class.
4. Make a list of circular and square shaped items you use almost every day. Illustrate them. Put your illustrations on our "Everyday" bulletin board.
5. Keep a list of figures or items you see during a week which are circular or square, such as road signs, household items, personal items, school items, and hospital items. Try to make categories for the different items. At the end of the week, compare your findings with those of your classmates.

Theme: The Sea—What Is It?
Learning Alternatives:
1. Read one or more of the following books, or read a similar book of your own choosing:
   Moby Dick
   Kon-Tiki
   The Old Man and the Sea
   The Sea Around Us
   Captains Courageous
   After you have read the book, do one or more of the following activities:
   a. Draw a series of illustrations in the medium of your choice which depict the author's ideas about the sea.
   b. Prepare a script of the book which can be pantomimed or dramatized by members of the class. Highlight the author's concept of the sea in the script.
   c. Make puppets related to the characters of your book. Develop a script about the most exciting part of the book and put on a puppet show for your class or younger students.
   d. Make a map showing where the events of the book occurred. Design ways of illustrating major events on the map. Share your activities with your class or with younger students, or share them with people in hospitals, nursing homes, or community centers.
2. Contribute to a bulletin board and learning center area by bringing in postcards, photographs, books, and artifacts about the

sea. Organize categories for these materials and label them.

3. Identify the major bodies of water in the world. By reading, interviewing people, or viewing films and filmstrips available at the audiovisual center, complete the following:
   a. Draw a map with the bodies of water located on it.
      1) Determine what major wars have been fought on the waters and label these on the map.
      2) Determine trade routes used on the waters and plot these on the map.
      3) Plot the routes of some early explorers on your map, and locate areas where landings have been made by U.S. astronauts.
   b. Select a city or a village located on a body of water. Gain information by reading, interviewing, or using other media.
      1) Write a paper or illustrate in some way how the location is influenced by the water near it.
      2) Assume you are a person who lives in the town or village and makes a living from the sea. Using information gained through your research about the city and how the sea influences it, present a puppet show or other dramatization about yourself, your city or village, and your work on the sea.
      3) Make a list or describe how life in the city or village might be different if it were not located on a body of water.
   Consult with your teacher or classmates about ways you can share what you have done.

Topic: Soil, Leaves, Bugs
Learning Alternatives:

Develop more understanding about bugs and their characteristics by doing the following:

1. Collect sow bugs from cool, dark, moist places, such as under logs or stones and in leaf litter.
2. Collect several leaves of varying kinds (e.g., beech, oak, maple, pine, dogwood) and place each kind in a closed container with 8 to 10 sow bugs. If no other containers are available, try plastic bags filled with air. Containers should have plenty of moisture in them. Keep containers away from direct sun.
3. Keep a record of changes in sow bugs (number, size), the number of days taken to eat the leaves, type of leaves used, and other observations.
4. After several days of observations, data collection, and record keeping, compile your data and observations and any of those your classmates might have into a chart showing daily changes.
5. Develop at least two hypotheses about sow

bugs, based upon your data and observations.
6. Discuss your hypotheses in class and conduct other investigations if hypotheses need further verification.

Topic: Making Salads
Learning Alternatives:

1. Develop your own way of showing the following:
   a. The definition of salad
   b. The origin of the word salad
   c. Several types of salads
   d. Changes in prices over the past 3 years in ingredients needed to make a salad
   e. Nutritional benefits of various salads
2. Select several countries and find the following information:
   a. The major salad eaten in the country
   b. The ingredients of the salad
   c. Whether or not such salads are common in the United States
   d. When the salad is usually eaten during the meal in the particular country

For alternatives to numbers 1 and 2 above, decide ways of sharing your findings with classmates and others.

3. Either by yourself or with one or two interested classmates, choose a salad and make it. Keep a record of the following:
   a. Steps you used to make the salad
   b. Ingredients used and their costs
   c. Time required to make the salad
   d. Specific nutritional benefits of the salad
   e. Your culinary reactions to eating the salad

Skill: Locating Places on Maps and Globes
Learning Alternatives:

1. Draw a diagram of your classroom. Locate your desk and your friends' desks on the diagram. Also place some of the following on your diagram: teacher's desk, learning center locations, class library, animal and plant areas. Identify east, west, south, and north on your diagram. Share your map-diagram with your classmates, and then put your diagram on the "Our Classroom Map" bulletin board. (You might want to include locations in the school— office, cafeteria, library, play areas—on your map-diagram.)
2. Contribute to a "Places We Have Visited and Lived" map with your classmates. Select, draw, or construct a map of the United States or the world. Pinpoint places on the map where you have visited and/or lived and pin a small flag in these places. When everyone in class has completed the activity, participate in a discussion about how you located places on the map. You could also discuss your favorite place or the place you liked least and why.
3. Use a dictionary or a book about maps and find the definitions of these words: *longitude* and *latitude*. Write the words and definitions in your

map and globe notebook. Use a map or a globe and practice locating latitude and longitude locations. You can practice with a friend. When you feel confident about longitude and latitude, take the short check-up test on "Using Longitude and Latitude Skills" which the teacher will give you.

PRESCRIBING LEARNING EXPERIENCES FOR STUDENTS

The link between the curriculum plan and the instructional activity, as depicted in the conceptual model found in Chapter 1, is the process of prescribing objectives and learning alternatives for individuals or groups of students.

Prescription is intended to make possible the best relationship between an individual student and a curriculum plan. One way of conceptualizing this relationship is shown in Figure 5. *A* represents the curriculum plan, *B* represents the individual student, and *C* represents the congruence between the curriculum plan and the individual student. The left diagram depicts the situation that exists when the plan is totally unsuited to the student. In the middle diagram, there is a casual relationship between the curriculum and the student, as depicted by the area labeled *C*. This is probably the typical relationship between students and the curriculum in most school programs. The ideal relationship is represented by the diagram on the right, where there is total congruence between the curriculum plan and the student. The achievement of such congruence is dependent upon the prescription process. The process is aimed at providing successful curriculum and instruction experiences for the individual student.

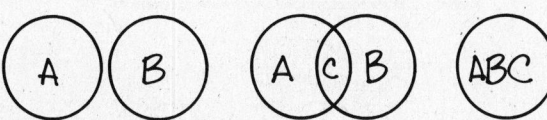

Figure 5. Relationship between individual student and curriculum plan.

Teachers and students can engage in many kinds of prescription activities. All should include provisions for regular and frequent student-teacher conferences. Conferences are essential for allowing teachers to check on student progress and to suggest changes in activities as needed. They may be scheduled in advance (e.g., through a weekly conference board) or may occur each time a student finishes a particular segment of work.

In situations where one teacher is scheduled with a large number of students daily, such as in a departmentalized secondary school, conferences are important but much more difficult to schedule on a regular basis. Some teachers have been able to find workable alternatives to holding regular individual conferences; for example, conferences might be held with groups of students working on the same objectives or unit of work, or there might be a sign-up board where certain blocks of time during the week are reserved for conferences, and students sign up when they feel a conference is needed. Conferences need not be long (sometimes five minutes or less) and need not be very frequent for some particularly self-directed students.

A few prescription activities are listed below. Other ideas can be found in the management chapter (Chapter 9) in this book. Prescription and management processes are closely related.

1. A teacher might write daily or weekly prescriptions (Figure 6) for each student and place the prescription sheet in the individual student's folder.

Barry		4-15-75
Name		Date

Prescription Complete science experiment... Number 20 on page 265.

Margie		5-5-75
Name		Date

Prescription 1) complete objectives 3-4 in "Cooking Unit." 2) Begin agreed upon objectives in "Needlepoint Package."

Jane	Math	5-15
Name	Subject	Week

Day	Objective	Alternative	Material
Mon	12	1) Complete pages 52-53 of text;	Text
		2) Play Math Bingo at Math Learning Center	Math Center

Figure 6. Daily and weekly prescription sheets.

2. A student might be assigned to a particular learning center from among those available. The prescription might be for learning alternatives found on specific task cards at the center (e.g., complete task cards 1 and 6), or for the learning center in general. If the latter, instructions for what to do and how to use the center would be available at the center.

3. Students and teachers can use contracts for prescription purposes. The student might contract to complete certain objectives and learning alternatives in a teacher-made contract, or he might develop his own contract and thus prescribe objectives and learning alternatives for himself.

4. A learning package, or certain parts of a package, might be assigned to or chosen by students. The objectives and learning alternatives found in the package would then become student prescriptions.

5. Many teachers strive to make available several learning alternatives appropriate for accomplishing instructional objectives. These varied alternatives can be used in prescribing by assigning objectives to a student and then allowing him to choose the learning alternatives in which to engage to accomplish the objectives. The alternatives might be found at learning centers, in teacher-developed contracts or prescription sheets, or in learning packages.

6. A management board can be designed for prescribing (Figure 7). The purpose of the board is to communicate what activities individual students should engage in for a particular time period. Students' names are placed on hooks according to where they are to spend their time.

7. Several commercially prepared or well-known national projects in individualized instruction contain prescriptive elements. Student prescriptions are based upon preassessment or diagnostic data or upon sequential skill development. Most of the programs provide prescription forms to use with students. Some programs use computers to provide student prescriptions, based on frequent individual test data.

Figure 7. Management board used for prescribing.

5

Creating And Using Classroom Learning Centers

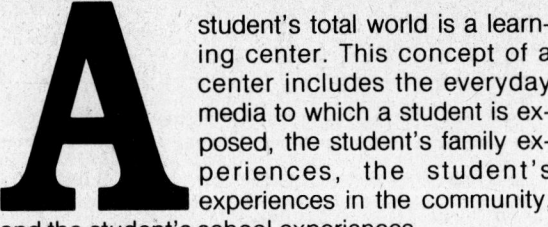

student's total world is a learning center. This concept of a center includes the everyday media to which a student is exposed, the student's family experiences, the student's experiences in the community, and the student's school experiences.

Even though this conception of a learning center is a valid one, it is too global for a discussion of individualizing instruction; therefore, rather than using the broad term *learning center,* we prefer to use *classroom learning centers* as a specific type of center for individualizing and personalizing curriculum and instruction experiences in a classroom environment.

Classroom learning centers are specified areas in the classroom designed by the teacher, by the teacher and students, or by students. They contain a variety of learning alternatives and media to enhance the development of concepts, themes, topics, skills, or student interests. Centers are means of achieving individualization and must be de-

signed for learners with varying abilities, interests, values, and learning styles. This definition applies to *classroom learning centers* as the term is used in this chapter; hereafter, the terms *center, learning center,* and *classroom learning center* will be used synonymously.

WHY CLASSROOM LEARNING CENTERS
The development and use of classroom learning centers is based upon beliefs about students and how they learn. Table 5 contains some beliefs about students and the implications of these beliefs for the development of centers.

TYPES OF LEARNING CENTERS
Basically there are three types of learning centers:
- Enrichment Centers
- Skill Development Centers
- Exploratory and Interest Centers

Enrichment Centers
Enrichment centers are designed to provide alternatives for all students in a classroom

Table 5

BELIEFS ABOUT STUDENTS	IMPLICATIONS FOR CENTERS
Students are curious and will explore without adult direction.	Develop centers for exploration of interests, subject matter, topics, and skills.
Motivation and interest are increased when students share in planning goals, content, and processes.	Have students participate in planning, implementing, and evaluating centers, and have specific centers for interest development and sharing.
Active participation and exploration in a classroom environment filled with alternatives facilitates a student's growth.	Alternative centers are desirable: skill development centers, interest and fun centers, exploration centers, interdisciplinary centers, reading centers, listening centers, construction centers.
Students are capable of making significant decisions about what and how they learn.	Center purposes and designs should contain a variety of learning alternatives and media to capitalize upon student abilities and desires for choice.
Student learning is enhanced by opportunities to apply information to new situations.	Learning alternatives in centers should help students gain and apply new knowledge and skills.
Students develop at their own rates and in their own styles.	Centers should offer a wide variety of learning alternatives (including media and materials); students will choose those alternatives most consistent with their own learning styles.
Cognitive development proceeds from concrete experiences to abstractions based upon those experiences.	Centers can be places where manipulatives and other learning materials for concrete experiences are easily accessible.
Excessive direction by adults leads to student conformity, apathy, and genuine disinterest.	Centers should maximize opportunitites for student self-management and self-direction based upon student abilities to be self-directive.
Students who lack success in school have negative views about most experiences schools have to offer.	Centers should have a range of learning alternatives to accommodate varying abilities.
Students learn to accept responsibility by making decisions and by accepting responsibility for those decisions.	Students should help in designing centers and have choices within and among centers.
Students are capable of monitoring and evaluating their own progress.	Teachers and students develop techniques for students to manage their own learning progress. Teachers help students understand the importance of choices and their consequences for learning.

engaged in a common unit of instruction. For example, a class could be engaged in a unit of study on the Far East. Enrichment centers could be developed to represent each country of the Far East. Students could work in the center(s) of their choice.

or

For the same topic, there might be related centers that stress content, process, or skills:

1. *Content Related Centers*
   a. The economics of Far Eastern countries
   b. The cultures of Far Eastern countries
   c. The products of Far Eastern countries
   d. Education in Far Eastern countries
2. *Process Related Centers*
   a. Preparation of foods native to Far Eastern countries
   b. Creative writing using pictures or artifacts of the Far East as story starters
   c. Drawing, painting, and model construction related to life in the Far East
3. *Skill Related Centers*
   a. Using maps of Far Eastern countries to develop map reading skills
   b. Reading stories from Far Eastern countries for developing reading skills

Enrichment centers provide a means for prescribing center experiences for individual students based upon teacher-student assessment. This approach assumes that the teacher assesses student knowledge and interest as a part of a unit of study and then assigns students to appropriate centers. For example, an English or language arts class might be studying the concept of "man versus nature." Learning centers could be developed using novels, short stories, poems, plays, or movies related to the concept. The teacher might assign students to the center containing the genre (e.g., poetry) with which they have the least experience, or students might be allowed to choose the center containing the genre they like best.

It is important to note that enrichment classroom centers are designed to be used following the teacher's introduction of an area of study to students. The centers help extend, enrich, and clarify a student's knowledge, skills, and values regarding selected curriculum areas.

Skill Development Centers

Skill development centers are designed for use following initial instruction in specific skills by the teacher. Instruction in skill development in an individualized program is planned mainly for small groups of students or individual students according to previous assessment. Once introductory instruction related to the skill has occurred, students spend time in centers where manipulatives, media, and other resources related to the particular skills can be found. Games (commercial and teacher-made) are often efficient and enjoyable ways to reinforce skills.

Many teachers maintain a skills progress chart which indicates the progress of each student in relation to skills to be learned. For example, a teacher might print skill names on library pockets and then glue the pockets on a wall chart in sequential order (Figure 8). Cards with students' names (Figure 9) would be inserted in the pocket corresponding to the skill being worked on by the students. The teacher could then tell at a glance which students were working on which skill and who was ready for instruction in a particular skill at any given time. This technique also aids in making learning center assignments. A student's name is moved from one pocket to the next only after he masters a skill, thus ensuring that he completes a needed skill before moving on to a new one.

More specific examples of managing student progress and of skill development centers are presented later in this chapter.

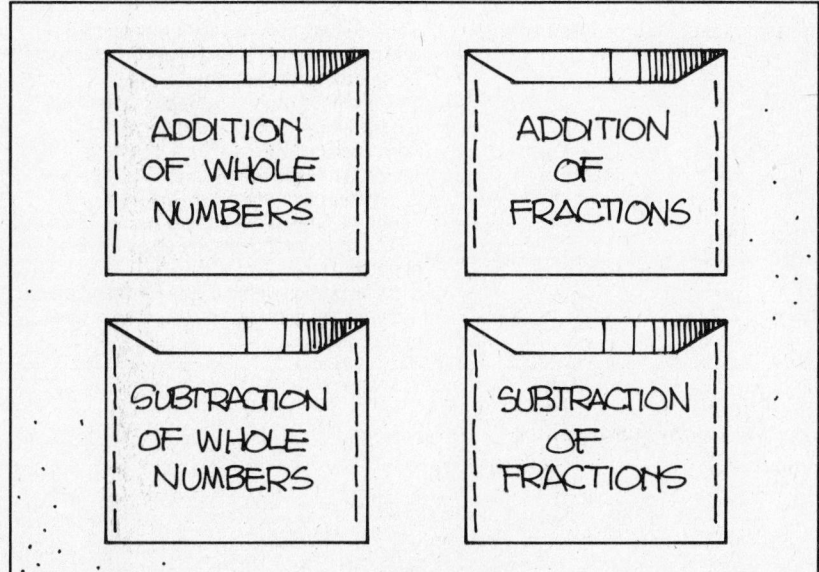

Figure 8. Sample wall chart using library pockets.

Figure 9. Sample pocket card.

Interest and Exploratory Centers

Interest and exploratory centers are designed to capitalize upon students' present and anticipated interests. The centers are designed also to introduce subject matter that is not a part of the general classroom curriculum. Many teachers arrange for students to develop their own exploratory and interest centers. Planning, developing, and evaluating centers provides students with opportunities for individualized problem-solving experiences. Interest and exploratory centers provide excellent opportunities for personalizing instruction.

Table 6
Variations on the Enrichment Center

TYPE	PURPOSE	SAMPLE TITLES
Single subject	For studying various concepts or skills within one subject area	Mathematics Spelling Writing Reading Geography Science
Multisubject	For interdisciplinary study, related subjects study, or for organizing centers in a classroom with limited physical space	Reading and Language Arts Social Studies and Language Arts Mathematics and Science Career Exploration, History, Geography, and Civics
Extension; improvements	For extending and reinforcing a concept, topic, theme, or idea related to classroom instruction	Individual Sports Team Sports Artists of the 20th Century The Jazz Age South America Sculpting Our Environment Gourmet Cooking
Project	For providing ideas, problems, activities, and materials for students to develop projects related to classroom instruction (any subject area or unit of instruction)	Model Making Scrapbook Making Drawing, Painting Collage Making Map Construction
Programmed instruction; kits and laboratories	For extending understanding of classroom instruction through programmed materials or learning kits and laboratories	SRA Reading Kits Language Master Bowmar Cassette Kits Reading for Meaning
Problem solving	For emphasizing learning processes rather than content	Such centers are typically interdisciplinary and contain open-ended problem situations for students to solve: for example, 1. Unfinished stories to be completed by the student who must justify his composition in terms of the beginning character development, plot, and theme; 2. Geographic facts (e.g., location of a country's largest city) about which students must draw inferences and make and test hypotheses; 3. Math games with multiple solutions which require an explanation of the solution used by the student.
Independent study	For an in-depth study or an individual project related to classroom instruction (topic usually elected by student)	All subjects

VARIATIONS ON CENTER TYPES

The three basic types of classroom learning centers discussed above—enrichment, skill development, and exploratory and interest—can and do have many variations. These variations have been identified by other authors and are practiced by many teachers in individualized programs; however, we believe that all variations can be categorized under the three types of centers cited in this chapter. The variations, their purposes, and specific examples of related learning centers are listed in Table 6, 7, and 8.

Table 7
Variations on the Skill Development Center

TYPE	PURPOSE	SAMPLE TITLES
Skill extension; skill improvement	For extending and reinforcing a skill or skills related to classroom instruction	
Single skill	For practicing and reinforcing one skill	Reading Graphs Sentence Writing Decoding Speed Reading Basic Carpentry Metric System
Multiskill	For practicing and reinforcing related skills; for application of interrelated skills	Preparing a Meal Planning Trips Mathematics Manipulatives and Games Reading Story Writing
Testing and checking	For taking and checking pretests, and for checking other assigned work (e.g., answers to practice mathematics problems)	All subjects

Table 8
Variations on the Exploratory and Interest Center

TYPE	PURPOSE	SAMPLE TITLES
Independent	For generating independent investigations not directly related to the planned classroom curriculum	All subjects
Hobby, enjoyment, fun	For encouraging students to develop and share personal interests; to allow students to engage in enjoyable activities not directly related to the curriculum	Photography Fishing Model Planes Needlework Painting
Career exploration	For allowing students to learn about and simulate various careers	Agriculture-Business and Natural Resource Careers Business and Office Careers Communications and Media Careers Construction Careers Environmental Control Careers Fine Arts Careers

COMPONENT PARTS OF LEARNING CENTERS

Depending on purposes, space limitations, and teacher and student personalities, classroom learning centers can be developed in all sizes and shapes, with the learning alternatives in them being limited only by the creativity and ingenuity of the persons constructing them. Nevertheless, in order to be most effective in contributing to the total individualized program, each center needs:

1. *A title and instructions.* These should be displayed prominently and discussed with the class before the center is used. The instructions:
   a. explain what students can do at the center;
   b. specify how many students can use the center at one time;
   c. specify what will be done with products created at the center.
2. *Necessary furniture, materials, and media selected on the basis of purpose for the center.*
3. *Learning alternatives.* Learning alternatives within centers should:
   a. be related to an objective or objectives, except in interest or exploratory centers, where there might be an objective for the total center rather than for each learning alternative;
   b. be diverse, ranging from easy to difficult and from concrete to abstract in order to accommodate varying interests, abilities, and learning styles;
   c. be highly motivational to encourage students to work independently (e.g., games, films, animals);
   d. be changed periodically so that students continue to have new choices;
   e. provide opportunity for students to apply what they have learned.
   Alternatives are usually written on task cards and placed in a container easily accessible to students.
4. *Procedures for Assessment.* As in any approach to individualizing, assessment of student progress should be based on the objectives for the student. Often students can check their own progress in centers, thus obtaining immediate feedback and freeing the teacher for instruction. Whatever means for assessment are used, they should be made clear to students in advance.

ARRANGING CLASSROOM ENVIRONMENTS FOR LEARNING CENTERS

Individualized classroom environments are created by many conditions and decisions. Creating conducive environments for classroom learning center activities depends upon:

- Furniture arrangement
- Storage and accessibility of supplies, materials, and equipment
- Space and location for quiet areas, activity areas, independent study, and small or large group instruction
- Space and equipment needed for display of student products and creations
- Free and inexpensive materials, supplies, and equipment needed to supplement school allotments
- Creation of needed materials, charts, storage units, display boards, room dividers, and screens
- Collection and arrangement of learning materials for centers

ALTERNATIVE ARRANGEMENTS

Learning center arrangements are not restricted to one particular type of classroom architecture. They can be designed for open space as well as for more traditionally constructed classrooms. Alternatives for arranging a typical classroom to accommodate learning centers are depicted in Figures 10, 11, and 12.

Learning center designs and storage areas also have different forms (see Figures 13 and 14).

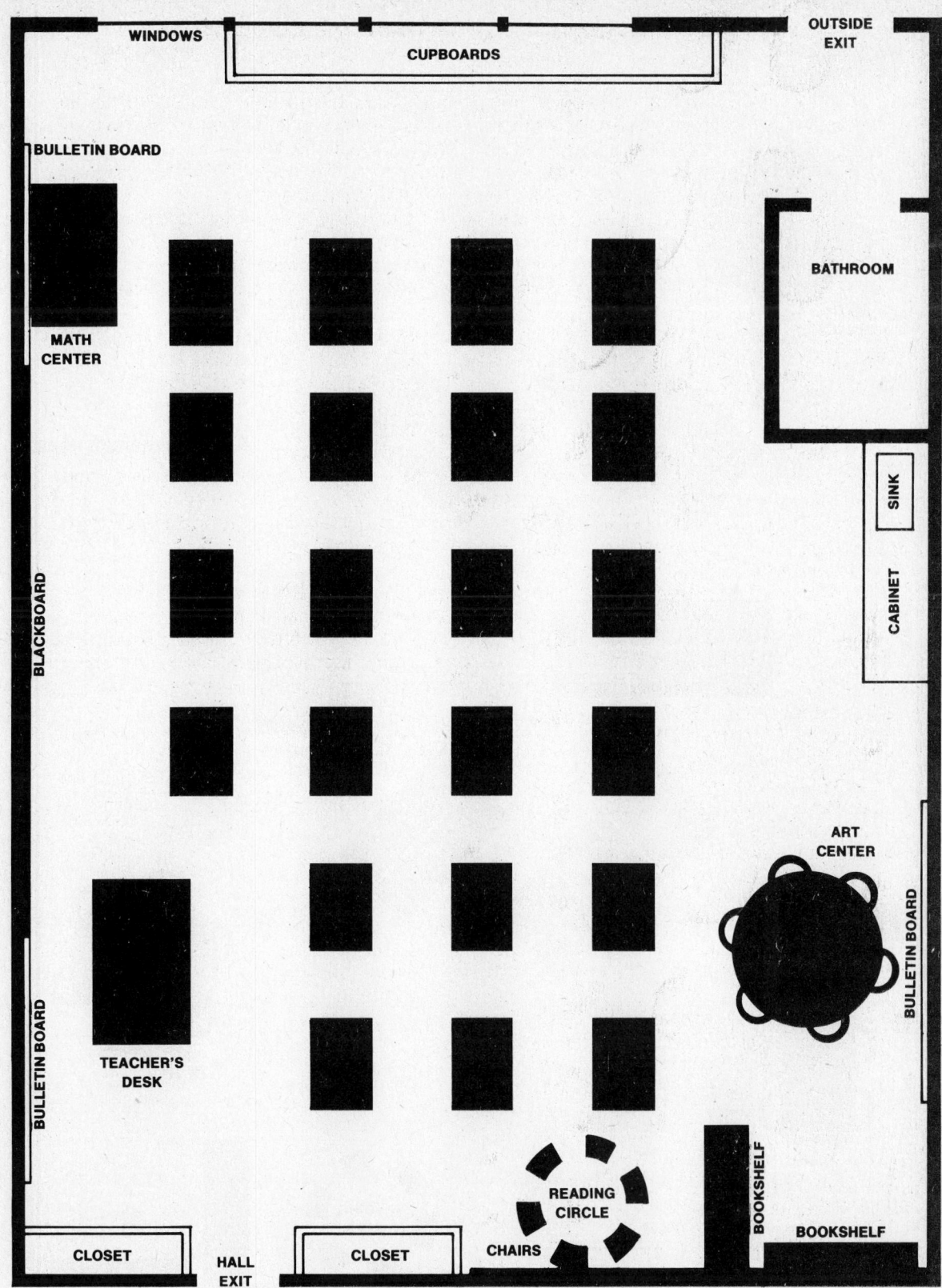

Figure 10

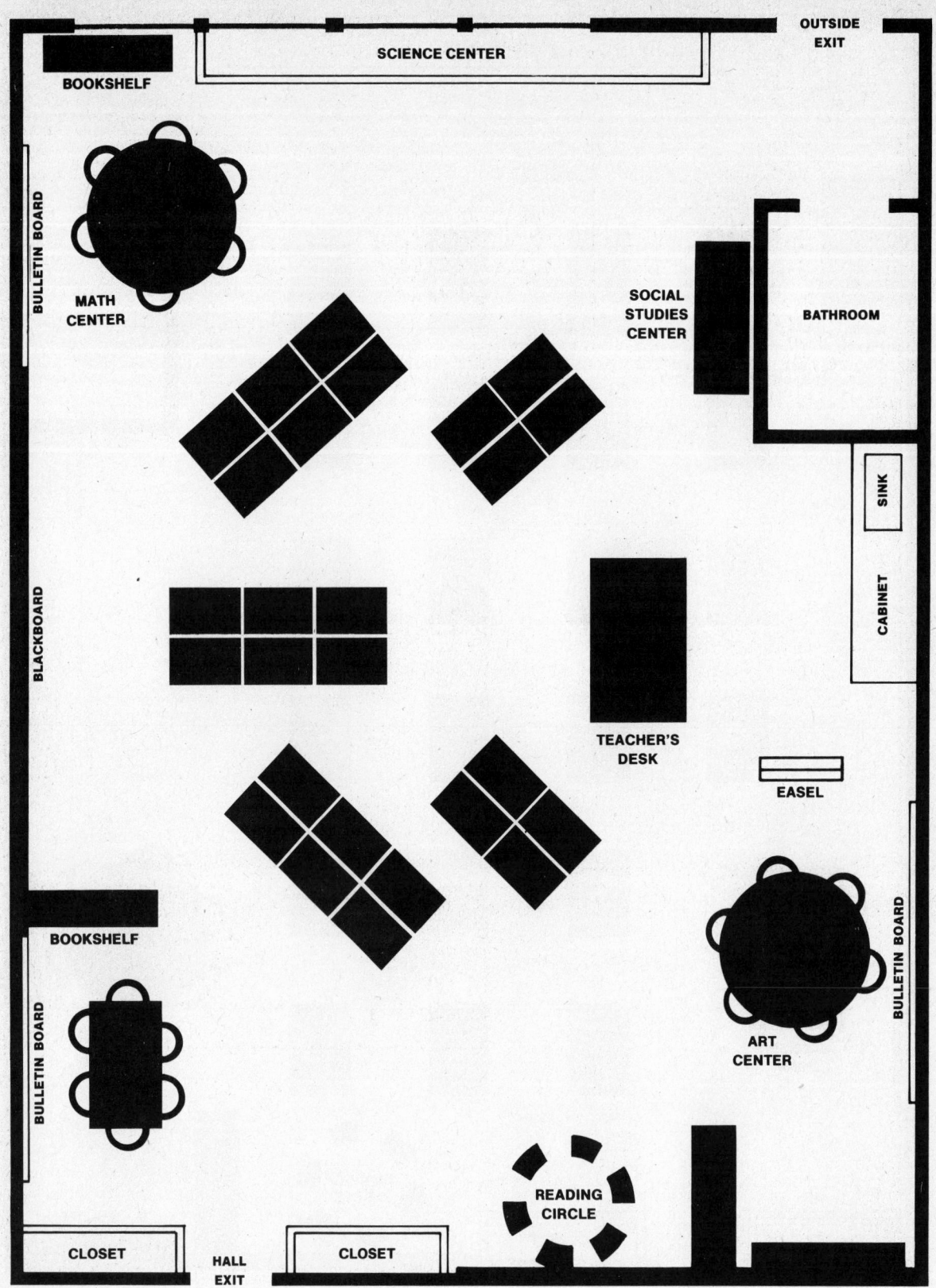

OUTSIDE
EXIT

SCIENCE CENTER

BOOKSHELF

BULLETIN BOARD

MATH
CENTER

SOCIAL
STUDIES
CENTER

BATHROOM

SINK

BLACKBOARD

CABINET

TEACHER'S
DESK

EASEL

BOOKSHELF

ART
CENTER

BULLETIN BOARD

BULLETIN BOARD

READING
CIRCLE

CLOSET

HALL
EXIT

CLOSET

Figure 11

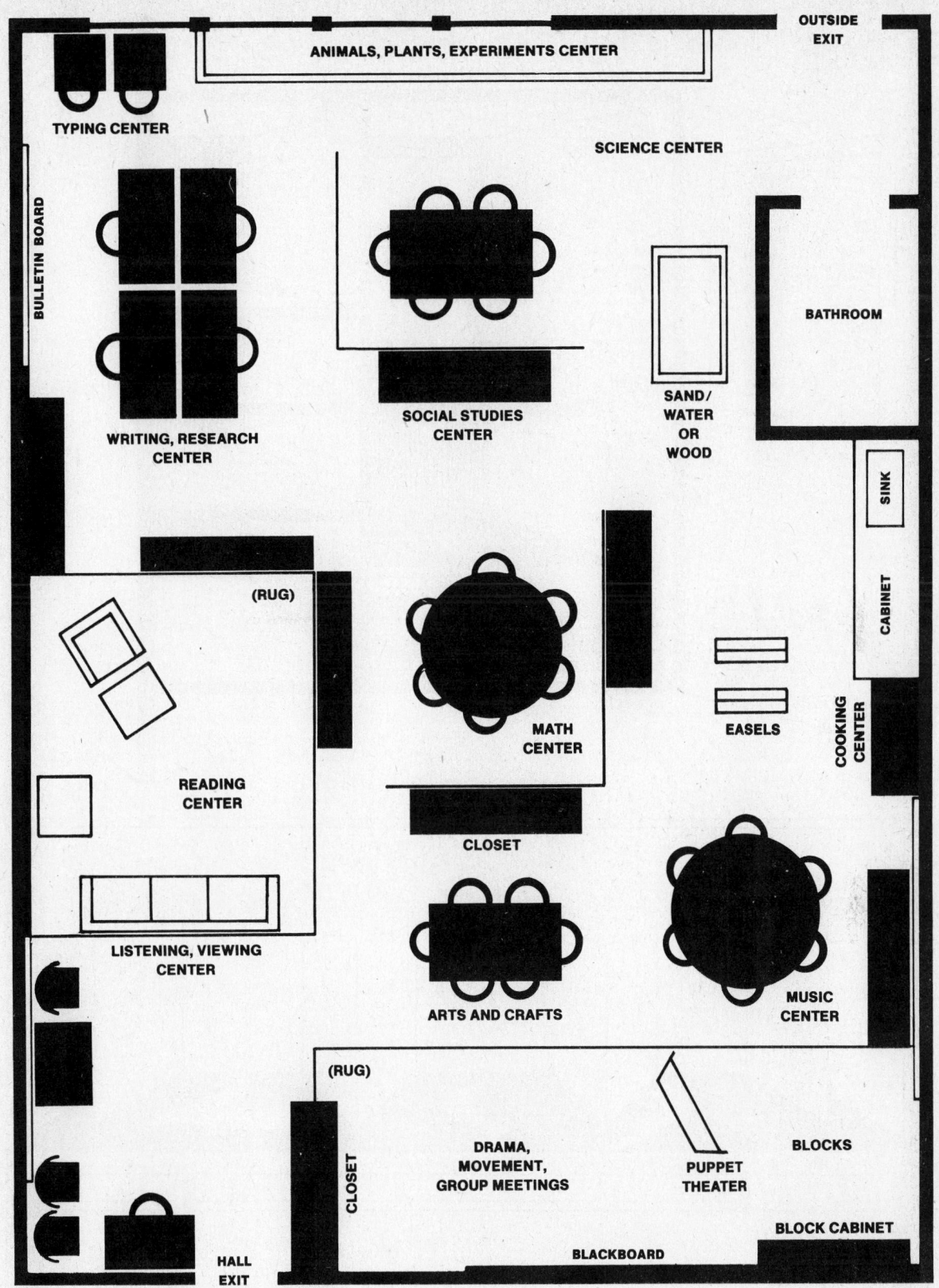

OUTSIDE
EXIT

ANIMALS, PLANTS, EXPERIMENTS CENTER

TYPING CENTER

SCIENCE CENTER

BULLETIN BOARD

BATHROOM

SAND/
WATER
OR
WOOD

SINK

SOCIAL STUDIES
CENTER

WRITING, RESEARCH
CENTER

CABINET

(RUG)

MATH
CENTER

EASELS

COOKING CENTER

READING
CENTER

CLOSET

LISTENING, VIEWING
CENTER

ARTS AND CRAFTS

MUSIC
CENTER

(RUG)

CLOSET

DRAMA,
MOVEMENT,
GROUP MEETINGS

PUPPET
THEATER

BLOCKS

HALL
EXIT

BLACKBOARD

BLOCK CABINET

Figure 12

Figure 13. Learning center designs.

62

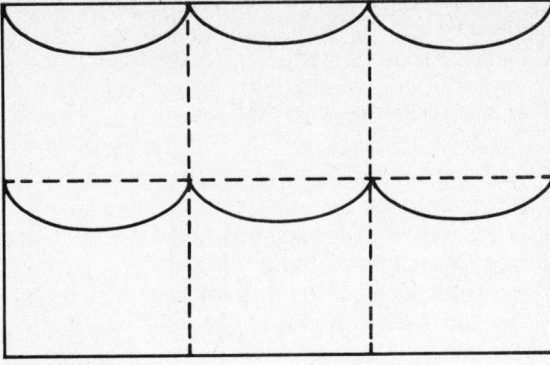

A. POCKETS.

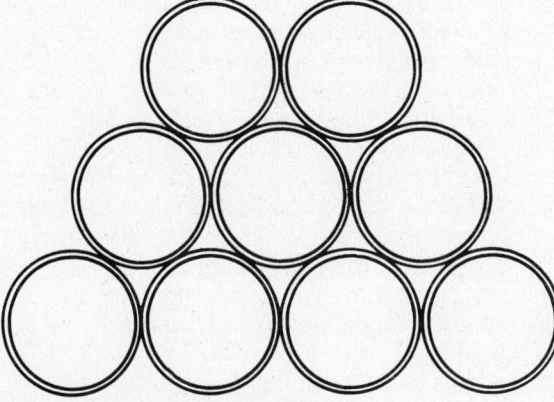

B. CANS OR ICE CREAM CARTONS.

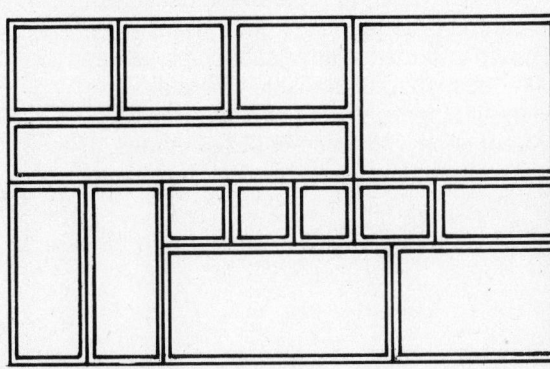

C. STACKED BOXES.

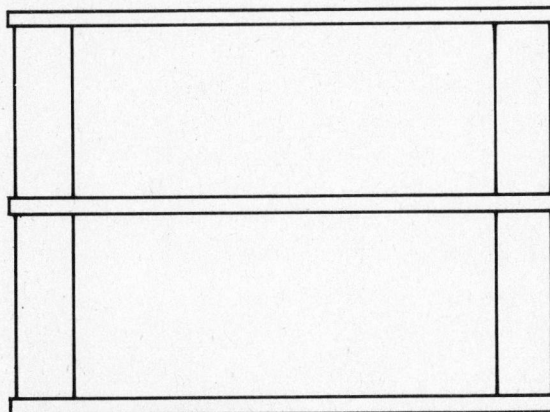

D. BOARDS AND BRICKS.

Figure 14. Storage areas.

EXAMPLES OF RESOURCES FOR LEARNING CENTERS

READING CENTERS
Comic books
How-to-do-it books
Newspapers
Magazines
Student writings
Single-copy books and
    magazines
Mystery books
Sports books
Animal books
Plant books
Adventure books
Romance books
Cookbooks
Art books

SCIENCE CENTERS
Plants
Leaves
Rocks
Animals
Microscopes
Binoculars
Magnets
Batteries
Light bulbs
Books on plants, animals,
    electricity, rocks, planets,
    stars, space travel,
    astronauts, famous
    scientists, inventions and
    discoveries
Liquid measuring containers
Dry measuring containers
Scales
Linear measuring devices
Aquarium
Terrarium
Bird cage
Simulation games
Compass
Stellar map

MATHEMATICS CENTER
Abacus
Mathematics games
    (teacher-
    made, student-made,
    commercial)
Pegboards
Paper money
Adding machine
Rulers
Slide rule
Measuring tape
Liquid measuring containers
Dry measuring containers
Graphs and charts
Graph paper
Stock market reports
Athletic team and individual
    statistics
Commercial advertisements
    with prices

CONSTRUCTION, ART, AND PROJECT CENTERS
Old magazines
Construction paper
Paste and glue
Stapler
Scissors
Hammer
Nails
Tacks
Sand
Wood
Plastic
Flour
Handmade looms
Easel
Paint brushes
Storage bins and pegboards
    for supplies and
    equipment
Paint (tempera, finger,
    watercolor, oil)
Clay
Trays
Sponges
Pipe cleaners
Soap
String
Yarn
Shoe boxes
Light bulbs and bottles
Model planes, cars, boats

SOCIAL STUDIES CENTER
Collection of old documents,
    music, photographs,
    greeting cards,
    recordings, clothes,
    firearms
Maps (local, state, national,
    international)
Globes
Time lines
Class time capsule
Newspapers
Magazine
Historical biographies
Autobiographies

COMMUNICATIONS CENTER
Creative writing ideas,
    including finished and
    unfinished stories,
    artifacts, photographs,
    music
Flash cards
Dictionaries
Thesaurus
Crossword puzzles
Scrabble game
Examples of various kinds of
    writings
Recordings
Lists of colloquial and slang
    expressions
Dialect materials
Workbooks
Programmed instruction
    materials
Individual learning packages
    for skill development
Nonverbal activity cards
Puppets

MANAGEMENT OF STUDENT PROGRESS IN LEARNING CENTERS

There are several factors to be considered in developing management processes for a classroom learning center: ages of students; student abilities for self-direction, self-management, and self-evaluation; type and purposes of the center; facilities available for record keeping; space for the learning center; learning alternatives available in the center; and others. These same factors are probably important to consider for any approach to individualization discussed in this book; therefore, Chapter 9 is devoted entirely to some overall considerations and approaches to the management of student progress.

Management of centers should address itself to such questions as: What students use which centers? When do they use them? How is progress toward objectives monitored and charted?

Ten ideas for consideration in managing classroom learning centers are:

1. Use a pegboard or board with hooks to display name cards of students who are assigned to or choose a center.
2. Post a schedule of the days of the week showing which students will be in the center on what days.
3. Make a chart with student names and indicate what days of the week and time(s) they are scheduled to be in the center.
4. Make a chart that indicates learning alternatives, tasks, skills, or objectives to be accomplished or which are available in the center, and list student names under headings as they complete objectives or alternatives.
5. Provide a file folder for each student for keeping management information.
6. Develop individual prescription sheets for each student. Provide spaces for: name of student, title of center(s) to which assigned, objectives to be completed in the center(s), learning alternatives engaged in, dates and times assigned to center(s), and dates objectives and learning alternatives were begun and completed.
7. Post charts or lists for students to sign for days and times they choose to spend in the center(s).
8. Have students keep personal journals in which they indicate what they are doing in centers. Journals can be used for self-evaluation, as well as for evaluation conferences between student and student, student and teacher, and student and parent, and among student, parent, and teacher.
9. Use shoe boxes, card files, jewelry boxes, tin cans, manila envelopes, or similar containers with center-related labels (e.g., title of center, center objectives, and center alternatives). Ask students to complete slips of paper or index cards with appropriate information (dates, times, problems) and place in container.
10. Design a chart, poster, or space on a chalkboard to identify on-going instructional modes in class (e.g., learning packages, contracts, or learning centers) and provide such information as relationships between modes, options available in modes, requirements in various modes, and sequence within and between modes.

CHECKLIST FOR CREATING AND USING LEARNING CENTERS

1. Examine the educational mission and decide upon the type of center.
   a. Is a classroom learning center appropriate to the educational mission or purpose? Is some other individualized approach more appropriate?
   b. What purpose(s) will the center serve?
   c. Is an enrichment center, skill center, or interest center best for the educational mission?
2. Specify objectives.
   a. What objectives of the classroom curriculum and instruction plan can be accomplished in the center?
   b. How do space allocation and design affect the objective to be included in a center?
   c. How do the objectives relate to the abilities and interests of the students?
   d. What alternatives are available for communicating objectives to students (e.g., posters, objective cards)?
3. Choose the optimum space and decide upon a design for the center.
   a. How much space can be allocated to the center?
   b. Is this the only classroom center or will there be others?
   c. How does the physical development of the students affect space consideration?
   d. What kinds of furniture and equipment are needed for the center?
   e. How does furniture and equipment for the center affect available space?
   f. How will the location of the center affect other classroom activities?
   g. Does the center need certain environmental conditions (e.g., plants in a science center need to be near light or windows)?
4. Secure needed furniture and materials.
   a. What furniture and equipment are needed?
   b. Are furniture and equipment available in the classroom? School? School system?
   c. Are there other local sources for obtaining furniture and equipment?
   d. Can students contribute, lend, or make necessary furniture and equipment?
   e. What instructional materials are needed?
   f. Are the materials available in the school system?
   g. What are other sources besides the school system for obtaining free and inexpensive materials?
   h. Can students contribute or solicit free and inexpensive instructional materials?
5. Design learning alternatives.
   a. Are the alternatives consistent with the purpose or objectives of the center?
   b. Are the alternatives explained in such a way that the student knows:

1) What to do?
2) Where to find information and what media to use?
3) What to do with results or products from the alternatives?

   c. Is there a wide assortment of alternatives to accommodate varying abilities, learning styles, and interests?
   d. Does the center include various media and materials (e.g., games, books, filmstrips, construction activities) to accommodate the intent of the learning alternatives?
   e. Are the alternatives written on task or activity cards and made easily accessible to students?
6. Write instructions for student use of center.
   a. How many students can use the center at one time?
   b. What can students do at the center?
   c. Are students assigned to the center or when can they use it?
   d. Are objectives for each learning alternative clear to students?
   e. Are all needed instructions for learning alternatives available to students?
   f. Are assessment procedures (including self-tests when appropriate) clearly established and available to students?
   g. What do students do with products made in the center?
7. Devise a management system.
   a. What alternatives are available for a management system for the center?
   b. Are there special requirements or materials needed for the system?
   c. Is the management system appropriate for the age and ability levels of the students for self-management activities?
   d. Does the system maximize student self-management and ease of record keeping for the teacher?
   e. Is the management system compatible with the evaluation philosophy of the school?
   f. What arrangements are necessary for the teacher and student to consult about student progress and evaluation?
   g. What scheduling procedures are needed in the classroom for the management system?
8. Set up the center.
   a. Are all materials, furniture, equipment, and other necessary accessories available for the center?
   b. When and how will it be best to put all the parts of the center together?
9. Orient students to the center.
   a. Are students well informed about purposes, procedures, and management of the center?
   b. Do students understand the relation of the center to other instructional activities in the classroom?

ROLES OF TEACHERS AND STUDENTS IN DEVELOPING AND IMPLEMENTING CENTERS

STEPS	ROLE OF TEACHER	ROLE OF STUDENT
1. Examine mission of center and decide on type.	Primary responsibility for decisions about type of center, when to change center.	Advisory responsibility.
2. Specify objectives.	Primary responsibility for decisions in skill and enrichment centers; advisory responsibility for decisions about exploratory and interest centers.	Primary responsibility for objectives for exploratory and interest centers; advisory responsibility for skill and enrichment centers.
3. Choose optimum space; design centers.	Assess classroom space opportunities and limitations; decide on maximum number of centers.	Help design centers for maximum efficiency and motivation.
4. Secure needed furniture and materials.	Assess what is available through schools; assess student contributions and make inclusion and exclusion decisions; guide in solicitation of free and inexpensive materials, furniture, and other accessories.	Contribute materials; solicit free and inexpensive materials, furniture, and accessories.
5. Design learning alternatives.	Primary responsibility for learning alternatives for skill and enrichment centers; shared responsibility for exploratory and interest centers.	Shared responsibility for learning alternatives for exploratory and interest centers; advisory responsibility for skills and enrichment centers.
6. Write instructions for student use of centers.	Primary responsibility except for centers developed by students.	Responsible only when involved in developing centers.
7. Devise management system.	Primary responsibility for efficient use of centers; primary responsibility for prescribing use of centers; responsibility for monitoring, evaluating, and charting individual progress toward objectives.	Advisory responsibility for management; shared responsibility for evaluating and keeping up with own progress and outcomes; shared responsibility for choosing learning alternatives for exploratory and interest centers.
8. Set up centers.	Shared responsibility.	Shared responsibility.
9. Orient students.	Responsible for thorough orientation.	Participate in orientation.

Examples Of Classroom Learning Centers

CURRENT EVENTS CENTER
Possible Learning Outcomes
1. Identifiying important people in the news.
2. Describing significant current events.
3. Identifying major parts of a newspaper.
4. Identifying and comparing major news media.

Center Learning Alternatives
1. Examine the photographs of important people in the news. Identify each one by looking in magazines, newspapers, or watching the news on TV.
2. Using the pictures of people in the news, sort them into categories such as sports, politics, military, and entertainment.
3. Make up at least one riddle about a person in the news. Put the riddle in the classroom riddle book or on the bulletin board.
4. Look at examples of caricatures and begin your own collection. Begin a scrapbook of your classmates' best-liked caricatures. Be sure to identify each one.
5. Draw a caricature of a person in the news. Put the drawing in the caricature pocket in the classroom newspaper learning center.
6. Listen to the news on TV or radio for one week. Make a list of the major topics discussed each day.
7. Begin a scrapbook of news important to you. Include magazine or newspaper clippings or news stories of daily events.
8. Begin a collection of cartoons about events in the news.
9. Draw cartoons about current events.
10. Examine a newspaper and list all the major sections, such as sports, comics, entertainment, and business. Make a chart or matching game showing each section.
11. Examine the collection of newspaper clippings and sort it into categories.
12. Call the local newspaper and find out if a group of students may come to visit the newspaper office and what they can expect to see.
13. Write a letter to the editor, a want ad, a weather report, a news or sports story— anything that might be found in a newspaper.
14. Begin a weekly newspaper for the class. Include all the important parts of a newspaper.
15. Take a survey to find out where most people learn about current events: newspapers, magazines, radio, TV, or another source.
16. Choose one current event and collect information about it from as many sources as possible. Prepare a short report.
17. Compare a newspaper with a major news magazine. How are they alike? How are they different?
18. Plan a radio or TV news broadcast to present to the class. Help plan a daily or weekly news show for the class.
19. Watch TV or listen to the radio and choose favorite news broadcasters.

Learning Resources and Equipment
1. Attractive sign for the center.
2. Many different kinds of newspapers.
3. Radio.
4. Television set (commercial and/or student-made using cardboard box and roller inside with student drawings).
5. Magazines.
6. Graphs and charts.
7. TV and radio schedules.
8. Photographs of people in the news.
9. Scrapbooks.
10. Newsprint and other supplies and materials for making a newspaper.

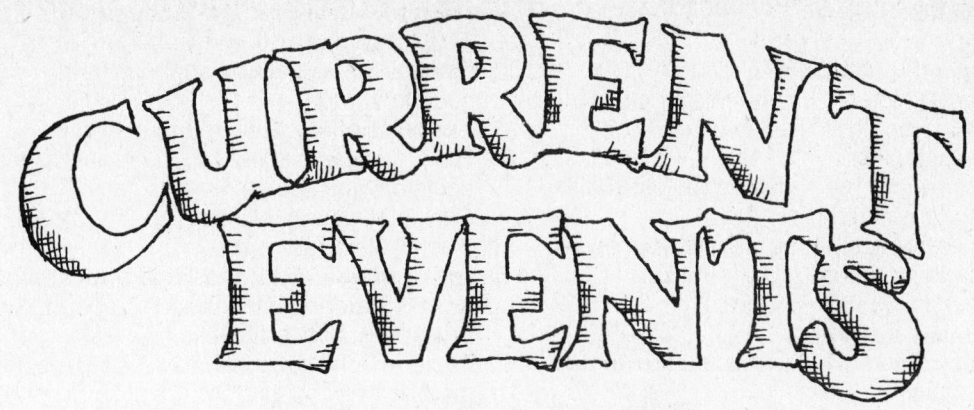

CURRENT EVENTS

At this center you can:

1. Listen to a news broadcast.
2. Read about current events.
3. Start a news scrapbook.
4. Do task cards.
5. Begin a newspaper.

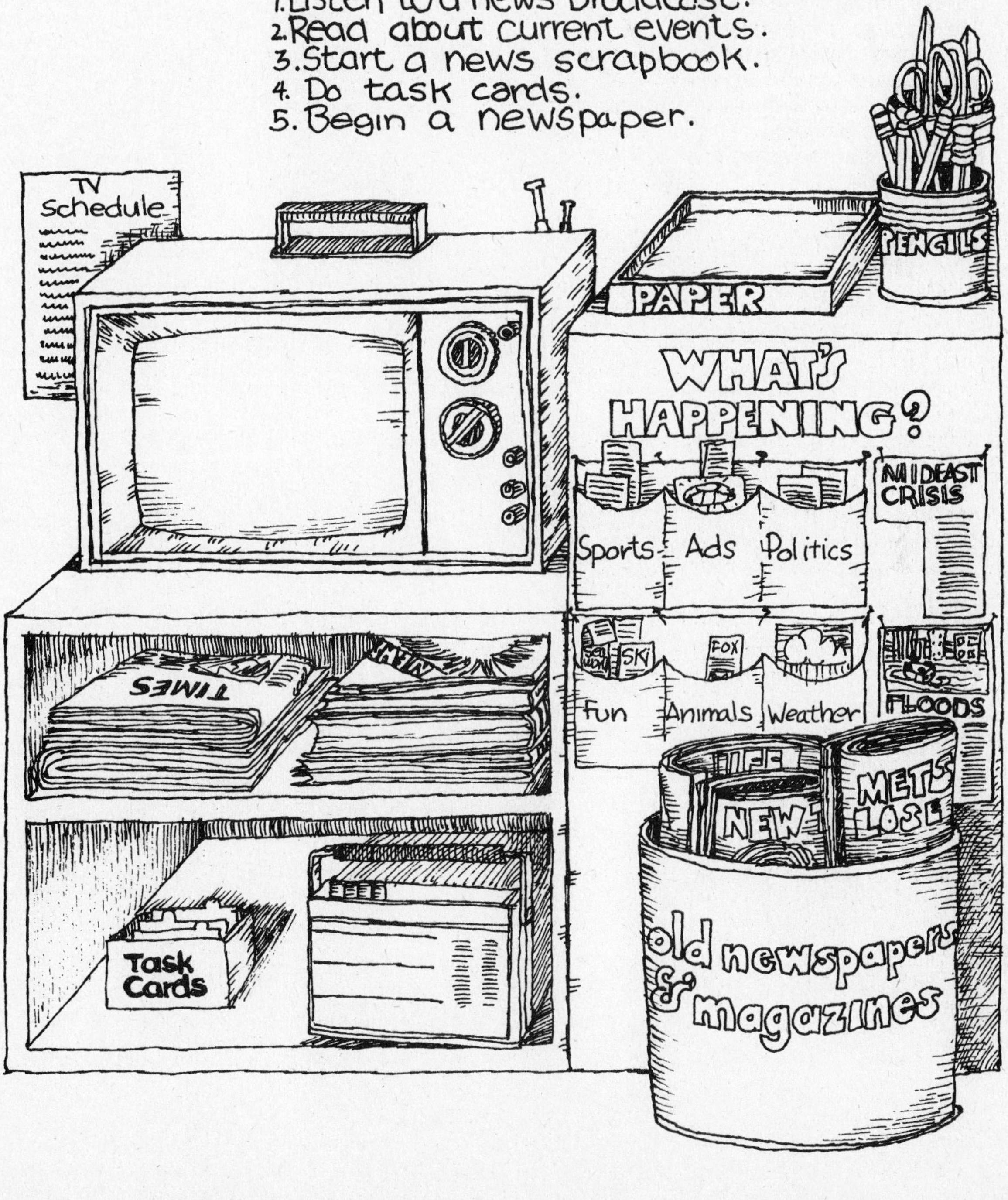

TV Schedule
PAPER
PENCILS
WHAT'S HAPPENING?
MIDEAST CRISIS
Sports
Ads
Politics
SKI
FOX
Fun
Animals
Weather
FLOODS
TIMES
METS LOSE
NEWS
old newspapers & magazines
Task Cards

SCULPTURE CENTER

Possible Learning Outcomes

1. Identifying (a) type of sculpture, (b) materials used, and (c) methods used in different sculpture examples.
2. Matching correctly the names of sculptors with examples of their work.
3. Creating original sculptures utilizing a variety of materials and methods.

Possible Center Activities

1. Create many different types of sculpture from a variety of materials.
2. View films and filmstrips; examine books, slides, photographs about sculpture and sculptors; examine actual sculptures.
3. Do research reports and booklets on sculpture and sculptors.
4. Play sorting, classifying, and matching games with sculpture pictures.
5. Invite a local sculptor to class to discuss and demonstrate his work.
6. Organize a class sculpture exhibit.
7. Do task cards.

Learning Resources and Equipment

1. An attractive sign for the center.
2. Task cards dealing with sculpture and sculptors.
3. Examples of actual sculpture of all types.
4. Films, filmstrips, books, photographs, slides on sculptors and sculpture.
5. Clay, play dough, plaster, wax, styrofoam, plastic, plexiglass, soap.
6. Variety of wire, metal and wood scraps, spools, dowels, cardboard tubes and scraps, straws, dried peas, and toothpicks.
7. Papier-mâché materials, newspaper, paste, paint.
8. Plastic knives, string, glue, nails, hammer, etc.
9. Old magazines, scissors.

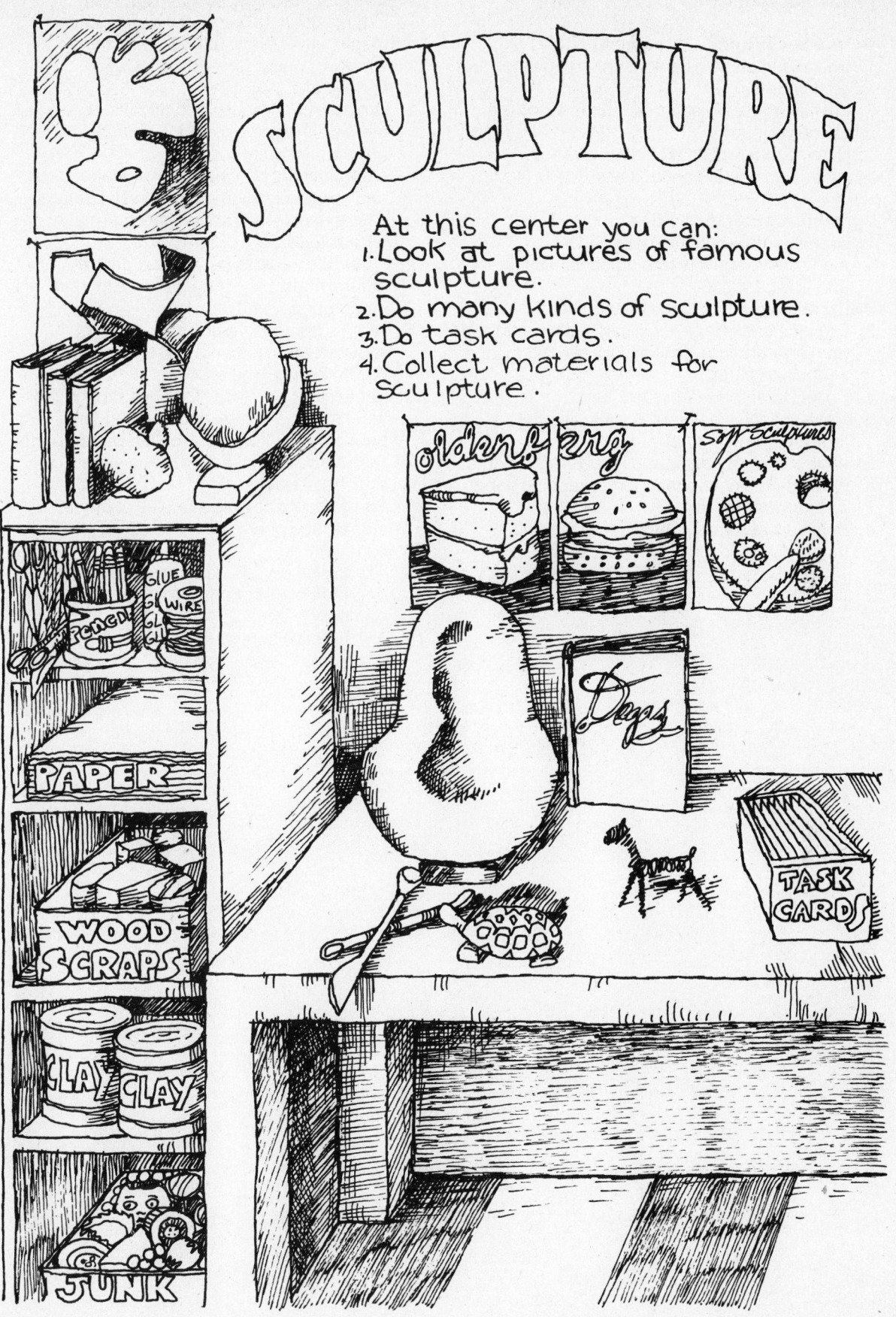

SCULPTURE

At this center you can:
1. Look at pictures of famous sculpture.
2. Do many kinds of sculpture.
3. Do task cards.
4. Collect materials for sculpture.

PRINTING CENTER

Possible Learning Outcomes

1. Describing and/or demonstrating printing techniques.
2. Identifying the object or technique used for various prints.
3. Naming different items that are printed.
4. Producing useful printed items.

Possible Center Activities

1. Examine printed items (newspapers, magazines, fabric, wrapping paper, stationery, greeting cards).
2. Experiment with various printing techniques.
3. Examine books, articles, films, and filmstrips on printing techniques, the history of printing, and famous art prints.
4. Collect examples of printed items.
5. Make collections of fingerprints, lip prints, footprints, and animal tracks.
6. Write stories or poems and illustrate with prints.
7. Print fabric, books, stationery, wrapping paper, and monoprints.
8. Begin a weekly or monthly newspaper or magazine.

Learning Resources and Equipment

1. Examples of printed items: newspapers, magazines, fabrics, books, stationery, wrapping paper, fine art prints, and fingerprints.
2. Examples of precut wood and linoleum blocks, lithograph stones, and metal newspaper type.
3. A commercial printing set of alphabet letters and numerals mounted on dowels, a stamp pad, examples of rubber stamps, and a typewriter.
4. Fruits and vegetables, various gadgets, natural materials, string, cardboard, glue, and inner tubes.
5. Various fabrics, papers, inks, brayers, scissors, glue, tempera and finger paints, plastic knives, and sponges.
6. Books, articles, films, filmstrips on printing techniques, the history of printing, and background information on famous art prints.
7. Task cards with directions for a variety of printing activities.
8. Bound books to hold samples of prints, stories, and poems, and records of printing experiences.
9. A resource person from the local police department (fingerprints) or the newspaper to visit the class.
10. An attractive sign for the center.

PRINTING CENTER

At this center you can:
1. Look at printed items.
2. Make many different kinds of prints.
3. Collect examples of prints.

FABRIC SCRAPS

PRINT

PAINT

INK INK

JUNK

IT'S ABOUT TIME CENTER

Possible Center Activities

1. Practice placing hands of clocks at designated times.
2. Using mimeographed sheets, let student practice reading hands on clock faces.
3. Move the big clock's hands according to the poster's listed times.
4. Experiment with the stopwatch: time friends on the playground.
5. Using the globe, discover that daytime in one part of the world means nighttime in another.
6. Think creatively by writing reasons people need clocks and a uniform time system.
7. Using a television schedule from the newspaper, arrange the clock hands to times different programs come on the air.
8. Using a bus schedule, examine times to leave or arrive at different cities.
9. Use worksheets to determine: How many minutes in one hour? In two hours? In one half hour? How many seconds in three minutes? In one half minute?

Learning Resources and Equipment

Poster board and markers
Clock
Alarm clock
Stopwatch
Hour glass or egg timer
Globe
Mimeographed sheets
Maps
Library books
Encyclopedias
TV and bus schedules
Task cards

What Time Is It?

Name _____   Date _____

Draw My Hands

Name _____   Date _____

4:10

11:30

9:35

5:00

12:00

1:11

IT'S ABOUT TIME

I have hands!
I have a face!
I can tell you
something!
Practice
setting
my
hands
to
4:05
2:30
10:50
8:03
12:13
6:30

4:45
7:07

Television
schedule

Bus
schedule

How many
minutes:
1 hour
3 hours
½ hour
60 seconds
How many
seconds:
3 minutes
4 minutes
½ minute

greenwich

Activity
cards

PLANT CENTER

Possible Learning Outcomes

1. Identifying the parts of a plant.
2. Identifying at least one function of each part of a plant.
3. Naming at least four factors influencing the growth of plants.
4. Matching different fruits with their seeds.

Possible Center Activities

1. Do a variety of experiments listed on task cards.
2. Examine examples of fruits, seeds, plants, and soils.
3. Collect examples or pictures of fruits, seeds, and plants.
4. Record experiments in graph, story, or picture form.
5. Make a terrarium.
6. Put together puzzles on the parts of a plant.
7. Look at books and filmstrips on growing plants.
8. Plant and care for a variety of seeds and plants.

Learning Resources and Equipment

1. An attractive sign for the center.
2. A resource person from a local nursery or florist to visit the class.
3. Materials to make a terrarium: glass jar, cover, gravel, charcoal, soil, plants, and water.
4. Puzzle of parts of plant; matching game with parts of plant and corresponding words.
5. Bound books to hold records of experiments, artwork, stories, poems.
6. Many examples of growing plants, seeds, fruits, and soils.
7. Pots, other containers, digging tools, and watering can.
8. Magazines, seed catalogs, paper of all kinds, crayons, pencils, marking pens, string, glue, scissors.
9. Books, filmstrips, films on plants and seeds.
10. Task cards with ideas for experiments such as:

    Light:
    Two similar plants; cover one with a paper bag. *Or,* plant with large leaves; tape a cardboard shape on one leaf.
    Water:
    Three similar plants; water one every day, one every week, one not at all.
    Soil:
    Plant seeds in clay, sand, gravel, potting soil.
    Air:
    Cover a leaf with petroleum jelly. *Or,* seal a plant up in a jar, leave a similar plant in the air.
    Root:
    Half submerge a carrot or sweet potato in tap water. Put others in distilled water, water with added plant food. *Or,* examine a nearby hillside; look at areas covered with plants and bare areas.
    Stem:
    Cut a carnation stem or celery in half lengthwise halfway up. Put one section of stem in red water, the other in blue.
    Fruit and seeds:
    Cut open various fruits and vegetables, examine the seeds, plant them to see what grows.
    Flower:
    Put two plants, one with flowers and one without, outside on a warm spring day.

PLANT CENTER

Things to do:

1. _____
2. _____
3. _____
4. _____
5. _____
6. _____
7. _____

TASK CARDS

FOOD

SOIL

PLANTS GROW BLOOM HOW TO

AQUARIUM CENTER

Possible Learning Outcomes
1. Identifying the parts of the aquarium and one function of each part.
2. Identifying each type of fish present in the aquarium.
3. Knowing books about fish.
4. Learning facts about the care of aquariums and tropical fish.

Possible Center Activities
1. Construct aquarium.
2. Observe fish.
3. Examine fish pictures.
4. Play word and numeral fishing games.
5. Play parts of aquarium matching puzzle.
6. Do fish art activities.
7. Look at fish books and filmstrips.
8. Write stories or poems about fish.
9. Listen to fish stories.

Learning Resources and Equipment
1. A variety of stories and scientific books on fish and aquariums.
2. Tank, glass top, pump, filter, charcoal, glass wool, heater, thermometer, gravel, plants, fish, food, and net.
3. A variety of papers (construction, writing, drawing, tissue, foil, cellophane), pencils, crayons, marking pens, scissors, glue, tempera, and finger paints.
4. A bound book to hold stories, poems, and artwork about fish.
5. A fishing game with large tag board fish bearing numerals from 20 through 40. The fish are in an old tank, have paper clips on their heads, and are caught with a magnet on a fishing pole.
6. A fishing game with small tag board fish bearing words. These fish are in a glass bowl and are caught with a net.
7. A puzzle matching the parts of the aquarium with the corresponding word for each picture.
8. Pictures of various fish to count, classify, identify, or use as inspiration for creative writing.
9. Filmstrips or loops and projector.
10. Tapes or records of fish stories and a recorder or phonograph.
11. A resource person from a local pet shop or aquarium to visit the class.
12. An attractive sign for the center.

MICROSCOPE CENTER

Center Learning Alternatives

1. Go to the lab cabinet marked "microscopes" and choose a compound microscope. When taking the microscope from its case, carry it with both hands. Hold the arm of the microscope with one hand and place the palm of the second hand under the base of the microscope. Bring the microscope back to the center. Set the microscope down gently with the arm pointing toward you and the stage away from you. If you are not familiar with the arm, base, and stage of the microscope, review them on the diagram in this center.

2. View the film loop, *Using the Microscope, Part I: Parts and Functions.* Next, turn to exercise 2 in *Biology Investigations.* Proceed to read Part I, "The Parts of a Microscope," and find each part in italics on your own microscope. Make a chart showing the parts of the microscope on the left side and each part's function on the right side. Turn to page 5 of *Investigations of Cells and Organisms* and check your chart against the parts and functions found on this page.

3. In this activity you will trace a ray of light from the window of your classroom, through the various parts of the microscope, to your eye. Turn to page eight of *Biology Investigations* and do the exercise entitled "Reviewing Principles."

4. Now that you understand the parts and functions of the microscope, it is time to actually use it. Observe one of the following films: *Compound Microscope,* or *The Microscope.* Now turn to page six of *Biology Investigations* and do Part 2, "Use of the Microscope." If you have no questions, go on to activity 5.

5. In the last activity you made a "wet mount" slide by placing a drop of water on a slide, adding the newsprint letter, and placing a cover glass over both the water and letter. This is the standard procedure for preparing a temporary slide for viewing under the compound microscope. To review this technique, turn to page 43 of *An Introduction to Field Biology* and read the exercise. Now view the film loop entitled *How To Make and Use a Slide.* If you understand this procedure thoroughly and have successfully prepared a "wet mount" slide, go on to activity 6.

6. Now that you know how to carry a microscope, how to focus a microscope, and how to prepare a slide for viewing under the microscope, it is time to learn how to determine the size of an object under the microscope. Turn to page 7 of *Laboratory Investigations in Biology* and do the exercise entitled "Measuring Microscopic Objects." You will find a plastic ruler for your use on the table in front of you. When you finish this activity go on to activity 7.

7. Choose two of the following four exercises found in the book, *Investigations of Cells and Organisms* to perform:
   Exercise 5, "Cell Structure—Onion Cells"
   Exercise 6, "Cell Structure—Elodea Cells"
   Exercise 7, "Cell Structure—Human Epidermal Cells"
   Exercise 8, "The Cell as an Independent Organism"
   You will find all the needed materials in the microscope center.

8. Now let's review what you have learned about the compound microscope by doing the self-instructional program entitled, "To Use a Microscope—A Self-Teaching Program." This material is located in this center.

9. This activity is a self-test on the use of the compound microscope. It is found on pages 50 and 51 of *An Introduction to Field Biology.* Take this self-test. If you miss any of the questions, go back and repeat activity 8. When you answer all of the self-test questions correctly, you may go on to the quest activities found in the "quest task" box. The quest activities are over and above your regular work. They do not have to be done unless you have an interest in doing them.

THE COMPOUND MICROSCOPE

PURPOSE: To introduce you to the compound microscope and to give you some practice in its use.

OBJECTIVES: You should be able to do the following:

1. Carry a microscope correctly
2. List microscope parts and their functions.
3. Compute total magnification of the various objectives
4. Measure size of objects under microscope
5. Prepare a "wet mount" slide and view it
6. Correctly care for the microscope.

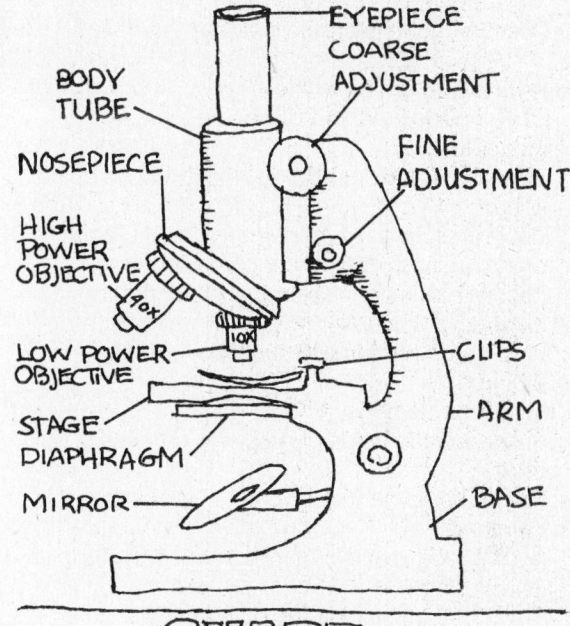

CHART

PART	FUNCTION
1. EYEPIECE	1. _____
2. COARSE ADJUSTMENT	2. _____
3. FINE ADJUSTMENT	3. _____
4. BODY TUBE	4. _____
5. NOSEPIECE	5. _____
6. OBJECTIVE	6. _____
7. STAGE	7. _____
8. DIAPHRAGM	8. _____
9. MIRROR	9. _____
10. CLIPS	10. _____
11. ARM	11. _____
12. BASE	12. _____

EGG CENTER

Possible Learning Outcomes

1. Describing or demonstrating three functions of eggs.
2. Naming animals that lay eggs and animals that do not.
3. Recognizing new words about chickens, eggs, and hatching.
4. Describing the hatching process.

Possible Center Activities

1. Observe the hatching of hen eggs in an incubator.
2. Take part in various cooking experiences using eggs.
3. Decorate hen eggs, paper eggs, and L'eggs containers using a variety of materials.
4. Record hatching, cooking, and decorating experiences in story, poem, or graph form.
5. Play matching game with animal and egg pictures.
6. Make candle eggs.
7. Put sequence cards of hatching process in order.
8. Play word game with chicks in L'eggs container.
9. Look at books and filmstrips about animals that lay eggs.

Learning Resources and Equipment

1. An attractive sign for the center.
2. An incubator, fertilized hen eggs, feed, water, a large box, and a calendar for recording the hatching process.
3. Sequence cards on the hatching process.
4. Pictures of animals and pictures of their eggs to match.
5. A L'eggs container holding tag board chicks bearing words about eggs, chickens, and hatching.
6. A tag board hen with matching words.
7. Hen eggs for cooking, other ingredients, an electric frying pan, other utensils, recipe charts for scrambled eggs, boiled eggs, fried eggs, deviled eggs, and other recipes using eggs.
8. Hen eggs, old candles, paraffin, pot, hot plate for candle making.
9. Hen eggs, vinegar, dye, wax crayons, cups, spoons for dyeing.
10. Construction paper, tissue paper, crayons, chalk, paint, fabric scraps, ribbon scraps, glue, empty egg cartons, L'eggs containers, cardboard for art projects. Pictures and/or examples for ideas.
11. Books and filmstrips or films about animals that lay eggs.
12. Bound books to hold records of hatching, cooking, and decorating experiences, poems, stories, and artwork.

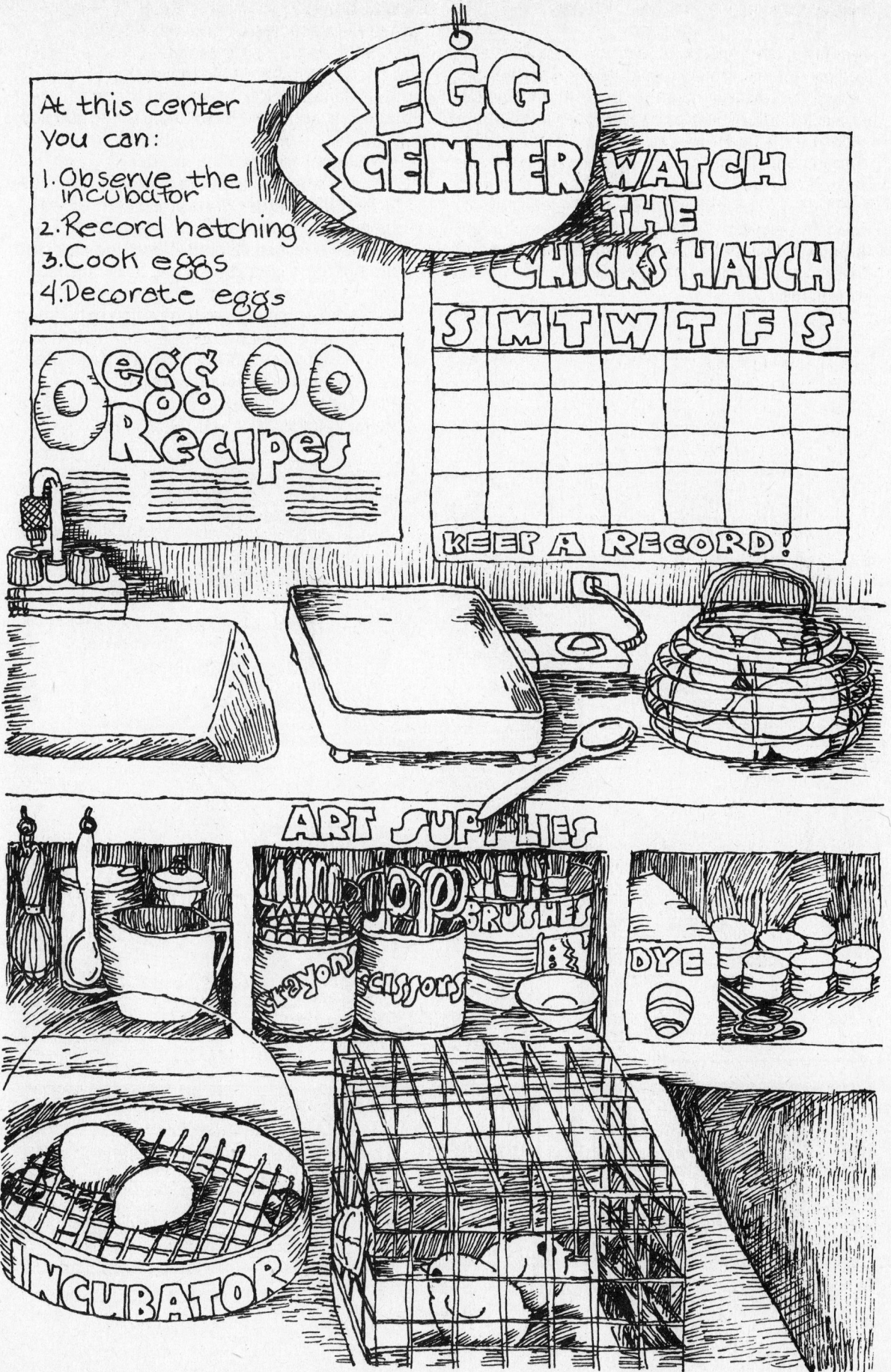

AMERICAN REVOLUTION CENTER

There are three groups of learning alternatives for this center. Alternative 1 (written in *black*) is designed to provide a common base of information for all students. The *blue* activities are intended to expose the student to a literary or audiovisual interpretation of one aspect or personality of the Revolution. They require some written output from the student. The *red* activities are the least structured. In carrying out these activities, the student must locate his or her own resource materials and develop a personalized expression of his or her knowledge.

Instructions

This learning center is about the American Revolution. Before beginning work at the center, you should read about the Revolution in your social studies book and take part in class discussions about the Revolution. When you come to the center
1. Do alternative 1 (written in *black*).
2. Choose one *blue* learning alternative from the activity task cards. When you have finished it, have a conference with your teacher.
3. Choose one *red* alternative from the task card file and carry it out. When you have finished it, have a conference with your teacher.
4. If you have time, choose one of the enrichment packages and work through it, *or* design your own enrichment activity and carry it out after consultation with your teacher.
5. Place all written work in your individual record-keeping folder.

Record-keeping Sheet for
The American Revolution Learning Center

Students' Names	Black Activity Completed	Blue Activity Completed	Teacher Conference	Red Activity Completed	Teacher Conference

★ ★

Contract
for
The American Revolution
Learning Center

I,_____ , Contract to complete the following activities in the American Revolution Learning Center:

1. Complete the *black* colored activity card.

2. Choose one *blue* colored activity card and complete it.

3. Have a conference with my teacher to go over the *blue* activity.

4. Choose one *red* colored activity card and complete it.

5. Have a conference with my teacher to go over my *red* activity.

Student's name_____

Teacher's name_____

Date_____

★ ★

Contract
for
The American Revolution
Enrichment Package

*I,*_____ *, have completed all assigned activities for the American Revolution Learning Center and have chosen to work on the enrichment package*_____ *.*
In working on this package I will do the following things:

1. Complete the assigned reading for the package.
2. Fill out Worksheet A and go over it with my teacher.
3. Choose and carry out a suggested activity or, with my teacher's approval, design and carry out my own activity.
4. Have conferences with my teacher when appropriate.

Student's name_____

Teacher's name_____

Date_____

89

Comic Consequences

Your name_____

Title of comic strip_____

1. What makes the story funny? _____

   _____

   _____

   _____

2. What is the main character like?_____

   _____

   _____

   _____

   _____

3. How is the character like real people? _____

   _____

   _____

   _____

   _____

   _____

4. Do you know anyone who is like this? _____ Who is it and how are they like this? _____

   _____

   _____

   _____

   _____

5. How would this story be told by you if it had really happened to someone?_____

   _____

   _____

   _____

   _____

   Would your story be funny? _____ Why, or why not? _____

   _____

   _____

   _____

   _____

READING INTEREST CENTERS

A. Free Reading

Possible Learning Outcomes
1. Creating positive attitudes toward reading.
2. Increasing vocabulary and speed through reading practice.
3. Increasing comprehension.

Materials Needed
1. Newspapers
2. Comic books
3. Adventure books
4. Short stories
5. Word puzzles
6. Several short and informative books and magazines on high-interest topics
7. Fashion magazines

Instructions
Here are several books, magazines, and other materials that might be of interest to you. Spend the next hour choosing and reading those materials that are of most interest to you. When you have finished, write a few notes in your journal about what you read.

B. Comic Strips

Possible Learning Outcomes
1. Teaching sequence as an idea.
2. Supplementing a study of stereotypes with comic strip examples.
3. Giving an example of story telling in pictures.
4. Encouraging self-expression and teaching interpretation.

Materials: comic strips.

Instructions
Below are several envelopes containing entire comic strips from the newspaper. The pictures are mixed up. Take the pictures from the envelope and arrange them in order to tell the story as it may have appeared in the newspaper. When you have finished, raise your hand and the teacher will come to check it for you. Then take one of the mimeographed sheets and answer the questions on it. Fill out one of these sheets (page 90) for each comic strip you complete.

C. Comparatives

Possible Learning Outcomes
1. Learning the concept of difference.
2. Increasing understanding and language ability through comparison.
3. Knowing English comparatives and superlatives.
4. Increasing self-expression.

Materials Needed: books and magazines.

Instructions
1. Using the magazines, cut out pictures that illustrate the following comparisons (You may use any pictures you choose.):

a. small	smaller	smallest
b. long	longer	longest
c. happy	happier	happiest
d. good	better	best
e. pretty	prettier	prettiest
f. fat	fatter	fattest

2. Have someone else at the center look at your choices while you look at theirs. Do you agree with their choices? Why, or why not?
3. Use your magazines to find comparisons other than the ones listed in the center. Write them.
4. Make comparisons of some things with which you are familiar. Do at least five of these. (*Example:* I like lemon cake, but I like angel food cake better, and I like chocolate cake best of all.)

D. Brotherhood—The Family of Man

Possible Learning Outcomes
1. Supplementing a social studies unit by giving thought to problems shared by all mankind.
2. Using terms and ideas concerning mankind.
3. Encouraging positive relationships among students.

Materials Needed
1. A copy of *The Family of Man*.
2. Three or four dictionaries.
3. Friendship poems.
4. Pictures of people of different races (posters and magazines).

Instructions
1. Look through *The Family of Man* and write your reactions.
2. Read the poems about friendship. Write your reactions to some of the poems, answering these questions:
   What is friendship to you?
   Who are your friends?
   How do these poems relate to your friendships?
3. Look closely at the posters and books in the center. We have in our class people representing different races. How are the races alike? How are they different? Why do you think these differences are there? What do you know about other races?
4. Use the dictionaries to look up the definitions of the words below. Then write a brief story, using these words to talk about the people you know.

   friend   mankind   loyalty   race   humanity

E. Ads

Possible Learning Outcomes
1. Knowing the importance of good word usage in communicating an idea.
2. Realizing the value of ads in our commercial society.
3. Increasing vocabulary and language skills.
4. Helping students become more familiar with newspapers and magazines.

Materials Needed: newspapers and magazines.

Instructions
1. Find several advertisements and answer the following questions about them:
   a. What words appear most often to help sell a product (*example:* guarantee)?
   b. What kinds of things are being sold?
   c. Who is trying to sell the items?
   d. Cut out one of the ads you have found and rewrite it the way you would sell it.
   e. Do any of these ads make you want to buy something? Why?
   f. What kind of information do ads give you?
   g. Which ads do you like best? Why?
   h. Which ads are most believable? Why?
   i. What is the advantage of a colorful ad with attractive pictures?

F. Famous People

Possible Learning Outcomes
1. Clarifying values.
2. Practicing expressing beliefs and opinions.

Materials
1. Newspapers.
2. Magazines.
3. Pictures.
4. Posters.

Instructions
Select one famous person from the people in the pictures and books in the center. Read about the person, then answer the following questions:

1. What has the person done to become famous?
2. What is the person like?
3. Why are people interested in her or him?
4. Did the person have to work hard to become famous? If so, what did he/she have to do?
5. Do you like and admire this person? Why?
6. Would you like to be similar to this person when you grow up? If so, in what ways?

Developing And Using Individual Learning Packages

This chapter is divided into five parts. In the first part, we present a definition of learning packages and list several viable characteristics of these packages. A model of the components of learning packages is developed in the second part of the chapter. Each component is listed and briefly described. The third part of the chapter is a discussion of distinctive approaches to the use of packages in the classroom and includes hints for making them successful. A planning guide for developing a package constitutes the fourth part, and the chapter ends with examples of learning packages for social studies (racial attitudes), ecology, sports (basketball), math (multiplication), spelling, and measurement.

When you finish this chapter you should be able to:

1. Define learning packages.
2. List and explain the components of learning packages.
3. List and discuss two ways of using learning packages in the classroom.
4. Develop a learning package that meets the criteria set forth in this chapter.
   a. Select an important skill, concept, or idea that can be used for instructional purposes in the classroom.
   b. Write instructional objectives appropriate for the skill, concept, or idea you have chosen.
   c. Develop learning alternatives that call upon a variety of resources and media and are consistent with the instructional objectives.
   d. Develop procedures for assessing (pretest and posttest) the individual student's work with the learning package.

A RATIONALE FOR LEARNING PACKAGES

Individual learning packages are designed to allow a student to learn a particular concept or skill, or pursue an area of interest at his own learning pace. They contain learning alternatives that allow the student to choose activities most compatible with his own learning style.

Packages are usually in printed form and are organized around a specific content area (concept, theme, topic, or skill). They proceed through a logical sequence of instructional objectives and learning alternatives designed to help the students accomplish the objectives.

Developing learning packages is a curriculum development activity that can be engaged in by one teacher, a team of teachers, or a systemwide curriculum development committee. Learning packages can be obtained through package banks and from commercial publishers.

Learning packages
1. Can be used by one student or a group of students.
2. Provide opportunity for students to plan their own time for learning.
3. Provide opportunity for students to develop concepts and skills at an individual pace.
4. Place emphasis upon students' self-management and self-direction.
5. Require students to choose alternative strategies for learning.
6. Promote creative and divergent thinking.
7. Can be used to help students clarify values.
8. Maximize utilization of existing learning resources, including textbooks, audiovisual materials, and human and community resources.
9. Enable teachers to use their professional expertise in a curriculum development enterprise.
10. Provide an inexpensive means for developing a classroom instructional program.
11. Allow the teacher to become a facilitator and manager of the classroom learning environment.

A MODEL FOR PACKAGE DEVELOPMENT

A learning package is a specific form of a curriculum plan; therefore, its format includes most of the component parts of a curriculum plan discussed in previous chapters in this book. The components are identified here to illustrate how they are applied to one of the alternative approaches to individualization.

1. *Title.* The title is a creative choice made by the individual or the group developing the package to give the learner the major idea of the package in a concise form.
2. *Concept, Theme, Topic,* or *Skill.* The identification of the organizing element of the package.
3. *Introduction or Rationale.* Students using a package will need to have a general notion about the package. The introduction or rationale gives students an overview of the following types of information:
   a. The major instructional purpose of the package;
   b. How the package will benefit students;
   c. Where the package fits in or relates to other experiences the students have in class;
   d. Instruction as to the use of the package if such information is not contained elsewhere.
4. *Instructions.* If there is a separate section for student instructions, some questions that might be answered in this component are:
   a. Should students use their own paper for writing materials for the package or will worksheets or activity sheets be provided?
   b. Should students give the teacher parts of a package as they are completed or wait until the total package is finished?
   c. How will the students' efforts be evaluated? Will there be a pretest?
   d. If other students are working on the same package, is it permissible to work with them?
5. *Instructional Objectives.* These are statements that indicate specifically what the student will accomplish upon completion of the package.
6. *Pretest.* The form of preassessment recommended for use with packages is a pretest. A pretest is optional with a learning package, depending upon the purposes of the package. If the purpose is to lead students through a sequential development of skills or concepts, then a pretest (or some form of assessment) is highly desirable. On the other hand, if the package is more interest centered, then the pretest is not crucial.

   The pretest is used to assess students' abilities in relation to instructional objectives. The pretest is administered before the student begins a learning package. If the student demonstrates an ability on the pretest to meet the instructional objectives, then he need not continue with the activities of the package; rather he might begin work on the next package in the sequence.
7. *Learning Alternatives.* Learning alternatives are the means by which students accomplish instructional objectives. A package should contain more than enough alternatives to accomplish the objectives.

   Often some alternatives are required of students while others are designed as optional choices. Alternatives should include the following information:
   a. What are students to do?
   b. What media should students use?
   c. What should students do with any product of the learning alternative?

Examples of learning alternative statements are:

   Bring 3 different leaves from trees near your home to class and add the leaves to the Leaf Bulletin Board. Using appropriate resource materials, identify the names of the trees from which you took the leaves and label your leaves on the bulletin board.

or

   Go to the learning station in our classroom on leaves. Select one of the books at the station and find pictures of 3 leaves you like. Draw the leaves, color them, and add them to our Leaf Bulletin Board. Label the leaves you draw.

   As many learning alternatives as possible should be created for each instructional objective. The more learning alternatives created, the more likely individual learning needs of students will be met.

   Learning alternatives for instructional objectives should also represent various modes of learning, such as
   a. Reading
   b. Listening
   c. Interviewing
   d. Viewing a film or filmstrip
   e. Drawing
   f. Painting
   g. Building
   h. Role playing
   i. Dramatizing
   j. Peer teaching

8. *Posttest.* The posttest is included at the end of the package and is derived from the instructional objectives. Items on the test should relate directly to the statements of instructional objectives in a package. Teachers who use pretests often use the same test for posttesting purposes.

Some instructional objectives are so stated that the evaluation is based upon the product developed in the learning alternative. For example, the instructional objective might be for the student to be able to write a paragraph with no more than three grammatical errors. One of the learning alternatives is to watch three situation comedies on television and write paragraphs about the type of humor found in each. The three paragraphs could then be evaluated to determine if any one of them meets the criterion of the objective.

For an item on a posttest this same objective might read: Go to the Creative Writing Center in our classroom and choose one of the 25 pictures in the pocket labeled Story Starters. Write a paragraph about the picture you have chosen.

Developers of learning packages have used a variety of formats and a variety of names (e.g., Unipac, LAP, IIU), but four of the parts listed above are essential to any package. They are:

1. identification of concept, theme, topic, or skill
2. instructional objectives
3. learning alternatives
4. assessment

Examples of learning packages at the end of this chapter further illustrate each component.

USING LEARNING PACKAGES TO INDIVIDUALIZE INSTRUCTION

Learning packages can be used in an individualized program both for enrichment and for teaching those concepts and skills a school faculty believes to be essential for their students.

Packages Used for Enrichment

Using packages for enrichment may suggest that the total group of students in a teacher's assigned class is engaged in a common unit of instruction. Let us assume that the unit deals with the theme of war as a form of conflict. Packages can be written to include topics related to the theme. For example: *Similarities and Differences Between World War II, the Korean Conflict, and the Vietnam War; Changing Concepts of War Heroes; Morality of War;* and *Economic Bases of Wars.* Similarly, if a class were doing a unit on ecology, packages could be written on *Conflict Between Energy and Ecology; Role and Responsibility of Individuals for Saving the Environment;* and *Home, School, and Community as Environments.* This approach to the use of packages enables students to select areas they wish to study according to their own interests and needs. The package supplements and enriches the indivdiual student's study of the theme or concept. In addition, packages used for enrichment can be included in an independent study program.

Packages Used to Develop Essential Skills and Concepts

Perhaps the most common way of preparing and using learning packages is to base them on a series of concepts, themes, topics, or skills related to a subject or curriculum area and to use the packages as the basis of the planned curriculum. These packages may be sequential, as for example those developed for mathematics instruction. Others may not require sequential development, as might be true in a language arts classroom. To illustrate, let us consider the following list of suggested learning package titles:

MATHEMATICS	LANGUAGE ARTS	SCIENCE
1. Addition of Whole Numbers	1. American Short Stories	1. Astronomy
2. Subtraction of Whole Numbers	2. Making a Film	2. Botany
3. Multiplication of Whole Numbers	3. Creative Writing	3. Environmental Studies
4. Division of Whole Numbers	4. Humor in Poetry	4. Meteorology
5. Introduction to Fractions	5. Who Am I?	5. Microscopic Biology
6. Addition and Subtraction of Fractions	6. Transformational Grammar	6. Oceanography
7. Multiplication and Division of Fractions	7. Letter Writing	7. Practical Chemistry
8. Introducing Decimals	8. Freedom	8. Physiology
9. Addition and Subtraction of Decimal Fractions	9. Courage	9. Special Geology
10. Multiplication and Division of Decimal Fractions	10. Man and Nature	10. Maps and Globes

PLANNING GUIDE FOR DEVELOPING LEARNING PACKAGES

1. Learning package title: _____

2. Concept, theme, topic, skill: _____

3. Introduction or rationale: _____
   _____
   _____

4. Instructions: _____
   _____
   _____

5. Instructional objectives: _____
   _____
   _____

6. Pretest: _____
   _____
   _____
   _____

7. Learning Alternatives:

Instructional Objective Number 1:

   (1.1) _____

   (1.2) _____

   (1.3) _____

   (1.4) _____

   (1.5) _____

Instructional Objective Number 2:

   (2.1) _____

   (2.2) _____

   (2.3) _____

   (2.4) _____

   (2.5) _____

Instructional Objective Number 3:

(3.1) _____ THIS CARD IS FROM ONE AT A TIME © 1976 GOODYEAR PUBLISHING COMPANY INC.
_____

(3.2) _____
_____

(3.3) _____
_____

(3.4) _____
_____

(3.5) _____
_____

Instructional Objective Number 4:

(4.1) _____
_____

(4.2) _____
_____

(4.3) _____
_____

(4.4) _____
_____

(4.5) _____
_____

8. Posttest: _____
_____
_____
_____
_____

We can observe from the listings that the titles in mathematics follow a sequential outline of development. In contrast, the titles in English or language arts and in science follow an interest-centered or topical outline.

When packages are developed in either sequential order or around interests, themes, topics, or skill areas, they can be used as the main basis for organizing curriculum and instruction experiences in the school or classroom. Such an approach provides for organizing instruction on the basis of packages developed by one teacher, a group of teachers in one school, a systemwide package development project, or by purchasing commercially prepared packages.

Let us refer again to the package titles listed above:

1. In an arithmetic or mathematics class, the suggested titles would represent the basal mathematics program. Other titles or materials might be used for enrichment purposes. Students would work with the packages in the indicated order at their own speed. The packages would contain pretests to enable the student and teacher to know whether or not the student needed the package. Need would be based upon previously stated criteria which indicate acceptable levels of knowledge on the pretest. With students working at their own rates under the guidance of a teacher, some would be far along in the sequence of titles (Introduction to Fractions, for example), while others would be somewhere else on the sequence continuum.

2. In the language arts and science classes, the titles would represent basic curriculum plans. Other packages or activities could be developed for enrichment or to meet a unique need or interest of one or more students. In the list of packages given above for science and language arts, the topics and skills are neither listed nor developed sequentially. Teachers and students could approach the use of the materials in several different ways; for instance,

   a. Through an assessment of interests, the teacher could prescribe the packages that best meet individual student interests.

   b. Through an assessment of skills, the teacher could prescribe packages that help students gain needed skills.

   c. Students could have freedom to learn from any of the packages by freely choosing those of interest and/or need to them.

OTHER HINTS FOR MAKING PACKAGES SUCCESSFUL

1. If you are using packages for the first time, introduce them carefully and slowly. Start with one package, perhaps even with only a few students. Develop a package for one unit or topic, and use it in place of the unit.

2. A package communicates intent and feelings. Make the package as personal as possible for the student. If you write the package, strive to make your personality come through in your writing. Avoid using impersonal statements such as "the student will," or "the teacher will." Instead, use "you," or "you and your friends or classmates."

3. Use illustrations, cartoons, funny drawings, jokes, pictures, and quotations when appropriate.

4. Packages for young students or for students with reading difficulties will need to be designed to include many pictures and illustrations and simple or single words. Someone will probably need to read directions or learning alternatives to the students. Some package information can be tape-recorded or explained by another student.

5. Be sensitive to the probabilities of students' being successful with a package. When deciding on the length of packages, consider (a) the experience and ability of the students in self-direction; and (b) how quickly successes or rewards (i.e., completion of the package) are required by the students. If the package is too long, many students might become discouraged or disinterested.

6. The development of enough learning packages to carry on a classroom program takes time. If one teacher is developing packages for one class of students, package development can be a time-consuming, though rewarding, experience. Working with other teachers to develop and use packages probably results in more efficient use of teacher time and in more creative, practical packages.

Examples Of Learning Packages

THE BLACK AND WHITE PROBLEM IN AMERICA

Introduction

This learning package is designed to acquaint you with the attitudes of blacks and whites toward each other in the past and in the present. It also will introduce you to the nature of the black experience in America through investigation of slavery and the dynamics of the black ghetto. Because you will be the determiner of the system of race relations in the future, this package also will help you to define your attitudes toward persons of the opposite race. More important, by completing this package you may gain greater understanding of the people you encounter each day.

This package serves as your social studies unit on race relations. As you progress through the activities, you may discover certain activities are not included that may prove helpful. Feel free to include these in the package and share them with fellow classmates and the teacher.

Instructions

The package contains five major objectives for you to complete. For each objective there are various activities you can perform to help you achieve the objective. You will be told how many activities to choose to do but not which activities to choose. Choose those that will broaden your understanding the most.

Each objective describes the manner in which you will demonstrate your accomplishment of the objective. When you have demonstrated your completion, indicate that to the teacher and show your completed work. After completing a conference on the work, you may proceed to the next objective.

Work on the objectives in the order they appear in the package.

You will need to supply your own writing materials. All articles, books, and tapes referred to in the learning alternatives can be found in our Race Relations Learning Center.

Objectives

1. You will be able to list and provide illustrations for at least four categories of white responses to the question "What place does the black man have in society?"
2. You will be able to list and provide illustrations for at least four categories of black responses to the question "What place does the black man have in society?"
3. You will demonstrate your understanding of slavery by giving three reasons to support your answer to the question "Was slavery harsh or kind?"
4. You will be able to define the concept "ghetto" and depict the nature of ghetto life by answering the question "What happens in a ghetto day?"
5. You will define your present position regarding race relations by answering the question "What is my relationship to the opposite race?"

NOTE: Any answers for the objectives may be either written or verbal and shared with an audience consisting of at least the teacher and anyone else the student wishes.

Activities

Objective Number 1: Complete any five of the following nine activities. Keep a notebook of your results.

(1.1) Read *The Klansman* by Thomas Dixon. Make a list of the white responses to blacks you see and try to distinguish among them as to common themes. If you choose this activity, 1.2 may be repetitive.

(1.2) View the film *Birth of a Nation.* Arrangements have been made to have it shown in the school media center. Treat the responses you see in the film in the same way listed in activity 1.1.

(1.3) View the TV show "All in the Family" and make a list of the attitudes toward blacks you hear. What do these attitudes convey about the black's place in society?

(1.4) Read *Intruder in the Dust* by William Faulkner. How does the lawyer see Lucas? How do most of the people of Jefferson see Lucas? How does the sheriff see Lucas? You may want to write down your answers.

(1.5) Read newspaper articles containing arguments for and against segregation in 1900, and for and against busing in the 1970s. Compare the arguments and see if there are any similarities in the attitudes toward race behind the arguments. Make a note of your observations.

(1.6) Interview white people you know—family (if white), friends, and even civic leaders—and ask them what the black's place in society is. Keep a record of your findings.

(1.7) Read the book *Black Like Me.* Contrast the ways the white people treat the author according to what color his skin is. Keep a list of the differences you see. Find other classmates reading this book and compare lists.

(1.8) View the movie *Guess Who's Coming to Dinner?* This movie is also available in the media center. What responses to the question asked in the title of the movie do you see? List them.

(1.9) Read the James Monroe article. What proposal is suggested? Why?

Objective Number 2: Complete any five of the following nine activities. Keep a notebook of the results.

(2.1) Read the essay written by Booker T. Washington. What is he saying about the jobs blacks want? What place in society is he ready to occupy?

(2.2) Read the essay by W. E. B. du Bois. How does he differ from Booker T. Washington? (If you read Washington; if not, think of what du Bois is saying blacks should strive for.)

(2.3) Listen to the tape of Martin Luther King. What is his goal? What will the achievement of this goal do for blacks? Does he include whites in his vision?

(2.4) Read the essay by Marcus Garvey. What solution does he propose? What effect would this have on race relations?

(2.5) Conduct interviews with family (if black), close friends, and even civic leaders to see how they respond to the question "What place do blacks have in society?"

(2.6) Read the novel *Wife of His Youth* by Charles Chestnutt. What color should blacks be to make it in society? What hope is there for "black" blacks?

(2.7) Read a copy of the *Black Panther* newsmagazine. What goals does it seem to advocate for blacks? How might these goals be achieved? What is your reaction to the goals? To the means for achieving them?

(2.8) Read *The Autobiography of Malcolm X*. How many different positions do you see Malcolm take on (a) who he is, (b) who white people are, (c) what blacks must do to get their proper place in society, (d) what that proper place is?

(2.9) Read Ralph Ellison's *Invisible Man*. What did white people expect of him? What were his responses?

Objective Number 3: Complete four of the following seven activities. Keep a notebook of your results.

(3.1) Read the book or view the film *The Autobiography of Miss Jane Pittman*. What are you told about slavery? How did it affect families? What talents did a slave need to have?

(3.2) Read *The Confessions of Nat Turner*. This book is not accurate history, but it is revealing of how the slave looked at slavery. What objections to slavery did Turner have? How did he respond to slavery? Did others feel the same way he did? Why?

(3.3) Read the newspaper accounts of slave incidents. Why were whites so afraid of insurrection? Why would slaves insurrect?

(3.4) View the two documentary films on slavery. What was the daily life of a slave like? What comforts did slaves have? What discomforts did they endure?

(3.5) Listen to the prepared tape of slave and slave-owner letters. How did the two views of slavery differ? How did the two views of slavery resemble each other? How do you account for the fact that not all slaves agree, nor all slave owners?

(3.6) Devise a short scene with four or five classmates which depicts what life as a slave might have been like, and present the scene to the class. Arrange a convenient time for your presentation.

(3.7) Read the article by V. B. Phillips. Why does he say slavery was kind? How does it relate to what you have seen about slavery?

Objective Number 4: Do one activity from Numbers 4.1 and 4.2. Do one activity from Numbers 4.3 and 4.4. Do one activity from Numbers 4.5 and 4.6. Keep your results in a notebook.

(4.1) Watch the "Cosby Kids" on TV. What does the neighborhood look like? How do their experiences differ from yours? How accurate do you think the show is?

(4.2) Watch "Sanford and Son," "Good Times," or "The Jeffersons" on TV. What does the neighborhood look like? How do their experiences differ from yours? How accurate do you think the show is?

(4.3) Read *Manchild in the Promised Land* by Claude Brown. Compare this book to the show you watched in 4.1 or 4.2. How do Claude Brown's experiences differ from yours, or the ones depicted on the TV shows? Which do you feel is closer to the reality of the ghetto?

(4.4) Read *Native Son* by Richard Wright. Compare this book to the show you watched in 4.1 or 4.2. How do the book's experiences differ from yours, or the ones depicted on TV? Why? Which do you feel is closer to the reality of the ghetto?

(4.5) View the documentary on the Newark riot. Why did the people riot?

(4.6) View the documentary on ghetto life. How would you react to the living situation shown? Why are there ghettos?

Objective Number 5: Complete as many of the following activities as you feel are necessary to complete the objective satisfactorily. Keep a notebook of results.

(5.1) List significant encounters you have had with individuals of the opposite race.

(5.2) Remember and list all the statements you have heard from family members or friends about the nature of the opposite race. Which ones do you accept as truth?

(5.3) List your close friends who are of another race.

(5.4) How many activities involving the opposite race do you voluntarily engage in?

(5.5) What is an opposite race? Why is it opposite?

(5.6) How often do people of another race visit your home? Why do they come?

(5.7) List experiences in which you were in a minority position. How did you feel?

(5.8) What responses discovered in objectives 5.1 or 5.2 have you expressed? Why?

(5.9) How do you think members of another race see you?

(5.10) What have you learned that you didn't know before about race by completing this package?

Further Instructions

The teacher would be interested in seeing your notebooks from all activities, but you are only required to hand to him/her your responses to the questions in the objectives. Arrange a conference so that you both may discuss your progress.

Evaluation

Evaluation consists of the responses given to the questions contained in the objectives. Responses may be verbal or written.

AN INTRODUCTION TO ECOLOGY*

Introduction and Instructions

Ecology is a word we hear nearly every day. It is the study of the relationship between living things and their environment. In the world today, the study of ecology has become a major science, but only recently. Pollution and extinction have made people take notice of how we are treating our world. Ecology is an area we must all learn more about. This learning package will help. You may do any activities you feel will make you knowledgeable about ecology. There are many topics that may interest you, and you may want to study them in detail. If one particular area of the package interests you for further study, see the detailed studies listed at the end of the package which you can pursue as individual projects. You may check with the teacher about your special interest.

Keep an ecology notebook. Put all of your answers and activities for the package in your notebook. We will use your notebook in our conferences and will use it to make decisions about your progress.

Objectives

1. You will write definitions for ten words related to our study of ecology, with accompanying illustrations or pictures to demonstrate your understanding. The definitions must be consistent with a standard reference book, such as a dictionary.

2. a. After completing the following learning alternatives, you will be able to draw a diagram of the water cycle which will explain where water comes from.

*This package is most appropriate for students who have some experience in self-direction.

b. You will be able to list three ways water becomes polluted and describe the effects of polluted water on the life of animals or people.

3. After completing the following learning alternatives, you will be able to list five animals whose natural habitats and characteristics have been changed by man, describe the changes, and explain what man did to cause the changes.

4. After completing the following learning alternatives, you will develop a plan for year-round use of a plot of soil which will not deplete the natural nutrients in the soil. You must be able to justify your plan.

5. After completing the following learning alternatives, you will list five ways in which you and your family can reduce pollution in our community. Within two weeks you will have begun practicing at least three of those ways.

6. After completing the following learning alternatives you will list in a chart four sources of energy, the good points and bad points about using each, particularly as they affect the environment, and the availability of each.

Learning Alternatives

1. *These alternatives will acquaint you with words used in the study of ecology and what they mean.* It would be a good idea to keep this list as a reference you can return to during other package activities.

   Complete all three of the following activities.

   a. Find the following words in the dictionary or encyclopedia and write their meanings below. Notice their roots.

   ecology: _____

   _____

   _____

   ecosystem: _____

   _____

   _____

   pollution: _____

   _____

   _____

   environment: _____

   _____

   _____

   recycling: _____

   _____

   _____

smog: _____

_____

_____

extinct: _____

_____

_____

endangered: _____

_____

_____

conservation: _____

_____

_____

energy: _____

_____

_____

population: _____

_____

_____

b. Try to imagine what these words mean to your everyday life and surroundings. Listen for the words on television and watch for them in books and magazines. Discuss what you hear and think in class when we have discussion time for ecology.

c. Find illustrations, or make your own illustrations, for these words. Add these to our Ecology Bulletin Board.

2. *These alternatives will help you understand the water cycle.* While you work on the alternatives think of these questions: Where does water come from? What uses does man make of water? How does water become polluted?

a. Read about the water cycle in your science book or encyclopedia. There are other books in the library. Write or record important information you find.

b. Make your own terrarium with a built-in water cycle to watch. Get a jar and place rocks, sand, then soil in the bottom. This is similar to the real ground. Place a small green plant in the jar and water it. Cover the top of the jar with a piece of glass or clear plastic, making it airtight. Place the jar in the sun, indoors. Watch it every day and see how water col-

lects at the top and "rains" on your plant. Record your observations on a sheet of paper.

c. Make a diagram showing how rainwater falling to earth gets to your drinking fountain at school.

d. Have you ever seen a polluted stream or river? Is this wrong? Think of two good ways you could help prevent water pollution.

(1.) _____

_____

(2.) _____

_____

e. Imagine you are an animal dependent upon unpolluted water. Create a story or play about yourself and how polluted water affects your life as an animal.

f. Watch television shows to find instances where water pollution has seriously affected animals and people. Add what you find to your notebook.

3. *These alternatives concern wildlife.* The tasks will help you understand how animals affect the environment and how the environment affects them.

a. View the film on wildlife and wildlife surroundings. Explain in your notebook the relationship between wildlife and the natural habitat and how man influences and controls this habitat.

b. Discover one type of wildlife found near your home. Where does it live? What does it eat? Would you want to capture it? Will it always be in your neighborhood?

c. Feed birds in your yard with stale food your family would throw away. What birds come to eat the food? Keep a list of the different birds you observe.

d. Write several reasons man has found value in killing animals.

_____

_____

_____

Do you think it is ever right to kill animals? Do you think it is ever right for animals to kill men? Why?

_____

_____

_____

e. Have you ever been hunting or fishing? Why did or would you go? Can anyone hunt anywhere or anytime? Who says when people may hunt or fish? The pamphlets from the Department of Wildlife Conservation might help you with these lists. They can be found in our Ecology Learning Center.

f. What is an endangered species? List three endangered species in our country:

(1) _____

(2) _____

(3) _____

Now list two extinct species:

(1) _____

(2) _____

4. *These alternatives are concerned with soil conservation.*

a. Take a walk, ride your bike, or ask someone to drive you through the countryside. Look at the land and notice how it is used. Are there bare areas, gullies, eroded areas, or large areas of cut trees? How do these affect conserving the soil? Draw an illustration of how soil conservation depends upon plants, animals, and people.

b. Build a mound of dirt somewhere. Take a pitcher of water, hold it steady, and pour it slowly over the mound. What happens? Now find a mound with plants or weeds growing in it. Pour water the same way. Is there a difference? This effect is the same as that of rainwater or streams flowing downhill.

c. Farmers grow food in the earth. Where do the vitamins and minerals come from? Can the nutrients in the soil ever wear out? What can farmers do about this? You might read Chapter 6 of our science book or view the filmstrip on soil conservation in the viewing center.

d. Find out how many people there are to feed in the world. How many of these people don't get fed? See if you can discover if any of the hungry areas of the world have soil conservation problems. If they do have problems, why?

e. Make plans to contribute to a class garden or to plant a garden of your own. Consider the following questions and record your plan in your notebook:

(1) What do you want to plant?

(2) When should it be planted?

(3) What kind of soil is best for the plants?

(4) How will the plants affect the soil?

(5) What should be planted next in this soil?

5. *These activities will help you understand waste and its effect on the environment.*

a. Visit the sewage treatment plant for your community. Go out to a junkyard or city dump. Why is the dump often termed "landfill operation"? Do you think your community is getting rid of its waste properly? Write a paragraph stating your position.

b. Begin saving newspapers, sacks, and other paper. Find out if there is a recycling center in town. If there is, take your paper there to be recycled. If there is no center, ask the mayor why there isn't. You can do the same with glass, and ask your neighbors and friends to save glass and paper too.

c. Name five things you now throw away which could be recycled or used again.

(1) _____

(2) _____

(3) _____

(4) _____

(5) _____

d. Who do you think are the biggest polluters and wasters in your community? Why? Do animals pollute?

e. What do the terms *decompose* and *organic* mean? What is a compost pile? How would you start one?

f. Go to the grocery store. Notice the way food is packaged. Decide what packaging is needed for the good of fresh food and what is useless packaging. Why does something wrapped in cellophane need to be in a cardboard box?

6. *These activities show you how the energy crisis relates to you and what you can do about it.*

a. Think of as many sources as you can of world energy. Make a list or illustrate these sources. Which of the sources do you or your family use?

b. Decide whether solar energy and water energy are less wasteful than coal and oil energy. Be ready to explain your decision. Why are coal and oil used more often than solar and water energy?

c. Ask your parents how much gasoline they use each week. Determine how much they pay for this gasoline and why it costs more now than it used to. Could you and your friends help conserve gasoline? Add your ideas to a class discussion or to some class project.

d. Read about or ask someone what the term strip-mining means. Also, see if you can find where most strip-mining is done today in our country and where most of it might be done in the future. Think about the question: What would happen if strip-mining were illegal? Discuss this in class.

1. Be prepared to share your notebook with the teacher when you schedule your individual conference.

2. Define the following words:
   a. endangered_____
   _____
   b. smog_____
   _____
   c. recycling_____
   _____
   d. ecology_____
   _____

3. Draw a diagram showing what happens to water in a terrarium. Write a paragraph explaining how that is like what happens to water in the earth's atmosphere.

4. List three things that can be done to stop water pollution.

5. In the left-hand column of the chart below list five animals that have had to change their environments or their characteristics because of man. Then complete the remainder of the chart.

NAME OF ANIMAL	TYPES OF CHANGES	HUMAN BEHAVIOR THAT CAUSED CHANGE
1._____	1._____	1._____
2._____	2._____	2._____
3._____	3._____	3._____
4._____	4._____	4._____
5._____	5._____	5._____

6. List three things you and your family now do to reduce pollution.
   a. _____
   b. _____
   c. _____

7. In the left-hand column of the following chart list four sources of energy. Then complete the remainder of the chart.

SOURCE OF ENERGY	REASON TO USE THIS SOURCE	REASONS NOT TO USE THIS SOURCE	HOW AVAILABLE IS THIS SOURCE?
1._____	1._____	1._____	1._____
2._____	2._____	2._____	2._____
3._____	3._____	3._____	3._____
4._____	4._____	4._____	4._____

Related Projects

If you have become interested in the subject of ecology, here are some related topics you may study and report on. If you have a special interest not listed here, ask the teacher for reference books and materials.

air pollution
noise and vision pollution
solar heat
nuclear energy
mass transportation
population growth
preserving the wilderness
the problems of DDT
food chain
balance of nature

Reference Materials

Books (reading level—4th through 8th):
Ecology: The Circle of Life by Harold R. Hungerford
Understanding Ecology by Elizabeth R. Billington
The Hole in the Tree by Jean George
Pioneers of Ecology by Donald W. Cox
Who Lives in this Log? by Wilda Ross
Ecology: The Science of Survival by Laurence Pringer
As We Live and Breathe by the National Geographic Society
Ecology by Shelley and Mary Louise Grossman

Films (166m—from 15 to 45 minutes):
Large Animals that Once Roamed the Plains
Before the Mountain was Moved
Cry of the Marsh
Pollution—It's Up to You
Man's Effect on the Environment
Once There Were Bluebirds
The Stream
What are We Doing to Our World? (Parts One and Two)
Problems of Conservation:
Air
Forest and Range
Mineral
Our Natural Resources
Soil
Water
Wildlife

BASKETBALL

Instructions

You may take a pretest on this learning package and receive credit for it without doing the activities. If you feel you have a good understanding of the game of basketball, ask the teacher for the pretest. If the pretest results show that you have a lot to learn about basketball, complete the required activities in the package and see your teacher to discuss evaluation. Decide with your teacher which activities you will do. This page will be filled out when you and your teacher meet and the darkened circles will indicate the activities you will do.

1. Definitions of Basketball Terms
   - ○ a. Illustration of five terms
   - ○ b. Video tape of five terms
2. Fundamentals of the Game of Basketball
   - ○ a. Basketball court
   - ○ b. Players and positions
   - ○ c. Diagram of offensive plays
   - ○ d. Diagram of defensive plays
   - ○ e. Illustration or video tape of one fundamental
3. Official Basketball Rules
   - ○ a. Learning center on official rules
   - ○ b. 24 or 30 second clock?
   - ○ c. Legalize dunking?
   - ○ d. Officiate a game.

Objectives

After completing this learning package, you will be able to:

1. Define the terms dribble, dunking, player control foul, traveling, screen, pivot, jump ball, double foul, and blocking with 100 percent accuracy.
2. Chart the dimensions of a regulation size basketball court on graph paper.
3. State physical and skill requirements for the guard, forward, and center positions.
4. Diagram three offensive and three defensive plays.
5. State and demonstrate two fundamentals each of passing, shooting, defensive movement, and rebounding.
6. Write the official rules concerning traveling, basket interference, goal tending, and post play fouls.

The following are terms used in the game of basketball:

blocking	player control foul	dribble
dunking	foul	free throw
held ball	holding	jump ball
pivot	traveling	screen

Learning Alternative 1

Choose five basketball terms. Define them and illustrate each term in picture(s).

Learning Alternative 2

Use the video tape machine (see teacher for instructions) to tape you and a sufficient number of students demonstrating five of the following:

a. a dribble
b. a dunk
c. a player control foul
d. traveling
e. a screen
f. a pivot
g. a jump ball
h. a double foul
i. blocking

Fundamentals of the Game of Basketball

Basketball is not only one of the fastest of all major sports, but is also one of the most exacting, requiring better physical condition and even more precision than most other sports. Despite the fact that certain individual abilities are required to become a good basketball player, team play is extremely important. There are five players on a basketball team—a center, two forwards, and two guards. The center is usually the tallest of these and has the longest reach and the best jumping ability. The forwards are usually the best shooters, and are slightly shorter than the center. The two guards are usually the quickest and best ball handlers on the team. They must be accurate passers and shooters.

Learning Alternative 1

Chart to scale the dimensions of a basketball court. Label boundary lines, lanes, and circles with appropriate names.

Learning Alternative 2

Compile a list of players from your favorite team (high school, college, or professional) who have played the guard, forward, and center position. Give your personal comments on why each player played his particular position. Research requirements for each position. Books and other materials can be found in our basketball learning center.

Learning Alternative 3

Illustrate and explain three offensive plays. You might read *Winning Basketball Plays,* in the learning center, for help.

Learning Alternative 4

Illustrate and explain three defensive plays. If you need help try reading *Basketball Fundamentals and Techniques.*

Learning Alternative 5

Illustrate or video tape one of the following fundamentals: passing, shooting, defensive movement, rebounding.

Official Basketball Rules

There are two officials in basketball: the referee and the umpire. The referee and the umpire meet with the captains at midcourt before the game to talk over the rules.

It is the responsibility of the two officials to stop play when a rule is broken. There are two classes of rule-breaking in basketball: violations and fouls. Each year, the National Collegiate Athletic Association (NCAA) publishes an official basketball rule book which explains and defines violations and fouls.

Learning Alternative 1

Complete the learning center activities on Official Rules.

Learning Alternative 2

Discuss the pros and cons of a 24 or 30 second clock in men's high school or college basketball in paragraph form. Give at least two arguments for and two against, and then argue for one side or the other.

Learning Alternative 3

Discuss the pros and cons of making "dunking" legal once again in high school and college. Write a mock debate on the subject between a small player and a very tall player.

Learning Alternative 4

Officiate one of the intramural games after school (see teacher about scheduling). Recall and record all mistakes you remember making.

Reference Materials

Bee, Clair Francis. *Basketball Fundamentals and Techniques.* Ronald, 1959.

Bee, Clair Francis. *Make the Team in Basketball.* Grosset and Dunlop, 1960.

Bee, Clair Francis. *Winning Basketball Plays.* Ronald, 1959.

Cooke, David C. *Better Basketball for Boys.* Dodd and Meade, 1960.

Fagan, Clifford B. *1974-75 Basketball Rules, Simplified and Illustrated.* National Federation of State High School Associations, 1974.

Gill, Amorgi. *Basic Basketball.* Ronald, 1962.

Steitz, Edward S. *The Official NCAA Basketball Rules, 1975.* NCAA Publishing Service, 1974.

Posttest

1. Define the following:
   a. traveling
   b. jump ball
   c. screen
   d. dribble
   e. double foul
2. Fill in the blanks with the appropriate word or words:
   a. Basketball is a game played by two teams of _____ players each.
   b. _____ is the position played by the tallest person on the team, usually with good jumping ability and the longest reach.
   c. The _____ are usually the best shooters.
   d. The _____ are usually the best ball handlers.
   e. You would use a zone defense if _____ _____ .
   f. You would use a man-to-man defense if ____ _____ .
3. Look at the pictures projected on the screen. Decide which pictures are of plays that are legal and which are of plays that are illegal in basketball. Briefly explain your answer.
   a. _____
   b. _____
   c. _____
   d. _____
   e. _____

MATH PACKAGE
Multiplication: 5th Package

Skill: 5's and more 5's

This package will help you to:
1. multiply any number between 1 and 20 by 5 with no more than 5 mistakes;
2. identify 10 everyday uses of the numeral 5 or multiples of 5.

This package is to help you learn more about the number 5 and its multiples. Your mathematics pretest indicated that you need practice in using this number.

Learning Alternatives

Do numbers 1 and 2 below and any others you think will help you accomplish the objectives of the package. All products of the package should be kept in your notebook for this package.
1. Become familiar with the materials, games, and worksheets in our classroom Math Learning Center. These resources will help you with this package.
2. Make a list of the uses of the number 5 in the United States monetary system. See if you can determine if there are other countries that have similar uses.
3. Keep a record of things you or members of your family purchase. Which items are a multiple of 5? What is the multiple?
4. Make drawings or cut out magazine pictures that illustrate the use of the multiple of 5 in telling time. Explain your drawings and selections in your notebook.
5. Use a tape cassette to practice multiplying by 5. Have a classmate check your tape.
6. Arrange for one of your classmates who has achieved the objectives of this package to help you understand multiples of 5.
7. Sign up to play "Five-O" with a group of classmates. You might need to make arrangements a few days ahead of time. The list is in the Math Learning Center.
8. Make a poster listing and illustrating as many ideas as you can think of which are based upon multiples of 5.
9. Imagine that tomorrow morning when you wake up, the number 5 and its multiples will no longer exist in our numerical system. What would this change in your daily life?

Postassessment

Arrange with your teacher for your post-assessment on the two objectives of this package. Bring your completed notebook for this package; it will be used as part of your assessment.

SPELLING PACKAGE NUMBER TEN

This package will help you to:

1. Correctly spell at least 10 of 15 words in this week's spelling list;
2. Demonstrate your understanding of the meanings of the words in this week's spelling list by
   a. defining each word;
   b. writing a story and using each word correctly;
   c. making drawings to illustrate correctly the meanings of the words;
   d. recording a story on a tape cassette using the words correctly.

Complete the following:
1. Study the following words. They are this week's spelling list.

boat	bayou	seagull
ocean	tide	porpoise
shrimp	seashells	Atlantic
blue	sand dollar	Pacific
sand	pelican	gulf

2. Ask the teacher for a pretest to help you know which of the words you can already spell and define correctly. If you missed no more than 5 of the words in the pretest, you can go on to the next group of spelling words.

Learning Alternatives

If you need further help with the objectives of this package, use some of these alternatives (remember to write which alternatives you do on your Spelling Record Sheet):

1. Go to the Spelling Learning Center. Practice spelling and defining the words with a partner, on a cassette recorder, or with some of the center games and worksheets.
2. Use a dictionary in our Research Center to help define the words.
3. Borrow a recorded tape that a classmate has prepared and had approved by the teacher. The tape correctly defines the words and uses them in a story.
4. When you know the meaning of each word, either draw your own illustration of the word or cut pictures out of magazines in our Materials and Things Center. You might make a collage of the pictures.
5. Find photographs or real objects that represent the words. Plan with classmates to prepare a display of as many objects and photographs as you can which represent the spelling words.

Postassessment

Arrange with your teacher to determine your postassessment of the two objectives for this package.

MEASUREMENT PACKAGE NUMBER TWO

Concept/Skill: Using the ruler

This package will help you to:
1. Identify all segments of a 12" ruler;
2. Use the ruler accurately in your own and assigned measurement tasks.

Instructions

Complete as many of the following learning alternatives as you think are necessary to prepare yourself for the postassessment part of this package.

1. How many ways do you know to use the word ruler? Make a list of these ways. Compare your list with those of your classmates and add your ideas to the Ruler Meaning Chart on the bulletin board.
2. Get a ruler used for measuring from the classroom supply center. Using the ruler, identify as many as you can of the different ways the ruler is divided. What is the smallest measurement on the ruler? The largest? Put this information under the category Rulers in your measurement notebook.
3. Answer the following questions about yourself:
   a. How many 12-inch rulers would it take to measure your height?
   b. If you were to measure your height, how many of the following would you be:
      (1) inches _____
      (2) 1/2 inches _____
      (3) 1/4 inches _____
      (4) 1/8 inches _____
      (5) 1/16 inches _____
   Place your answers in your measurement notebook.
4. How many things do you think you can measure accurately with a 12-inch ruler? Make a list of these things, or if you wish, illustrate them. Why did you select these items? Could you measure very small or very large items accurately with a 12-inch ruler? Why or why not?
5. Have you ever wondered who invented the 12-inch ruler and why? Use the materials in our Measurement Center to answer these questions. Put your findings in your notebook.
6. Take a 12-inch Measuring Kit from the Measurement Center. Each kit contains sample items to measure and an individual record sheet on which you should record the measurements. Practice measuring with your ruler using this kit or other kits. Measure at least three things you find in our classroom.
7. Bring five objects from home which you have measured with your ruler. Have five friends measure your items and see if their results are the same as yours. Keep a record of your measurements and those of your friends'.

Postassessment

Arrange with the teacher to take your postassessment. The postassessment for this package involves your measuring a scale drawing of our classroom with a 12-inch ruler. When you think you can do this accurately, let the teacher know.

7

Developing And Using Student Contracts

onnie is a bright eighth grade student who loves to do things to please teachers. She brings all assignments, completed and corrected, to each conference with a teacher. She is a delight and, of course, all teachers love her. But Mr. Leonard, Connie's language arts teacher, decided that Connie needs to be a more self-directed learner; therefore, at a conference with Connie, Mr. Leonard did not say what should or must be done. Rather, he helped Connie identify an area of interest to her and then promised to help find some resources. Together they thought of some activities Connie could do to help her learn. This was to be the only assignment Connie would get for two weeks. At the end of the conference, Connie managed a weak but apprehensive smile, and decided she would much rather have the teacher tell her what to do.

• Earl is a tenth grade student who was "socially promoted" all the way through school. Teacher comments in his record say things like: "Earl has a short attention span"; "Earl is immature"; "Earl disrupts students who really want to learn." Each day when Earl comes to math class, Mr. Keith has placed in his folder an assignment containing an objective and four activities. Earl and Mr. Keith have agreed that Earl will never have to do but two of the four activities, and that he can do the two of his choice. He simply initials the two he plans to do that day and leaves that, with any products from the completed assignment, in his folder at the end of the day. Math is now the only course Earl never skips.

• Mr. Warren, a high school science teacher, enjoyed all his classes except his first period chemistry class. In there, students were very argumentative and uncooperative. They would never work together or share information because of the intense competition for grades. So Mr. Warren announced to the class that any student could get any grade he wanted in the class, and that the grade of one person would have no bearing on the grades of others. Students were skeptical, but agreed to go along with the individual conferences Mr. Warren had scheduled. At each conference, Mr. Warren presented some ideas he thought the student should learn about and some student objectives based on those ideas. He also had a series of required and a series of optional learning alternatives for achieving a grade of A, another series of learning alternatives (fewer required) for achieving a grade of B, and still another series of learning alternatives for achieving a C. Each student signed a paper specifying which series of learning alternatives he or she would complete, and thus what grade he or she would receive. After this, Mr. Warren observed that it was easier for students to find partners for lab experiments.

The above vignettes help illustrate the use of instructional contracts as a means of individualizing instruction. Contracts are simply agreements between a student and a teacher (or in some cases, between a small group of students and a teacher) for specified educational activities, or mastery of an objective agreed on in advance, with a clear understanding of and agreement on the assessment procedures to be used. The contract may or may not have a grade designation.

Contracts
• help remove time as important variable in student learning, that is, they allow students to work at rates most comfortable for them;
• help students learn to manage their time;
• help the teacher provide individual prescriptions for a large number of students;
• help students learn to make choices about activities they will engage in;
• help involve students in curriculum planning.

Contracts are efficient means of prescribing for students, based on assessed need or interest, and usually are negotiated with students. The degree of student involvement in the negotiation of a contract should depend primarily on the level of self-direction of the student and, to a lesser degree, on the types of subject matter involved. Contracts range from being totally unstructured, with all objectives and learning alternatives decided by the student, to being so structured that students have no choices in the contract. Most are partly structured and fall somewhere between these two extremes.

Subject areas that are highly skill-oriented and highly sequenced are more likely to have contracts with nonnegotiated objectives than are courses not based primarily on skill development. But even when objectives are predetermined, there can be considerable choice for students among learning alternatives.

TYPES OF CONTRACTS

Type A (Structured Contracts): All component parts are predetermined by the teacher. The student and the teacher negotiate a contract from the predetermined components.

Type B (Partly Structured Contracts): Some components are predetermined by the teacher. Other parts of the contract are designed and developed by the teacher and the student. The teacher-student development stage of the contract serves as the negotiation of the contract.

Type C (Mutually Structured Contracts): No components are predetermined. Teacher and student cooperatively and mutually develop and negotiate all parts of the contract.

Type D (Unstructured Contracts): No components are predetermined. The student initiates and develops the parts and then negotiates those with the teacher.

Figure 15 suggests teacher and student roles in developing and using structured, partly structured, and unstructured contracts.

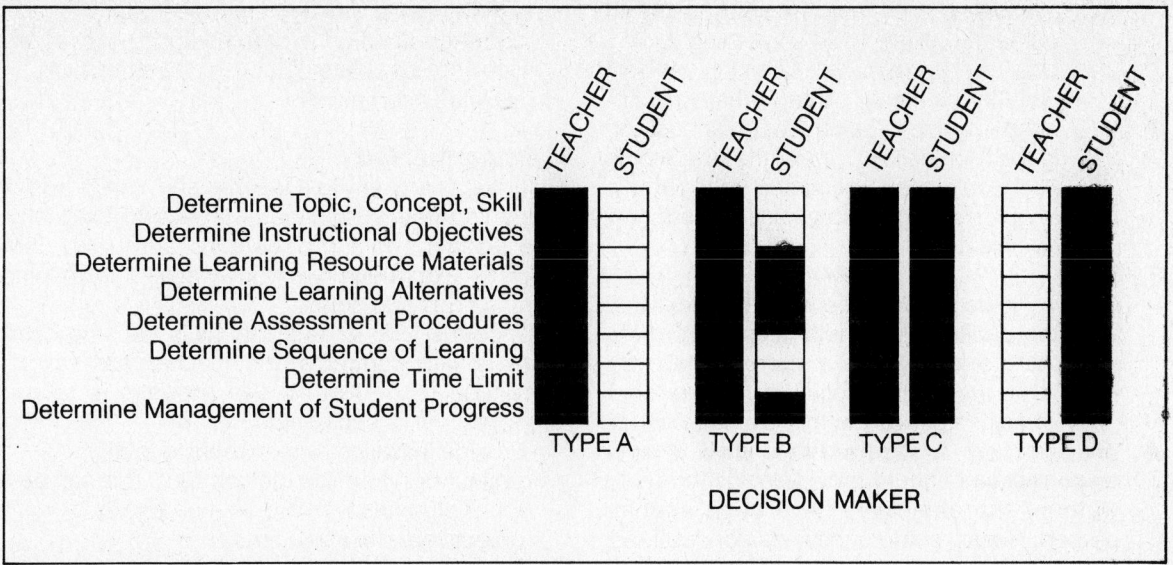

Figure 15. Teacher and student roles in contract development.

COMPONENT PARTS OF CONTRACTS

Below are listed the component parts of contracts. All contracts will not include all the following parts. The appropriate part of a sample contract is given as an illustration after the definition of each part. The sample contract to be developed is based on the concept of *Persuasion*.

1. **Objective or objectives** specify what is to be accomplished, the conditions under which the learning will be demonstrated, and the level of proficiency required for meeting the objective.
   Example
   a. Write a definition of "persuasion" which meets the criteria from any of the three dictionaries found in our classroom.
   b. Develop a procedure (audio tape, class presentation, written) for persuading someone to your point of view using at least three different types of persuasion.

2. **Resources** should include the books, film, filmstrips, and other media available, as well as any human resources who can help the student.
   Example
   3 dictionaries
   Books: *The Hidden Persuaders, Tom Sawyer*
   Person: Mr. Richards of the All-American Advertising Agency
   Filmstrip: "Columbus Sets Sail"

3. **Learning Alternatives** are the reading, writing, viewing, creating, interviewing, and other activities the student experiences to accomplish the objective(s).
   Examples
   Do the following three activities:
   a. Look up the word "persuasion" in the dictionary. Write the meaning on the top

of your paper so you will have it for easy reference.
b. Read Chapters 4 and 5 of *The Hidden Persuaders* and note any important ideas about persuasion which you find.
c. Interview Mr. Richards of the All-American Advertising Agency. Find as many as possible of the ways his agency uses to persuade people.

Do at least one of the following:
a. The dictionary has given you a definition of persuasion. Using your knowledge about what the word means, role play the following situations with other students:
   (1) A person tries to persuade people to vote for his candidate.
   (2) A person is persuaded to do something he does not want to do.
   (3) Someone tries to persuade someone else to buy a product.
   Try these again, this time using a different approach.

   Write a brief essay on the different ways you can persuade people to do things.
b. Read the chapter in *The Adventures of Tom Sawyer* on whitewashing the fence. How did Tom Sawyer persuade others to help him in his work? Write a story in which you use a trick to persuade someone to do something he or she normally would not want to do.
   or (optional, for the adventuresome)
   Think carefully about the term *whitewash*. See if you can determine how that term is commonly used today in our language and write a paragraph on how

"whitewashing" is sometimes used to persuade people to do something.

c. Look at the filmstrip "Columbus Sets Sail" in the media center. What was Columbus trying to persuade Ferdinand and Isabella to believe? Write the arguments you would use to persuade your parents to give you money to go somewhere new and exciting.

or

Try to persuade someone in the class that the capital city should secede from the state and become a state on its own. What arguments would you use to convince him or her that this is a better idea?

4. **Reporting Alternatives and Post-assessment** should provide evidence as to whether the objectives have been accomplished. Tests, conferences, demonstrations, and creations are examples of reporting alternatives. In addition, individual folders, worksheets, and pupil progress and evaluation forms are often appropriate. As in any approach to individualizing, assessment and reporting procedures should be specified in advance so that students know what is expected of them.

Examples

a. Write a definition of persuasion, or do a drawing or painting that communicates the definition of persuasion.

b. Find a classmate who considers himself a strong Democrat. In ten minutes try to persuade him to register as a Republican when he is old enough to vote, using at least three types of persuasion. Tape record the conversation and turn it in to your teacher.

In addition to the four component parts listed above, contracts usually have a plan for signatures of both parties and an expected completion date. Sometimes other items are included, such as times for student-teacher conferences and instructions to students. Examples of contracts can be found at the end of this chapter.

USING CONTRACTS

Contracts can be used for:

1. Daily assignments, with students given a new contract each day. These are often placed in students' folders before they come to class.
2. Determining grades. A grade contract enables the student to choose the grade he wishes to receive. He contracts to accomplish objectives and learning alternatives consistent with the requirements of his contracted grade.
3. Extended periods of time. Some contracts are intended to engage students in educational activities for several days or weeks. An extended independent study, a unit of work, or

a mini-course can be contracted. Such contracts usually include several objectives or one very complete objective and extensive learning alternatives.

Getting Started

If contracts are new to a teacher and/or a group of students, they should be approached gradually. The teacher's role in developing and using contracts is extremely important. Table 9 lists some contract dos and don'ts.

Once the teacher and the class become comfortable with contracts, the teacher has several functions to perform if the process is to run smoothly. He or she should:

1. Provide initial instruction relative to the objective(s) found in the contract. This can be for all students working on a particular objective at the same time.
2. Negotiate contracts. In the beginning this will involve writing most, if not all, the parts of the contracts (Type A); gradually, as students learn

Table 9
Contract Dos and Don'ts

DO

Start with very short (one or two day) contracts to give students experience in managing their own time.

Diagnose students and prepare some contracts in advance.

Thoroughly explain the role and function of contracts.

Negotiate contracts with students; sometimes it is best to start with only a few of the students in a class.

Help students set realistic deadlines for completion of work.

Renegotiate contracts with students if they are not functioning well with the one they have.

Continually analyze the contracts being used, as well as the process employed for using them.

Solicit student feedback.

Revise the process as required.

Gradually involve students in contract development.

DON'T

Expect all students to be able to use contracts effectively immediately.

Expect all students to like contracts initially (a contract is *one* alternative means for individualizing).

Assume that all instruction can take place through activities in the contracts (often contracts require students to attend instruction centers where the teacher is providing instruction related to the contract).

Use contracts without a good management system.

to manage their time, they can have a larger role in writing contracts. Eventually, some students will be able to write their contracts completely and will bring them to the teacher only for final approval and signatures.

3. Schedule student-teacher conferences to allow the teacher to keep up with the work of each student and to be aware of student reactions to and feelings about particular contracts. Some renegotiation of contracts, or parts of contracts, will often be required and can be accomplished during conferences.

4. Provide time for working on contracts. Some teachers designate times for students to work on contracts while others allow contract work at all times other than during teacher instruction or student-teacher conferences. The latter approach is more common when contracts are the only technique being employed for individualizing instruction.

5. Monitor progress, keep records. This includes keeping copies of contracts and developing means for recording progress. See Chapter 9 for specific examples of record-keeping procedures.

6. Provide resources and creative learning alternatives to be used in contracts. Contracts used only for making assignments in textbooks and workbooks usually do little to motivate students. Generally the more varied the resources and learning alternatives, the more likely students are to meet deadlines established for completion of contracts.

7. Relate contract work to other instructional techniques. Contracts can be written to include student work in learning centers, completion of specific learning packages related to the objective(s) of the contract, peer teaching and learning, and small group work. The latter is especially effective for developing creativity and problem-solving skills. For example, a small group of students might write and present a play, radio or television show, or an art show demonstrating what they have learned while working on their contract; or a learning alternative in a contract might require the student to use other students to develop and test certain hypotheses.

Examples
Of Contracts

Terrarium Contract

I. *Instructions*

Have you ever seen a beautiful garden inside a bottle and wished you could make one? Terrariums are very easy to make, fun and inexpensive. Once they are finished, they demand little or no care. They make wonderful gifts and can be put in small or large bottles, or jars—whatever you have around the house.

To complete this contract you will actually make at least one terrarium. It can be large or small according to your desire and the container(s) you are able to get. You will learn the ingredients that go into a terrarium, how much of each, how to plan a terrarium, and where to get your plants and mosses.

After reading through the contract, have a conference with your teacher before signing it at the end. She will decide with you how much you need to do, and the time you will have for completing the contract.

II. *Resources*

Books:

Baker, Samm S. *The Indoor and Outdoor Grow-it Book.*

Gilbert, Miriam. *Starting a Terrarium.*

Hoke, John, *Terrariums.*

Wickers, David, and John Tuey. *How to Make Things Grow.*

III. *Equipment*

Bag of small pieces of charcoal
Bag of vermiculite
Bag of potting soil
Filmstrip projector

IV. *Learning Alternatives*

1. Read one of the books in your classroom on terrariums. Make a report noting the different types of terrariums.

2. View a filmstrip about terrariums and write a short report.

3. Visit a local florist or garden shop where terrariums are on display. If possible, watch someone make a terrarium. Report on some of the different techniques used to make terrariums attractive.

4. Gather bottles that can be seen through easily, fish bowls, or clear plastic containers for your terrarium(s). You can use saran wrap for a lid. Keep in mind that you need to be able to get your hand into the bottle (tweezers could be used, but this is quite difficult). If you are unable to find a container, you can purchase a candy jar or bottle for under a dollar at your local dime or grocery store.

5. Using resource books in your classroom or library, make a list of small plants, ferns, evergreens, and mosses that grow abundantly in this area. Note the best places for finding these. Make a drawing of what they look like.

6. Visit a woods or creek bank near you to gather specimens for your terrarium. Be sure you can recognize poison ivy and oak before going so that you do not gather these plants. You will need something for digging and paper cups or cartons for your specimens. Be sure to dig up as many roots as possible so that you do not kill your plants. Mosses should be gathered with 1/4 to 1/2 inch soil intact. When you reach home, make sure your specimens are damp and place them in a plastic bag until you are ready to use them.

7. Using the books in your classroom, see how many of your plants, ferns, or mosses you can identify.

8. Plan your terrarium by making a drawing of your container showing the approximate size. Show the order in which you will put things in your container and approximately how much of each you will use. Indicate where you will put your plants and mosses. Try to include a hill or mountain, and/or a stream or pond, but don't clutter your terrarium.

V. *Making Your Terrarium*

Place your plants gently in the soil without crowding. Use a pencil or stick to firm the soil around the roots. Put your moss between the plants and add any other decorative touches you want to use. When you've finished, clean the glass if it is dirty above the ground, sprinkle gently with water, and cover. Moisture will collect inside so you need not water again for a month or so, depending on your container.

VI. *Agreement*

Circle the activities you agree to complete. Activities 4 and 6 are required. State how many terrariums you plan to make. Remember your contract can be renegotiated at any time.

Activities

1. Reading a book on terrariums
2. Viewing a filmstrip
3. Visiting a local florist
*4. Gathering your containers
5. Listing plants, ferns, etc.
*6. Gathering your specimens
7. Identifying your plants
8. Planning your terrarium

I will make _____ terrariums.

Date _____ Signed _____
(student)

Signed _____
(teacher)

ACTIVITES

This contract gives you many fun things to do on your own and with a friend. You are to complete _____ of these activities today.

Name _____

Date _____

ART

1. Make 2 big 🎃s.

2. Draw a picture book of what you did Halloween night.

3. Put the picture book inside the two big 🎃s and staple together.
Put your book with OUR BOOKS.

MATH

4. Write the numerals as high as you can.
*1, 2, 3, 4, 5, 6, 7, 8, 9, 10,

5. Show 1-10 on an abacus and show me.

READING

6. Read or look at a book. Tell a friend about the book.
Make a picture of the part you liked best.

SCIENCE

7. Watch the hamsters. Make a picture to show how they get their exercise.

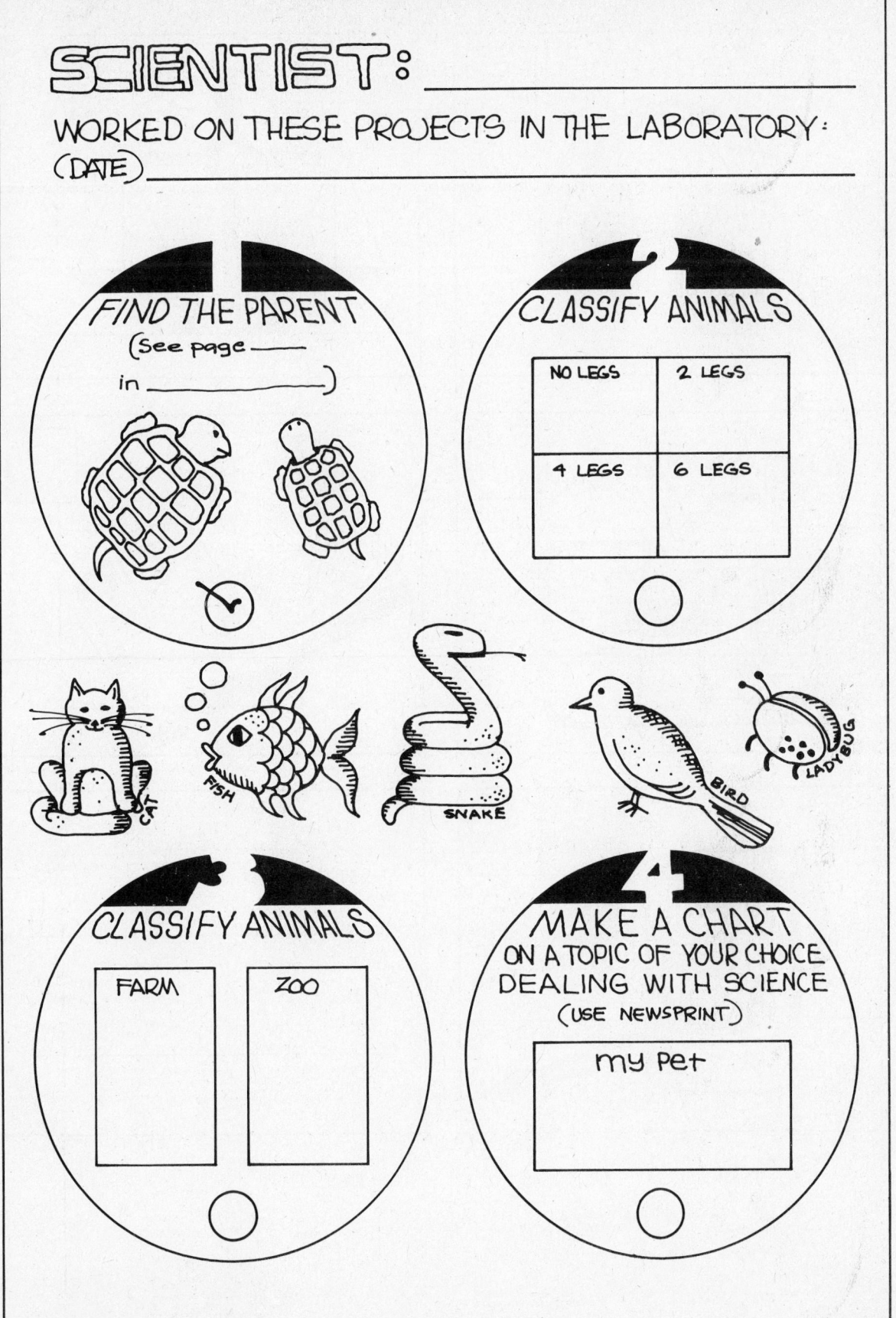

SCIENTIST: _____

WORKED ON THESE PROJECTS IN THE LABORATORY:
(DATE) _____

FIND THE PARENT
(See page ____
in _____)

CLASSIFY ANIMALS

NO LEGS	2 LEGS
4 LEGS	6 LEGS

CAT   FISH   SNAKE   BIRD   LADYBUG

CLASSIFY ANIMALS

FARM	ZOO

MAKE A CHART
ON A TOPIC OF YOUR CHOICE
DEALING WITH SCIENCE
(USE NEWSPRINT)

my pet

The student contracts to do one or more of these activities in the Science Learning Center. A check mark in the small circle at the bottom of a larger activity circle indicates that activity has been chosen.

Independent Contract

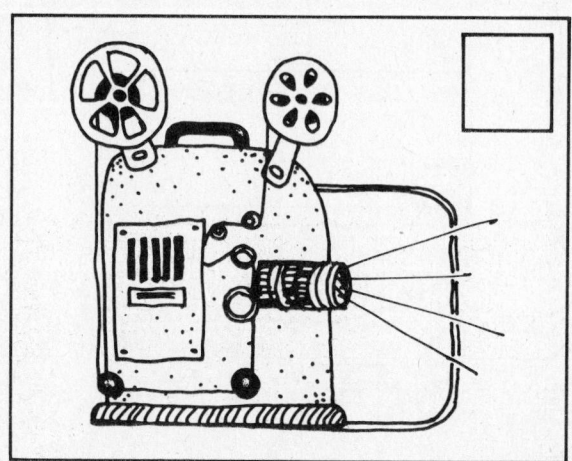

THIS CONTRACT IS FOR

_____
NAME

TO DO

_____
DAY

The student is given the contract, and he or she checks activities to do for a day or for several days.

Remember to save all your work to give the teacher. Color in the balloon when you've finished what it's told you to do.

THIS CONTRACT IS FOR _____

DATE STARTED _____ DATE COMPLETED _____

Time Schedule Contract
(To Be Completed Daily)

Week of _____

I contract to work in the learning centers indicated:

Hours

	9-10	10-11	12-1	1-2	Evaluation
Monday					
Tuesday					
Wednesday					
Thursday					
Friday					

ALTERNATIVES

Reading Center (5 times a week)

Math Center (5 times a week)

Independent Study (1 to 4 times a week)

Listening and Speaking Center (1 to 4 times a week)

Writing Center (1 to 4 times a week)

Art and Crafts Center (1 to 4 times a week)

Signed _____

(student)

Vocabulary Contract

Name: _____ Due Date: _____

Planning Date: _____

Subject: _____

Activities I will complete to help me learn my vocabulary words:

I. Knowing the words (select one):

    Game

    Putting word leaves in alphabetical order

    Making a word search puzzle

       My choice_____

II. Spelling the words (select one):

    Making new words from old ones

    Syllable classification

    Rhyming words

       My choice_____

III. Knowing the meanings (select one):

    Picture the words

    Game

    Write a poem or story with the words

       My choice_____

Signed: _____ _____
        (student)   (teacher)

Extra Activity: _____

Special Studies Worksheet #_____

I, _____,
accept the responsibility of completing this Special
Studies project.

Science Fiction
General Objective:
To become familiar with the literary form of a
    science fiction book.
Specific Objectives:
To locate the term *science fiction* in the dictionary
    and write its definition.
To locate an example of a science fiction book in
    the school library.
To read a science fiction book.
To list some of the reasons it is called a science
    fiction book.
To choose a topic and write a brief (1 to 2 pages)
    science fiction story.
**Learning Alternatives (check when
completed):**

1. Find the term *science fiction* in your
    dictionary and write the definition at the top
    of your paper.

2. Move to the library and find an example of a
    science fiction book. Ask the librarian if you
    need help.

3. Read the science fiction book. (Try to find
    one that is fairly short and "preread" it first.)

4. On your paper, below the definition, list at
    least four reasons it is called a science
    fiction book.

5. Choose a topic from your imagination and
    write a 1 to 2 page science fiction story.

Completed on:_____
                            (date)
Signed:_____
                        (student)

Contract

_____with_____
             (student)   (teacher)

Subject: _____

Contractual Conditions

What I want to find out: How I will show what I learned:

_____   _____

_____   _____

_____   _____

_____   _____

_____   _____

Due Date: _____

Consequences: _____

_____

Contract

_____with_____
             (student)   (teacher)

Subject: _____

Contractual Conditions

What I want to find out: How I will show what I learned:

_____   _____

_____   _____

_____   _____

_____   _____

_____   _____

Due Date: _____

Consequences: _____

_____

Strategies That Complement Individualization

The preceding chapters of this book described a process for developing individualized programs and presented alternative techniques, materials, and activities for implementing such programs.

As in any good idea, there are potential dangers in the concept of individualized instruction. One danger is that the term will be taken so literally that students will spend the vast majority of their time working alone. A related danger is that so much emphasis will be placed on sequencing and packaging content for skill and concept development that little attention will be given to the development of students' values, attitudes, creativity, levels of responsibility, and ability to relate to others.

Each of the approaches to individualizing described in preceding chapters can and should be designed to ensure student development in the cognitive, affective, and psychomotor learning domains. The purpose of this chapter is to provide additional alternatives that complement and enhance the individualized program and are specifically designed to

• promote student interaction with and understanding of others;
• develop creativity;
• provide experiences in democratic living, learning, and problem solving;
• provide opportunities for improved self-concept;
• provide opportunities for clarifying and developing values, attitudes, beliefs, and interests;
• provide opportunities for making decisions and assuming responsibility;
• provide opportunities for cooperative learning.

The six additional alternatives presented in this chapter are listed in the outer circle in Figure 16. Each alternative is described in the following pages.

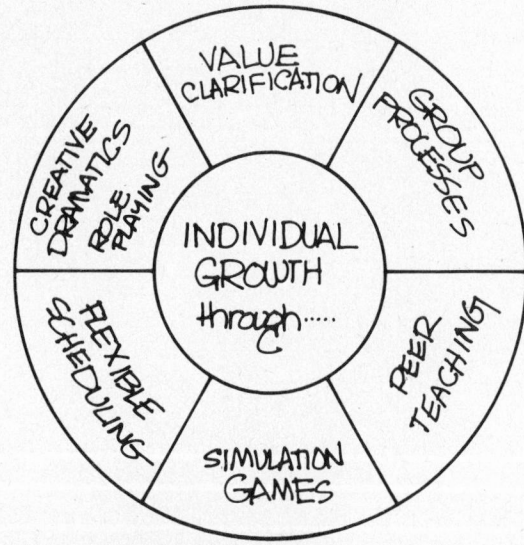

Figure 16. Strategies to complement an individualized program.

PEER TEACHING

It is an accepted axiom among teachers that they better understand certain concepts and skills after they have taught them. This idea forms part of the rationale for using peer teaching as an instructional technique; that is, students *really* understand a concept or master or extend a skill when they teach it to someone else.

Other reasons for using peer teaching—students teaching other students—are that it

• can provide insights about "learning how to learn";
• provides some of the additional human resources often needed in an individualized, personalized program;
• provides responsible, needed tasks that allow young people to practice adult roles;
• helps the student being tutored feel that he is important and cared for, and that his learning is important;
• helps move from nonindividualized and competitive to individualized and cooperative programs;
• often improves the self-concept of both the helper and the student being helped;
• works! Research continually confirms that most tutors experience success, and most students being helped respond to the attention being given to them with increased achievement.

Examples

Same-Age Peer Teaching is usually an informal, within-class program where students who have mastered a concept or skill are assigned or volunteer to help another student. Sometimes a teacher will post a list of students who have completed a particular objective, and students working on that objective are free to seek help from anyone on the list as the need arises.

Cross-Age Peer Teaching is usually a more formalized program and requires cooperation among members of a school staff, or possibly among two or more school staffs, as when high school students use free time or a study period to tutor in a school with younger students. Such a program is especially beneficial to young students who need older role models, and to adolescents who need to practice adult roles, or who need to be needed.

Cross-Cultural Peer Teaching may be for the same-age students or cross-age; the emphasis is on increasing contact with persons of other cultures/races. The assumption behind such a program is that increased contact will improve understanding and increase tolerance of persons who are culturally/racially different.

Requirements for a Successful Program

As in the implementation of any program, several steps must be taken to ensure the success of peer-teaching efforts. Figure 17 summarizes the steps necessary for implementing a successful program. First, there must be early involvement of all those concerned, administration, faculty, students, and parents. If any one of these groups decides that the program is not worth the time and effort, the program is not likely to survive.

Second, criteria for determining who will tutor and who will be tutored must be established. Questions of feasibility (e.g., Can we provide transportation for middle school students to tutor in an elementary school?) as well as relative benefits (e.g., Does a particular student need other experiences more than being tutored?) should be asked at this point.

Next, an overall system for program coordination should be developed. Such a system should specify who will do what, when they will do it, and where they will do it. This includes selecting the peer teachers and the students to be taught, making assessments and decisions about space utilization, developing and posting a schedule, and working out transportation plans, if any.

When all of these steps have been completed, those persons selected to do peer teaching should be trained. Minimum training should include: (1) ideas for icebreakers, getting acquainted; (2) ways to make the person being tutored feel good about himself and the work being done; (3) possible materials and resources; (4) ways of communicating with the teacher on progress being made by the student being taught.

At this point the peer teaching program can begin. A monitoring and evaluation system should be developed, including regular feedback from teachers, peer teachers, and students being taught. The information from this process can be used for modifying the program as needed.

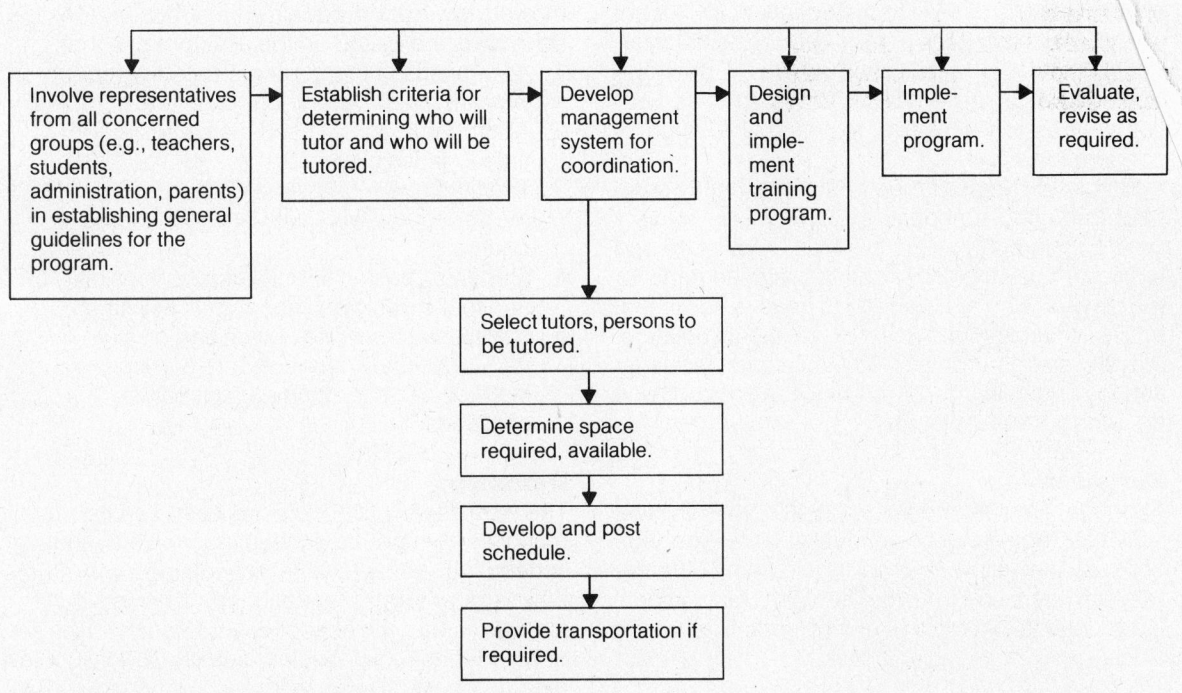

Figure 17. Steps in developing and implementing a peer teaching program.

SIMULATION GAMES

Simulation games represent various situations found in the real world, often with a segment of reality distorted in some way. They are designed with some educational intent, and provide a quick, efficient means of involving students in an area of study. They have rules of play, require social inter-action, and contain individual or group com-petition, although many games that appear competitive are designed to teach the value of cooperation.

Simulation games range from being highly com-plex, requiring computer programming, to very simple children's games such as "Cowboys and Indians." They typically contain assigned parts for the players, who are required to behave within that role and within the "reality" of the simulation. Players are confronted with situations requiring actions or decisions that influence the actions and decisions of other players.

Purposes
Although simulation games are seldom individual activities, they enhance an individualized program because they allow for learning on many different levels. They also can provide highly motivational introductions to a topic or unit of work, from which

students can make individual choices about fur-ther study. In addition, simulation games

1. Encourage students to learn from each other.
2. Provide opportunities for exploring the implications of socially acceptable and unacceptable behavior in a safe, nondestructive environment.
3. Create laboratories for developing problem-solving skills.
4. Give students experience in making decisions and examining the implications of those decisions.
5. Help students conceptualize and generalize from data they help generate.
6. Help students become active learners.
7. Provide the teacher with preassessment data about individuals and groups. Values, ability to relate to others, problem-solving skills, and leadership skills are often readily observable in simulation games.
8. Provide a feeling of realism often difficult to attain in a classroom when studying abstract subject matter. Complex problems are often easily understood by participating in simulation games.
9. Help relate affective and cognitive learning.

For descriptions, purposes, and publishers of specific simulation games, see Dennis M. Adams, *Simulation Games: An Approach to Learning* (Worthington, Ohio: Charles A. Jones Publishing Co., 1973).

FLEXIBLE SCHEDULING
Many schools with departmentalized curricula have adopted flexible schedules as a means of moving toward individualized instruction. Flexible schedules are based on the assumptions that:

1. All subjects in the curriculum do not require or warrant the same amount of time to complete.
2. All students do not need the same amount of time to finish a course.
3. The time needed for an individual student to master course work will vary from course to course.
4. Students can and should take responsibility for and make decisions about their learning.
5. Decisions about use of time and human resources (staff, students) are curriculum and instruction rather than administrative decisions.

Definition
The term *flexible schedule* has been used synony-mously with modular scheduling, flexible modular scheduling, variable time scheduling, and many other similar terms. Operationally, a flexible sched-ule means that the school day is divided into a set of time blocks, or modules, usually 15 to 30 min-utes in length. These modules are scheduled as deemed appropriate by the individual student and teacher, usually on a daily or weekly basis. Thus a

Student					
	MON	TUES	WED	THURS	FRI
9:00- 9:20	English	Social Studies Field Trip	Conference	Chemistry Lab	French
9:20- 9:40	English	Social Studies Field Trip	Bachelor Living	Chemistry Lab	French
9:40-10:00	Shop	Social Studies Field Trip	Bachelor Living	Chemistry	English
10:00-10:20	Shop	Social Studies Field Trip	Bachelor Living	English	English
10:20-10:40	Break	Break	Break	Break	Break
10:40-11:00	Shop	Math	Resource Center	Math	P.E.
11:00-11:20	Shop	Math	Resource Center	Math	P.E.

Flexible schedule.

student might spend 3 hours on a given day in his auto repair course to help rebuild the engine of a car, and no time in that course the rest of the week. Similarly, a student who is behind in math might schedule himself back into a math lab or open classroom for 8 to 10 hours per week until he advances as far as he wishes.

Some schools using flexible scheduling have open entry and exit times for courses, which means that students can finish a course in mid-year and begin another. This type of continuous progress without regard to years, semesters, and other arbitrary beginning and ending points requires that learning alternatives, materials, and objectives for courses be specified in such a way that a student can proceed through them at his own pace.

Flexible schedules usually reflect the following characteristics:

1. Schedules are set for a week's time, or less, rather than for a semester or a year.
2. Classes do not have standard lengths of time to meet; class time is determined by what is to be taught, and the means by which it will be taught.
3. Students regularly meet with teachers outside the scheduled class time, in both formal and informal groupings.
4. Instructional practices begin to become more individualized as advanced students move through a course rapidly while students less advanced in a particular subject take as much time as necessary for mastery.
5. Grades improve because students can stay in a course until they achieve the grade they want.

Problems

Most of the problems with flexible schedules relate to the implementation process rather than to the concept itself. Some potential problems are:

1. More work for teachers, particularly in the beginning, as they adjust to the schedule, prepare materials for students to use individually, and help advise students on how to schedule their time.
2. A computer is usually necessary to allow everyone to know what is being offered when, and to allow students to know when teachers have unscheduled time so that meetings can be scheduled.
3. Many students have difficulty assuming the amount of responsibility required in such a program, especially in the beginning.
4. Lack of parent and community support. This has been a particular problem when schools have allowed students not to schedule themselves into any planned school experience for certain parts of the day. Schools that have a "demand" flexible schedule, one that requires students to schedule themselves into some school activity for each module of the day, usually have received enthusiastic parent and community support and have found that students take far more courses than normal, sometimes as many as 10 or 12 per year.

VALUE CLARIFICATION

Each student has some feelings and values he or she uses in the selection of activities, interests, and goals in and out of school. Many values of a student are shared by his classmates and other persons. Other values are more personal, unique, and individual to a particular student or group of students. Some students have given serious consideration to the sources and consequences of their values. Other students are not sure of their values and do not comprehend the relationship among their choices, actions, and beliefs. Helping individuals and groups of students choose and clarify their values has become a priority goal in many school programs.

Purposes

The purpose of value clarification is to help students

- recognize and understand sources that contribute to value development;
- make value decisions;
- understand their own personal values;
- relate to people whose personal values differ;
- develop processes for making intelligent choices in all areas of living;
- recognize and cope with value conflicts;
- conceptualize the value systems of societies, cultural groups, and subcultural groups;
- understand the basis of value-related behavior and the relationships among choices, behavior, and consequences of choices and behavior.

Approaches

The process of clarifying beliefs, attitudes, or values is a highly personal and complex process. Varying approaches have been designed which enable teachers and students to focus upon values in a personal way. The approaches usually allow the individual student to reflect upon his own beliefs and to interact with other students and their beliefs.

Guidelines for Using Value Clarifying Activities
1. Avoid evaluating a student's values, moralizing to the student, criticizing the student, or imposing values upon the student.
2. Avoid requiring a student to participate in a particular activity.
3. Relate the activities to the content of a curriculum plan, or to on-the-spot events or occurrences in the classroom, the school, the nation, the world, or to student requests.
4. Use both spontaneous and preplanned situations and activities.
5. Enable students to make responses based upon their own beliefs.
6. Develop a nonthreatening and supportive classroom environment for students to express themselves.

Organizational Approaches to Value Clarification Activities
Seven general approaches to organizing for value clarifying activities in the classroom are:

1. Value clarification units, packages, contracts, or learning centers can be developed to help students understand the nature of values, realize some of their own values, and conceptualize the relationship between values and behavior.
2. Units of instruction in any subject in the school curriculum can include value clarifying activities.
3. Periods of time in the class schedule can be set aside to provide for value clarifying activities, exercise, and processes.
4. Mini-courses can be developed to enable students to understand the concept of values and to clarify values.
5. Counselors, guidance personnel, or teachers adept at value clarification can develop a schedule so that all students in a school have opportunities to participate in well-planned clarification programs and activities.
6. Teachers can work together to develop catalogs of clarifying questions and activities to use in their classrooms.
7. Teachers and students can use spontaneous incidents (e.g., arguments, fights, tragic events, happy events) as springboards to clarifying activities.

Resources for Understanding and Using Value Clarification in the Classroom

Several authors have compiled lists of practical and exciting possibilities for value clarification activities. Two of the sources available are:

Raths, Louis E., Merrill Harmin, and Sidney Simon. *Values and Teaching.* Columbus, Ohio: Charles E. Merrill Publishing Co., 1966.

Simon, Sidney B., Leland W. Howe, and Howard Kirschenbaum. *Values Clarification.* New York: Hart Publishing Co., 1972.

CREATIVE DRAMATICS AND ROLE PLAYING

Two popular methods that provide for individual and group expression, creativity, and development are creative dramatics—or spontaneous, nondirective dramatization—and role playing. The methods are similar in certain processes, but usually have different educational intentions.

Creative and nondirective dramatization are student-centered. In the case of creative dramatics, a student or students create plots, develop dialogue, cast parts, decide upon dramatization techniques, and supervise the production of the created situation. Nondirective dramatization takes its cue from both fiction and nonfiction selections in some published form. Students select what is to be dramatized under teacher guidance, group themselves to enact their selections, make production deci-

sions, and act out their chosen selections. This dramatization form is nondirective in the sense that the teacher does not direct the activities. Both of these methods promote creative abilities and provide for individual growth. Both can be used for certain skill and concept development in any subject area.

Role playing involves dramatization and provides opportunities for self-expression. The major thrust is to enable participants to dramatize their perceptions and solutions of problems. The problems can be selected from real life situations and spontaneous events, or they can be derived from common concerns, problems, and interests of a particular age group or a group of persons who share a common situation. Usually, teacher and students identify the context of the roles to be played, decide which students will play various required roles, and analyze and discuss the performance after the roles are played.

Variations

Creative dramatics, as used here, is distinguished from other classroom dramatic forms by its major purpose: to provide an environment in which the individual has the opportunity to create his own content and to have this content dramatized. The dramatization can be performed by one or several students, depending upon the requirements of the created situation. Creative dramatics experiences enable students to write stories and dramatize them, write plays and perform them, or develop situations that can be dramatized in a nonverbal form presented as a pantomime.

Spontaneous, nondirective dramatization of story content provides a setting in which students can survey and read story collections from various grade and interest levels. After reading as many stories as the individual student wishes, each student is given the opportunity to share the selection he enjoyed most with other members of the class. Titles of these stories and the number of characters in each story (both animal and human) can be listed on the chalkboard. When all the volunteers have discussed their selections, each student in the class is asked to choose from the list on the chalkboard a story he would like to read and then dramatize with others in a group. Groups are formed according to the number of characters required for dramatization. Sometimes it is necessary for a student to play more than one role in a dramatization in order to dramatize the best-liked selections. The drama groups reread the story together orally and then decide which group members will play the various characters in the story. Group members discuss their dramatization, rehearse, and then make their presentation before the class. No costumes or preplanned props are used. Any props or material needed to enhance the appearance of a character must be created from classroom resources. Emphasis is placed upon participation and enjoyment, not upon the quality of the dramatization itself.

This form of dramatization has been used effectively to increase individual student reading interests and abilities and to improve individual self-concept.

Spontaneous dramatization of problem situations is one role playing approach. This technique provides an opportunity for students and teachers to identify on-the-spot problems and concerns and to attempt solutions. Problematic situations can include name-calling, vandalism, classroom or school discipline, unjust rules and regulations, student-adult relations, or peer relations. The situation is briefly discussed with the class, and then students are asked to assume roles the incident requires. After student interpretations, perceptions, or solutions have been presented through role playing, a discussion is held to determine the effectiveness of the role-played solutions in relation to the problem. *Individuals who play roles are not evaluated. Their role interpretation is used as an alternative solution to the problem.*

Spontaneous dramatization of denouement is another role playing approach. The teacher or a student reads or relates a story of a typical life situation to a classroom group up to an exciting point, a dilemma situation, or the climax, and then students are asked to complete the story the way they think it should be through dramatization. No script is written; accent is upon student involvement and alternative interpretations. The quality of the acting is not important.

Spontaneous dramatization of curriculum content is an alternative for helping students understand information and concepts related to curriculum plans. Students can dramatize historical or contemporary events; science discoveries, life situations of scientists, or science phenomena; career and business situations; art and music activities; and other content from various curriculum areas. The purpose of this type of spontaneous dramatization is to offer an alternative approach for helping students learn content and skills they need in a particular curriculum plan. The major concern is with the accuracy of the content of the dramatization and not with the acting abilities of students.

CLASSROOM COMMITTEES AND TASK GROUPS

Individualizing can and does occur often through the use of committees and task groups in a classroom. Committees and task groups may be alternated with other individualized approaches, or they may be the primary means to individualize curriculum and instruction. Grouping is especially helpful in classrooms where few instructional materials are available for individualizing and when teachers feel they can best individualize by helping small groups of students.

Goals of Committee Work
I. In using committees, the teacher
   A. Provides for individual differences among pupils
   B. Provides opportunities for pupils to learn and improve needed skills and behaviors, such as,
      1. Following parliamentary procedure
      2. Using the library
      3. Utilizing community resources
      4. Taking notes
      5. Summarizing
      6. Evaluating
      7. Reading
      8. Writing
      9. Computing
      10. Experimenting
   C. Encourages pupil creativity

D. Achieves democracy in the classroom through democratic activities
E. Helps pupils select problems and goals of real interest for study
F. Helps pupils gain a sense of personal and group achievement
G. Creates an active, participating class
H. Acts as a guide and counselor to his pupils

II. In committee experiences, pupils have opportunities to
A. Become better acquainted with one another and to learn how to work well with others
B. Think independently and contribute their thoughts and ideas to group discussion
C. Learn the value of sharing experiences
D. Learn to listen to one another's ideas and insights
E. Discover helpful resources for problem solving and personal enjoyment
F. Grow in tolerance of others' ideas

III. In using committees, groups of students have opportunities to
A. Get acquainted through personal relationships and mutual efforts
B. Put into practice democratic principles
C. Participate in class and individual planning
D. Gain new ideas, interests, and information
E. Improve problem-solving skills and methods
F. Become more tolerant and less prejudiced toward other persons
G. Solve common problems
H. Plan for now and the future

IV. In introducing the committee idea, a teacher may use various approaches by
A. Defining ''committee'' with the class
B. Asking ''Why should we have committees?'' Have the class work together on the purposes and goals of the committees.
C. Discussing with the class the mechanics of committee work. Discussion areas might include: How can we organize? How can we select our leaders? How can we delegate responsibilities? How can we evaluate?
D. Showing a movie on committees in action followed by a discussion in planning for some committee work
E. Having an illustration of a committee at work

Kinds of Committees

In forming committees, a teacher may group pupils

- according to interest for unit work, learning centers, contracts, learning packages
- to study selected literature
- to write plans, skits, puppet shows
- to prepare bulletin boards and displays
- to work on needed skill development
- to care for the classroom
- to produce movies or video tapes

Selection of Committee Members

In using committees, a teacher may guide the formation of groups by:

1. Selecting committee members on the basis of the individual pupil's interest in curriculum plans. Pupils may indicate first, second, and third choices. This process may allow the teacher to balance the groups.
2. Having pupils form committees by choosing other students with whom they would like to work. It is often good to give first choice to pupils not usually selected among the first by others.
3. Selecting committees on the basis of pupils' abilities. The difficulty of a topic might also serve as a basis for grouping.
4. Allowing the chairperson to select members. The chairperson may be selected by the class or the teacher, and then he or she might select his or her own committee members.
5. Randomly grouping class members by rows in the classroom, alphabetical order, or any other means. This method might be the least desirable, but it works well for short-ranged tasks.
6. Forming committees according to the teacher's knowledge about psychological and social needs.
7. Grouping pupils on the basis of a sociogram which has been given after the pupils have become acquainted with each other.

Organization of Committees

I. In organizing a task group, members might want to
A. Determine what the responsibilities of group members are and select a chairperson and recorder, if necessary
B. Consider the overall purpose of the committee: to solve a problem related to a classroom unit; to design and complete a contract; to participate in a learning center; to work through a learning package; to plan for and produce a movie; to produce a

puppet show; to visit a nursing home and share experiences with persons at the home

   C. Divide the overall purpose into subunits, subtopics, specific tasks to be accomplished, or steps to be achieved

   D. Develop a plan of action or a set of procedures to use in accomplishing the overall committee purpose and the more specific tasks:

      1. Decide upon individual responsibilities and tasks in the committee

      2. Share ways of gathering information, keeping records, constructing, taking photographs

      3. Set completion dates for tasks

      4. Decide upon meeting times for the committee and ways of reporting progress

      5. Explore ways of sharing findings and products with classmates

   E. Plan with the teacher some means for assessing the committee's progress and achievement

II. In working on a task, problem, or activity, members might

   A. Select a chairperson and a secretary

   B. Define the purposes of their group

   C. Make a group plan. Make one copy for each member and one for the teacher.

   D. Collect and record information needed by the group

   E. Share information with group members

   F. Organize all the information collected by individual members

   G. Draw conclusions based upon the group's information

   H. Prepare any materials the group needs to share its findings

   I. Plan a presentation of the findings of the group for the class

   J. Make a presentation to the class

   K. Interact with class members and answer their questions

   L. Assess each individual's contribution to the group's purpose(s), the group's accomplishment of its purpose(s), the group's presentation to the class

III. In helping pupils improve the quality of group work, a teacher may need to

   A. Recognize that personality clashes may call for group reorganization or help from the counselor.

   B. Be alert to pupils' inabilities to read or use available materials. Direct pupils to other sources of information, such as, easier reading materials, television, films, and people

   C. Assess a pupil's ability to work in groups. If needed, help pupils develop skills and understandings of committee work.

   D. Evaluate pupils' abilities in using books, studying, and organizing materials. Teach those skills that are lacking.

   E. Understand that individual pupil problems in group work may stem from physical, social, and psychological needs or from sources outside the school.

Report of Committee Findings
In using committees, pupils may report by:

- explaining a mural or a diagram they have made
- having class members interview one or more committee members
- role playing
- developing projects—open house for parents, or a presentation to a civic group or to the P.T.A.
- writing summaries for the teacher and other classmates
- drawing a time line
- drawing pictures and charts
- drawing a map series
- presenting mock radio and television programs
- presenting a dramatization
- arranging for resource speakers
- presenting reports
- making scrapbooks or notebooks and displaying them
- sharing creative writings
- making model buildings or making wood and soap carvings
- having debates, forums, round-table discussions
- presenting monologues
- making bulletin boards
- presenting tape recordings
- making clay or plaster models and paper sculpture
- performing charades
- making flannel boards
- presenting illustrated talks at chalkboard or with opaque, filmstrip, and overhead projectors
- presenting puppet shows
- presenting shadow plays
- presenting photographic slide shows or committee-made movies

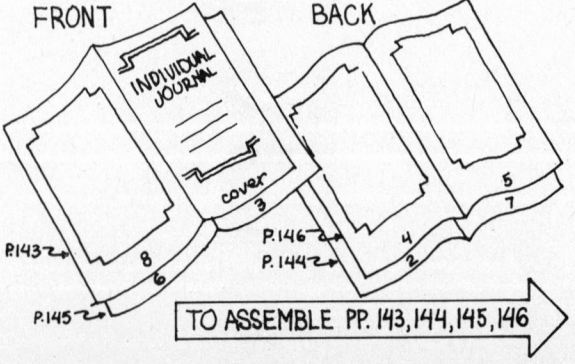

INDIVIDUAL JOURNAL

A Journal of My Progress in Group _____

Name(s) _____

Teacher _____

Class _____

- - - FOLD - - -

IX. Assessment of my Contributions to the Group

Self-Assessment	Group's Assessment	Teacher's Assessment

8

- - - CUT - - -

2

I. Unit Title

II. Class Objectives

III. Group Objectives

IV. My Objectives in the Group

V. Activities I Plan To Do in the Group

VI. My Interests in the Group

VII. Skills I Want To Develop in the Group

-------- FOLD --------

7

E. Art or Music Activities

Date	Activity	Comments

-------- CUT --------

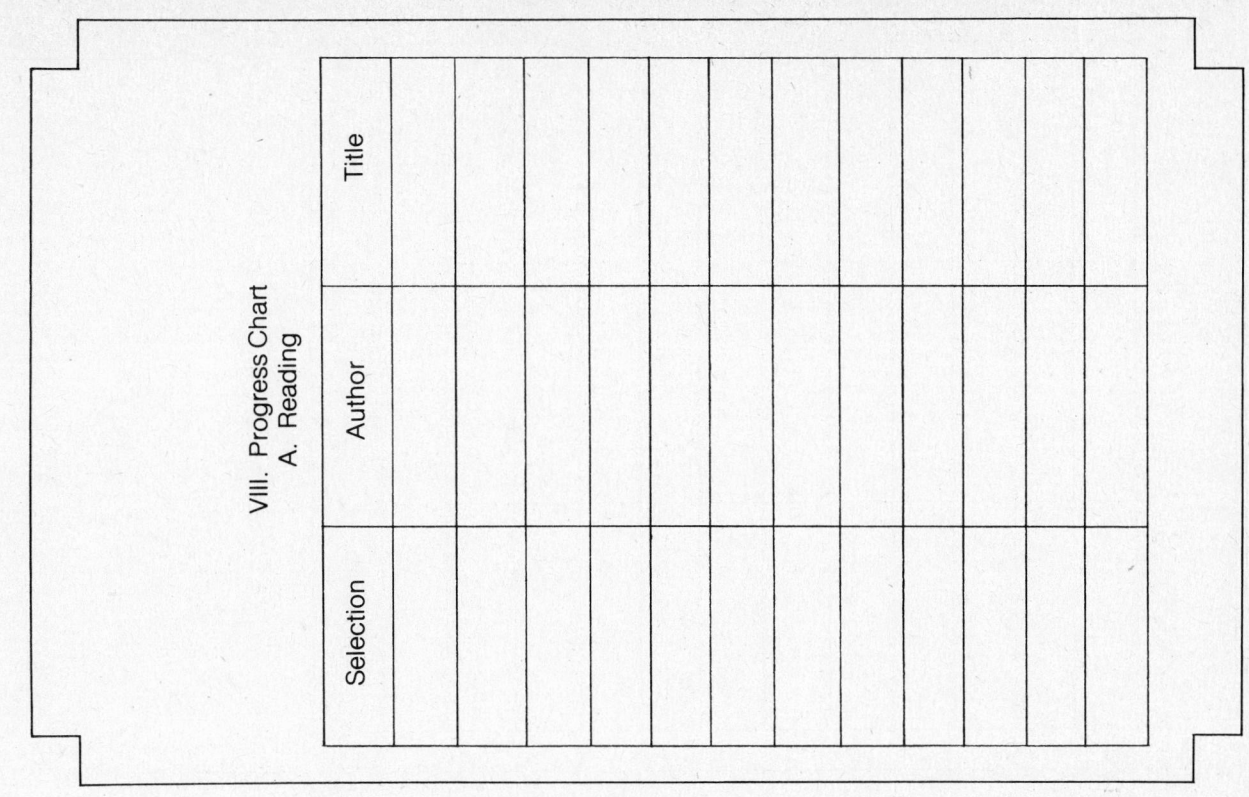

VIII. Progress Chart
A. Reading

Selection	Author	Title

3

D. Experiments and/or Construction
Activities

Date	Activity	Comments

6

CUT

B. Reports to the Group

Date	Topic	Comments

4

------------------------------- FOLD -------------------------------

C. Creative Writing and Drama Activities

Date	Topic and / or Title

5

------------------------------- CUT -------------------------------

Individual Evaluation for Task Group

Name _____ Date _____

1. So far, I have done the following to help the group define its purposes: _____
   _____
   _____

2. My specific contribution to the group task will be: _____
   _____
   _____

3. My progress so far is: _____
   _____
   _____

4. In completing my part of the group's task, I need help with the following: _____
   _____
   _____

5. I am presently using these resources: _____
   _____
   _____

6. I plan to complete my task by: _____

7. Other information my group and the teacher need to know about my task is: _____
   _____
   _____

Group Meeting Assessment Form

Name_____ Group_____

1. How do you feel the group meeting was today (circle one)?

   Not very good   Good   Very helpful   One of our
                                                               very best

2. How do you think the meeting could have been improved?_____

   _____

   _____

3. What was the objective of the meeting today? _____

   _____

4. How did you feel about the accomplishments of the objective (circle one)?

   Objective not   A little was   More than half   Objective
   accomplished   achieved   of the objective   achieved
                                        was completed

5. Did you feel good about your participation in the meeting? _____

   Why or why not?_____

   _____

   _____

6. Other comments: _____

   _____

   _____

   _____

Group Plan

Complete this form and give each group member and the teacher a copy.

  I. Group Title: _____

 II. Group Membership

    A. Chairperson or Leader: _____

    B. Secretary or Recorder: _____

    C. Other Members: _____

    _____

 III. Purposes, objectives, tasks, or problem area of the group: _____

    _____

    _____

 IV. Specific questions, subobjectives, or hypotheses of the group: _____

    _____

    _____

  V. Individual member responsibilities:

    _____

    _____

    _____

    _____

 VI. Chronology or time line for group tasks:

    _____

    _____

    _____

    _____

 VII. Possible sources of information:

    _____

    _____

    _____

 VIII. Proposed product or presentation of group's findings:

    _____

    _____

    _____

 IX. Means of assessing group efforts:

    _____

    _____

Group Progress Report

Title of Group _____ Date _____

For the week of _____

  I. The members of our group accomplished the following things this week:

_____

_____

_____

_____

  II. They used these resources:

          Name   *Resources*

_____

_____

_____

_____

_____

  III. They encountered these problems:

_____

_____

_____

_____

  IV. These members were unable to attend group meetings:

          Name   *Date*

_____

_____

_____

_____

  V. So far, group members seem to feel that the group's accomplishment is: _____

_____

_____

  VI. After this week, the following tasks remain to be accomplished:

_____

_____

_____

_____

9

Classroom Management In An Individualized Program

Classroom management is the means by which the teacher performs planning and record-keeping functions in an efficient manner that permits maximum individualization and student self-direction with minimum interruption to both the student and the overall classroom instructional program. The concept of classroom management encompasses all the processes involved in individualizing instruction: preassessment, prescription, engaging in learning alternatives, and postassessment. It communicates to teachers and students *who* will do *what, when,* and *where;* it further communicates what each student is engaged in and has already completed in a class.

WHAT DOES CLASSROOM MANAGEMENT MEAN TO TEACHERS AND STUDENTS?

Teachers say:

"Individualizing instruction makes it necessary to have a thorough system for management of student progress."

"Managing student progress involves record keeping."

"Record keeping is not evaluation, but it does flow naturally into evaluative processes."

"If individualized instruction is to meet its goal of helping the student learn at his own pace and level and in his own best learning style, management of the student's progress must also be individualized."

"The student should be allowed and encouraged to share in managing her progress in order to see her strengths and weaknesses. In this way, the student will become self-motivated in the achievement of her learning goals."

"Record keeping and managing student progress are continuous processes which involve the teacher and the student in accounting for and reporting individual growth and learning progress."

"The parents want to know how their child's school work is progressing and the student asks, 'What have I been learning?' The teacher wants to know how each child is progressing and also wants to have a way to report to administrators and parents."

"I need ways to schedule or assign students to learning centers and ways of best utilizing the limited amount of individualized learning materials in my classroom."

"Knowing which students are where and doing what is the key to success in an individualized program."

Students say:

"I like keeping track of my progress."

"Sometimes keeping my own records is extra work, but I can tell how much I've done and how much more I have to do."

"Most kids take it seriously. A few don't. The teacher has to help those who aren't serious."

"It makes you feel more like a first-class citizen."

"Checking into class the way we do makes more sense than the teacher calling the dumb roll."

"You need to know what you are supposed to do, and when, or some kids wouldn't do anything."

These comments by students and teachers illustrate that managing student progress in an individualized program involves determining

- *what* activities a student will do;
- *when* the student will do those activities;
- *where* the student will do those activities;
- *how* records will be maintained to indicate a student's progress in individualized activities and *how* these records will be used for student assessment.

Table 10
Managing Student Progress

DECISIONS ABOUT	DETERMINED BY
What educational activities the student can do	Purposes of the student Purposes of the teacher Objectives of a curriculum plan (e.g., unit, learning package, learning center, contract) Teacher-student planning Student's preferred learning style(s)
When the student will engage in activities	Objectives to be completed Learning alternatives available Results of diagnosis of students Schedule of classes "Fixed" activities in the school day (e.g., special classes, library periods) Space available for learning centers Space available for group work Space available for independent activity Materials available Length of time required to complete activities, tasks, experiments Day/week/month activities should be completed
Where the student will do activities	Appropriateness of doing activities at school or away from school Quiet study area locations Learning center locations Independent activity area locations Materials and media storage locations
How progress records will be kept and used for student assessment	Use of record keeping Records students will maintain Records teachers will maintain Methods employed in record keeping Means of reporting progress based on record-keeping information

To deal with these *what, when, where,* and *how* decisions, teachers need to consider

- ages and general abilities of students;
- student abilities and experiences in self-direction;
- student abilities and experiences in self-management;
- student experiences in self-evaluation;
- types and purposes of individualized approaches to be employed;
- facilities for record keeping;
- space for individualized activities and independent study;
- arrangements for grouping students for skill development activities, interest-centered activities, problem-solving activities, construction activities, and simulation and game activities;
- space required and available for individualized approaches (e.g., learning centers).

In addition, the *what, when, where,* and *how* of managing student progress can be determined as indicated in Table 10.

In summary, classroom management in an individualized program

- provides needed information for a more comprehensive understanding of the individual student;
- helps facilitate the classroom individualized program;
- provides information about individual student progress for both the student and the teacher;
- enables teachers to guide individual student learning more effectively;
- facilitates effective use of available classroom space and learning materials; and
- operationalizes alternative means of providing students with individual learning opportunities.

Examples Of Classroom Management Forms And Ideas

The examples contained in this section are primarily grouped according to functions. These are:

- prescriptions–assignments functions
- scheduling functions
- assessment–record-keeping–student progress functions

Some examples are designed to serve several functions.

Will the Real *You* Please Sign In?

Month_____

Week of _____

MONDAY	TUESDAY	WEDNESDAY	THURSDAY	FRIDAY

Week of _____

MONDAY	TUESDAY	WEDNESDAY	THURSDAY	FRIDAY

Duplicate a supply of sign-in sheets. Rather than calling roll, have students sign in the appropriate places.

Sign Here When You Have Done A(n)

SMALL GROUP DISCUSSION		SEMINAR		ORAL REPORT		SKIT	
Name(s)	Date:	Name(s)	Date:	Name(s)	Date:	Name(s)	Date:

Le Mans

Directions: Draw concentric circles around Le Mans each time you accomplish one of the objectives below. Number and date the circle. If you make it around five times in less than one week, you're a great driver!

1. Write correctly the conjugations of the four major tenses of the three types of verbs.

2. Use the *passé composé* and *imparfait* correctly in 10 sentences.

3. Correctly conjugate *aller, être,* and *savoir.*

4. Correctly use the verb tenses in the three types of "Si" clauses in 15 sentences.

5. Be able to list three uses of the subjunctive.

When you have completed the five laps, please take the posttest and give it to your teacher to mark.

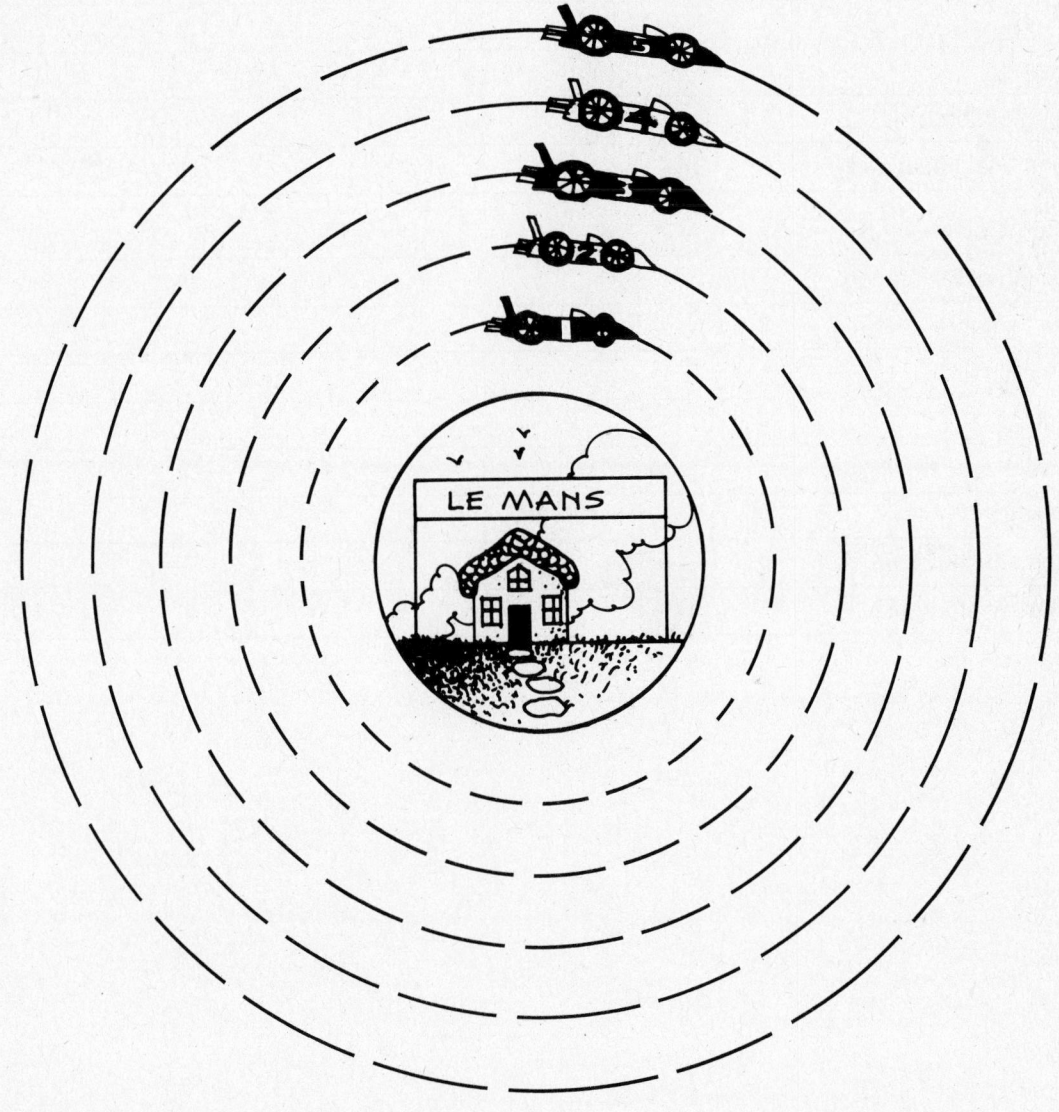

Name _____

Period _____

Date begun_____ Date completed _____

Industrial Arts Welding Center Progress Report

Name _____ Period _____

Date begun _____ Date completed _____

Directions: You must receive a notation of *S* (satisfactory) in each category after the second check before you may use the welder for project work. Always wear eye and body protection equipment.

Acetylene Welding	1ST CHECK	2ND CHECK	COMMENTS
Opening cylinders			
Adjusting regulators			
Lighting torch			
Adjusting flame			
Butt weld			
Lap weld			
Chipping			
Cutting off torch			
Putting equipment away			

Electric Welding			
Selection of heat range			
Project setup			
Striking an arc			
Butt weld			
Lap weld			
Chipping			
Equipment shutdown			
Equipment storage			

Student Profile

Name _____ Period _____

LEARNING PACKAGES COMPLETED

1. _____
2. _____
3. _____
4. _____
5. _____
6. _____
7. _____
8. _____
9. _____
10. _____

PROJECTS COMPLETED

1. _____
2. _____
3. _____
4. _____
5. _____
6. _____
7. _____
8. _____
9. _____
10. _____

LEARNING CENTERS APPROVED FOR USE

1. _____
2. _____
3. _____
4. _____
5. _____
6. _____
7. _____
8. _____
9. _____
10. _____

CONTRACTS COMPLETED

1. _____
2. _____
3. _____
4. _____
5. _____
6. _____
7. _____
8. _____
9. _____
10. _____

Individual Work-in-Progress Report

Directions: This report should be completed before each scheduled conference with the teacher and will remain on file in your folder.

Name _____

Class _____ Date _____

Activity _____

I ☐ have begun work,
  ☐ have completed the work,
  ☐ am working now,
  ☐ have not begun.

I expect to turn this activity in on_____
                                 (approximate date)

I have decided on the following reporting alternative:_____

_____

_____

I am having difficulty with the following aspects of the activity:_____

_____

_____

_____

_____

I am planning to add to or revise the activity as follows:_____

_____

_____

_____

_____

_____

_____

Signed _____

Learning Center Progress Chart

Name: _____

Directions: Use this chart to record the date each learning center activity was completed.

TITLE OF CENTER	ACTIVITIES	DATE COMPLETED

Learning Packages Cumulative Report

Name: _____

Directions: When you finish all objectives in an individual learning package, record the title of the package, the date completed, and the final grade.

TITLE OF PACKAGE	DATE COMPLETED	GRADE

Progress Chart for Learning Packages

Name: _____

Title of Package: _____

Directions: When working on a learning package, use this sheet to record your progress. As you finish your activities, indicate this below. When you finish all activities for a particular objective, enter the number of the objective and the date. Also indicate the method used in reporting. The teacher will enter your grade for each objective and the final grade. When you finish the total package, indicate this on the Learning Packages Cumulative Report.

ACTIVITIES COMPLETED	OBJECTIVES COMPLETED		METHOD OF REPORTING	GRADE
	NUMBER	DATE		
			FINAL GRADE	

Progress Report for Series of Contracts

Name: _____

Date contracts begun: _____ Date finished: _____

CONTRACTS	GRADE CONTRACTED FOR	GRADE ACHIEVED	REMARKS

Student's remarks concerning progress or general feelings about the series: _____
_____
_____

Teacher's reply: _____
_____
_____

Student's intentions concerning next series: _____
_____
_____
_____

Teacher's suggestions, modifications to, and / or approval of student's intentions: _____
_____
_____
_____

Progress Record for Round-Robin Learning Centers

Name: _____

CENTER NUMBER	TOPIC	ACTIVITIES COMPLETED	REMARKS
1			
2			
3			
4			
5			
6			
7			
8			
9			
10			

Topics might include Current Events, Advertisements, Reporting, Job Seeking, Women's Liberation, The Courts, Medicine and You, Income Tax, Poverty, Racial Prejudice, etc.

Before and After Continuum

Name: _____

Directions: Fill out one of these forms before you begin work on your contract and after its completion. Be frank and honest. This evaluation will not be considered in your grade. Use the following numbers in your evaluation:

1 = Very unsatisfied (displeased)
2 = Moderately unsatisfied
3 = Neutral
4 = Satisfied
5 = Very satisfied (excited)

I am _____ with the format of this contract.

I am _____ with the activities offered in the contract.

I am _____ with the reporting alternatives offered in the contract.

I am _____ with the teacher's statement of what I will gain from doing this contract.

I am _____ with the assessment techniques used by the teacher in this contract.

I am _____ about the learning alternatives offered in the contract.

I am _____ with the materials and media for this contract.

I am _____ with the facility with which I can locate and use these resources.

Learning Centers Daily Progress Record

Name: _____

Directions: This record will enable you and the teacher to maintain an up-to-date account of your work and will be used in an assessment conference. Complete this record daily and keep it in your folder.

LEARNING CENTERS	I	II	III	IV	V	VI	VII	VIII	IX	X
Date Begun										
Date Finished										
Activities Completed										
Easiest Center										
Hardest Center										
Most Interesting										
Least Interesting										

Other Comments: _____

_____

_____

_____

_____

_____

_____

Reading Center Progress Chart

Directions: Put an X in the box when you complete the numbered activities, which are written on the learning alternative cards. If you do the activity over because of too many mistakes, write your name again and recheck the activity number.

NAME	ACTIVITY #1	ACTIVITY #2	NAME	ACTIVITY #1	ACTIVITY #2

Student's Final Assessment of Progress

Directions: To be completed after the final contract activity and filed in your folder for the teacher's consideration.

Name: _____

Class: _____

Date: _____

Contract Title: _____

List of objectives contracted: _____

_____

_____

_____

_____

List and description of activities contracted: _____

_____

_____

_____

_____

_____

Grade contracted: _____

Assessment of instructional objectives: _____

_____

_____

_____

_____

_____

Assessment of the quality of my completed activities and reporting alternatives: _____

_____

_____

_____

_____

_____

Estimate of the grade that I deserve in accordance with the above criteria: _____

Conference Record of_____

Key:

Place
- H = Home
- S = School
- Ph = Phone

Nature
- R = Routine
- P = Problem
- E = Emergency

DATE	PLACE	NATURE	INITIALED BY	PARTICIPANTS	COMMENTS AND/OR RECOMMENDATIONS

Summary Sheet for Contract on _____

Name _____

Grade contracted for _____ Grade achieved _____

Date of contract _____

Reading completed (teacher's comments will indicate acceptability):

DATE STARTED	TITLE	AUTHOR	PAGE NOS.	DATE FINISHED	COMMENTS

Projects completed (teacher's comments will indicate acceptability):

DATE STARTED	PROJECT	MATERIALS USED	DATE FINISHED	COMMENTS

Reports completed (teacher's comments will indicate acceptability):

DATE STARTED	SUBJECT	METHOD AND MATERIALS	DATE FINISHED	COMMENTS

Conferences held:

DATE	NATURE OF CONFERENCE	NEED FOR FUTURE CONFERENCES OR COMMENTS

Evaluation Sheet for the Learning Package Entitled _____

_____

Name _____

Class _____ Date _____

CRITERIA	EXCELLENT	VERY GOOD	SATISFACTORY	SATISFACTORY LOW	UNSATISFACTORY
Following of Directions					
Adherence to Objective #1					
Adherence to Objective #2					
Adherence to Objective #3					
Resourceful Use of the Novel					
Evaluation of Conferences					
Completeness					
Use of Class Time					

Tabulation: _____

Final Grade: _____

Record Sheet for Individual Learning Package on _____

Name _____

Directions: This sheet will provide you and the teacher with a progress record for this package. After completing the necessary information, use the conference sign-up board to arrange a conference with the teacher. This record should be kept in your folder and filled in daily.

OBJECTIVES	ACTIVITIES COMPLETED	DATE COMPLETED	ACTIVITIES NOT YET COMPLETED	TEACHER-STUDENT EVALUATION
I				
II				
III				
IV				
V				

Individual Interest Research Paper Progress Record

Directions. This record will provide you and the teacher with information about your progress on your project. Keep this sheet in your folder.

Your Name: _____

Title: _____

Date Approved and Begun: _____

Date Completed: _____

Resources Used: _____

_____

_____

_____

_____

_____

_____

_____

_____

_____

Outline Submitted for Approval: _____

Rough Draft Submitted: _____

Final Draft Completed: _____

Final Assessment: _____

_____

_____

_____

_____

_____

_____

_____

_____

_____

Parental Permission Slip for Shop Activities

My son or daughter _____ has my permission to use the pieces of equipment indicated below after receiving proper instruction in the equipment's use. I realize my son or daughter has the responsibility of wearing the safety equipment provided. No equipment will be used until proficiency tests have been passed.

	YES	NO
1. Electric arc welder		
2. Acetylene welder		
3. Propane torch		
4. Electric grinder		
5. Table saw		
6. Saber saw		
7. Portable circular saw		
8. Soldering iron		
9. Drill press		
10. Router		
11. Band saw		
12. Belt sander		
13. Electric drill		
14. Valve grinder		

In Case of an Emergency

Doctor_____ Phone _____

Father's Name_____ Mother's Name _____

Work Phone_____ Work Phone_____

Home Phone _____ Home Phone _____

Neighbor's Name _____ Neighbor's Phone _____

I would like to alert the teacher to the following health problems my child has: _____

_____

_____

_____   _____
(Date)   (Signature of Parent or Guardian)

Contract Prescription Sheet

Name _____

Date _____ Class _____

GRADE RECEIVED	
GRADE CONTRACTED FOR	
TEACHER EVALUATION OF ACTIVITIES AND REPORTING ALTERNATIVES	
REPORTING ALTERNATIVES	
ACTIVITIES IN PROGRESS	
ACTIVITIES CONTRACTED FOR AND SIGNING DATE	
PRIMARY BEHAVIORAL OBJECTIVE	
CONTRACT TITLE	

This prescription sheet can be used by the student as an outline of activities he has contracted for and by the teacher as a record and progress report. It might serve as a general outline guide at the beginning of the student's contract project.

176

Individual Student Prescription Sheet

Student's Name _____

Date or Week _____

SUBJECT	ASSIGNMENT OR ACTIVITIES	MATERIALS NEEDED	ACTIVITIES COMPLETED	EVALUATION

Algebra Skills Sequence Chart

SKILL 10	Subtract poly-nomials		SKILL 20	Classify numbers
SKILL 9	Add poly-nomials		SKILL 19	Graph a system of linear equations
SKILL 8	Solve inequalities with one variable		SKILL 18	Graph a linear equation
SKILL 7	Identify axioms of real numbers		SKILL 17	Subtract poly-nomial fractions
SKILL 6	Solve problems with one variable		SKILL 16	Add poly-nomial fractions
SKILL 5	Solve equations of one variable		SKILL 15	Divide poly-nomial fractions
SKILL 4	Divide signed numbers		SKILL 14	Multiply poly-nomial fractions
SKILL 3	Multiply signed numbers		SKILL 13	Factor trinomials
SKILL 2	Subtract signed numbers		SKILL 12	Divide poly-nomials
SKILL 1	Add signed numbers		SKILL 11	Multiply poly-nomials

Cover the skill chart with acetate and use a wax pencil or felt pen to assign students to skills in which they need practice. When a student masters a skill, move his name to the next skill area on the chart.

Quadrilaterals

Name _____

Directions: When you have learned the characteristics of each special quadrilateral, write in the dates and place this form in your record-keeping folder.

THEOREMS AND PROOFS ON SQUARES

_____

THEOREMS AND PROOFS ON RECTANGLES

_____

THEOREMS AND PROOFS ON PARALLELOGRAMS

_____

THEOREMS AND PROOFS ON THE RHOMBUS

_____

THEOREMS AND PROOFS ON THE TRAPEZOID

_____

Circles

Name _____

Directions: When you have successfully completed the work on circles, write in the dates in the circle below and place this form in your record-keeping folder.

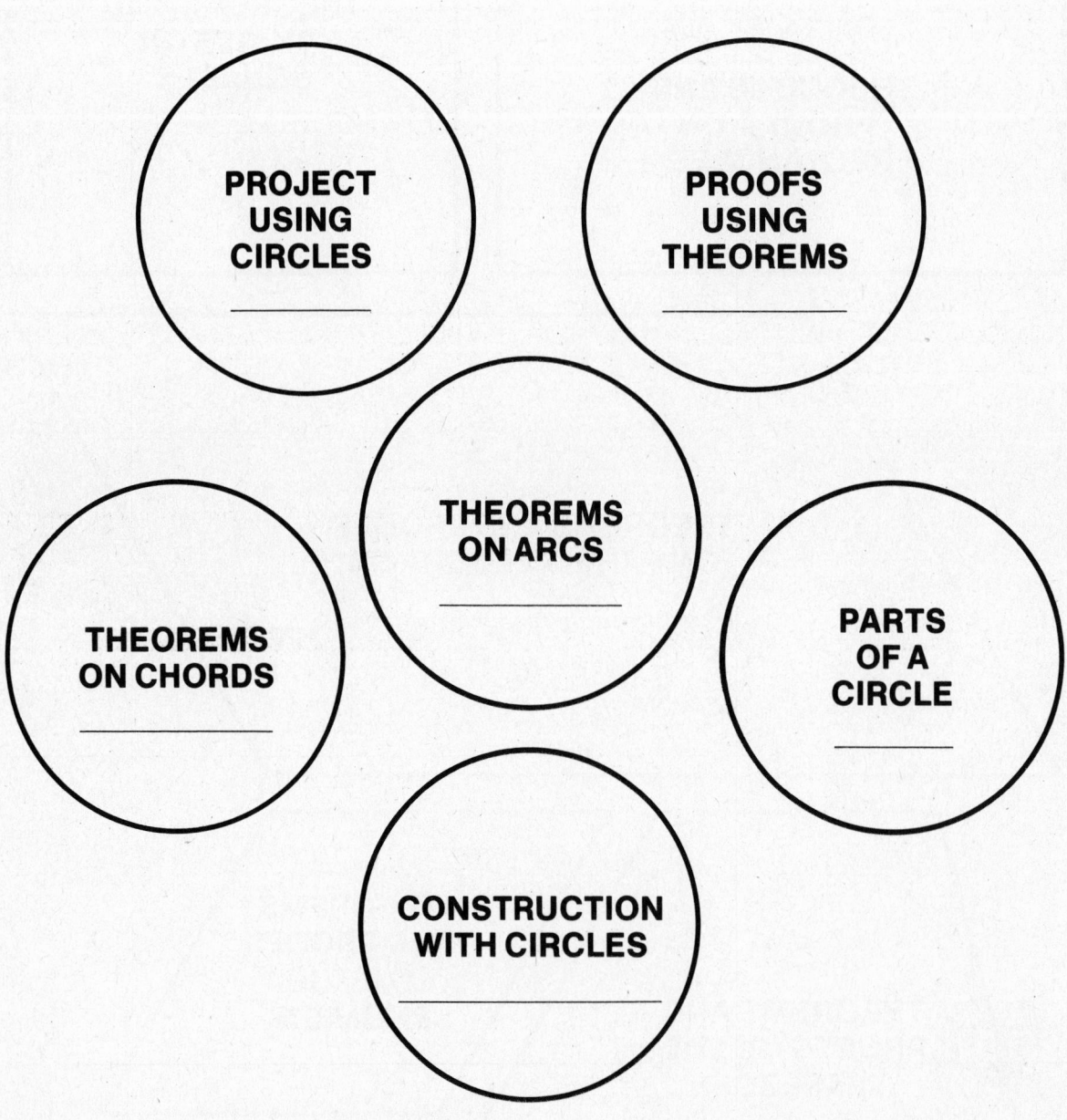

Triangle Congruences

Name _____

Directions: When you have successfully completed the work on each method of proving two triangles congruent, write the dates in the octagon below and place this form in your folder.

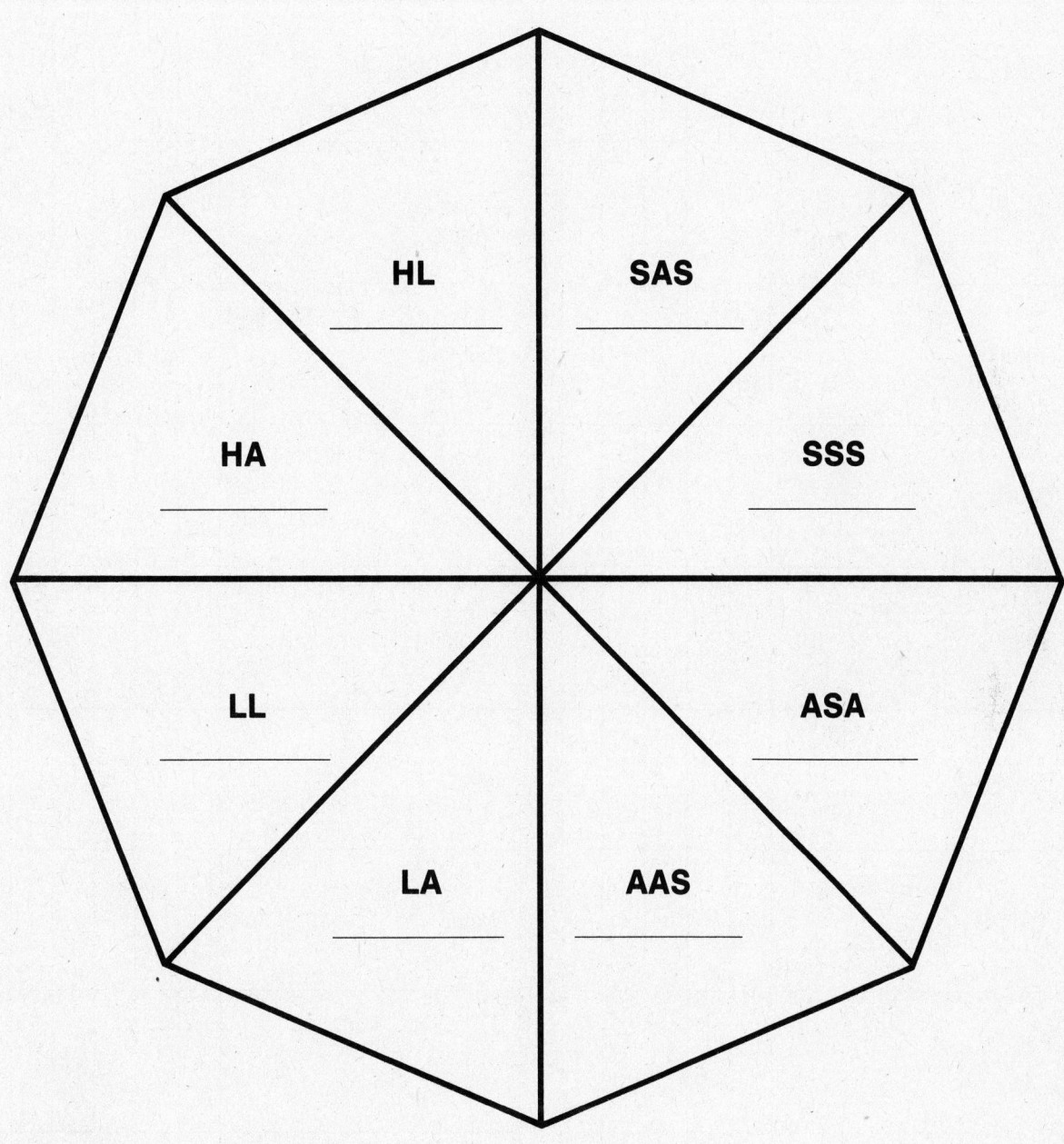

Learning Center Assignments

Name: _____

Date: _____

Name: _____

Date: _____

CENTERS	M	T	W	TH	F
Reading					
Graphs					
Poetry					
Printing					
Music					
Plants					
Cooking					
Blocks					

CENTERS	M	T	W	TH	F
Reading					
Measurement					
Creative Writing					
Painting					
Dance					
Cooking					
Sand					
Water					

Reproduce small charts indicating available centers. Use these charts to assign students to centers by giving a chart to each student daily or for a week.

Learning Center Daily Progress Report

Name: _____ Date: _____

Directions: At the end of each class period each day, fill out one of these reports. Indicate the title of the learning center and how much progress you made in the center. This will allow you to reflect on what you have accomplished and allow the teacher to plan assignments to learning centers for the next class period.

Title of Center: _____

Number of days assigned to it: _____

Activities completed today: _____

_____

_____

_____

_____

Activities yet to be completed: _____

_____

_____

_____

_____

Learning Center Daily Progress Report

Name: _____ Date: _____

Directions: At the end of each class period each day, fill out one of these reports. Indicate the title of the learning center and how much progress you made in the center. This will allow you to reflect on what you have accomplished and allow the teacher to plan assignments to learning centers for the next class period.

Title of Center: _____

Number of days assigned to it: _____

Activities completed today: _____

_____

_____

_____

Activities yet to be completed: _____

_____

_____

_____

_____

Math Grid

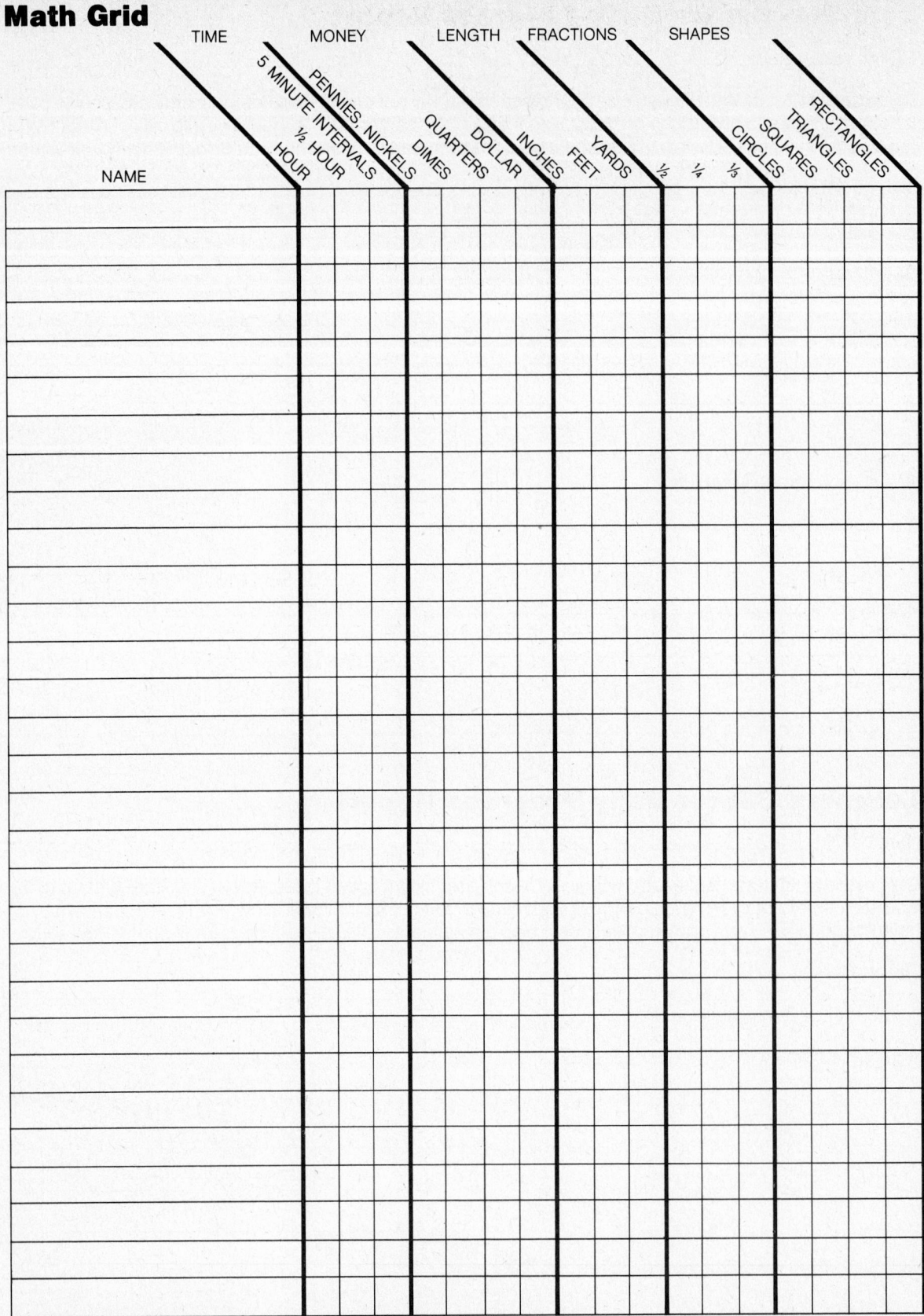

The Math and Alphabet and Beginning Sounds grids can be used to prescribe activities for students and to keep a record of what students have accomplished. One line can be drawn in the appropriate square to show that a student is working on a particular objective (/), and a second line can be drawn when the student completes the objective (X).

Often teachers add the date the objective was started and/or completed, or color code the marks in the squares. Such procedures make it easy to determine if students are working consistently or erratically, and should be a reminder if a student is bogged down for too long on one objective.

Alphabet and Beginning Sounds Grid

NAME

A B C D E F G H I J K L M N O P Q R S T U V W X Y Z
a b c d e f g h i j k l m n o p q r s t u v w x y z

Individual Interest Reading Areas

Directions: Below you will find space provided for the book, author, and your personal comments on any books you choose to read for your outside reading assignments. After you have completed each book, schedule a short conference with the teacher to discuss the reading. This record sheet should remain in your record-keeping folder.

DATE STARTED	DATE COMPLETED	TITLE	AUTHOR	COMMENTS (AFTER TEACHER CONFERENCE)

Basketball Objectives Sequence

Objective: Define *dribble, dunking, player, control, foul, traveling, screen, pivot, jump ball, double foul,* and *blocking* with 100% accuracy.

Students: _____

_____
_____
_____
_____
_____
_____
_____
_____
_____
_____

Objective: Chart the dimensions of a regulation size basketball court on graph paper.

Students: _____

_____
_____
_____
_____
_____
_____
_____
_____
_____
_____

Objective: State physical skill requirements for the guard, forward, and center positions.

Students: _____

_____
_____
_____
_____
_____
_____
_____
_____
_____
_____

Objective: Diagram 3 offensive and 3 defensive plays.

Students: _____

_____
_____
_____
_____
_____
_____
_____
_____
_____
_____

Objective: State and demonstrate 2 fundamentals each of passing, shooting, defensive movement, and rebounding.

Students: _____

_____
_____
_____
_____
_____
_____
_____
_____
_____
_____

Objective: Write the official rules concerning traveling, basket interference, goal tending, and postplay fouls.

Students: _____

_____
_____
_____
_____
_____
_____
_____
_____
_____
_____

A student's name is placed under the objective she/he is currently developing.

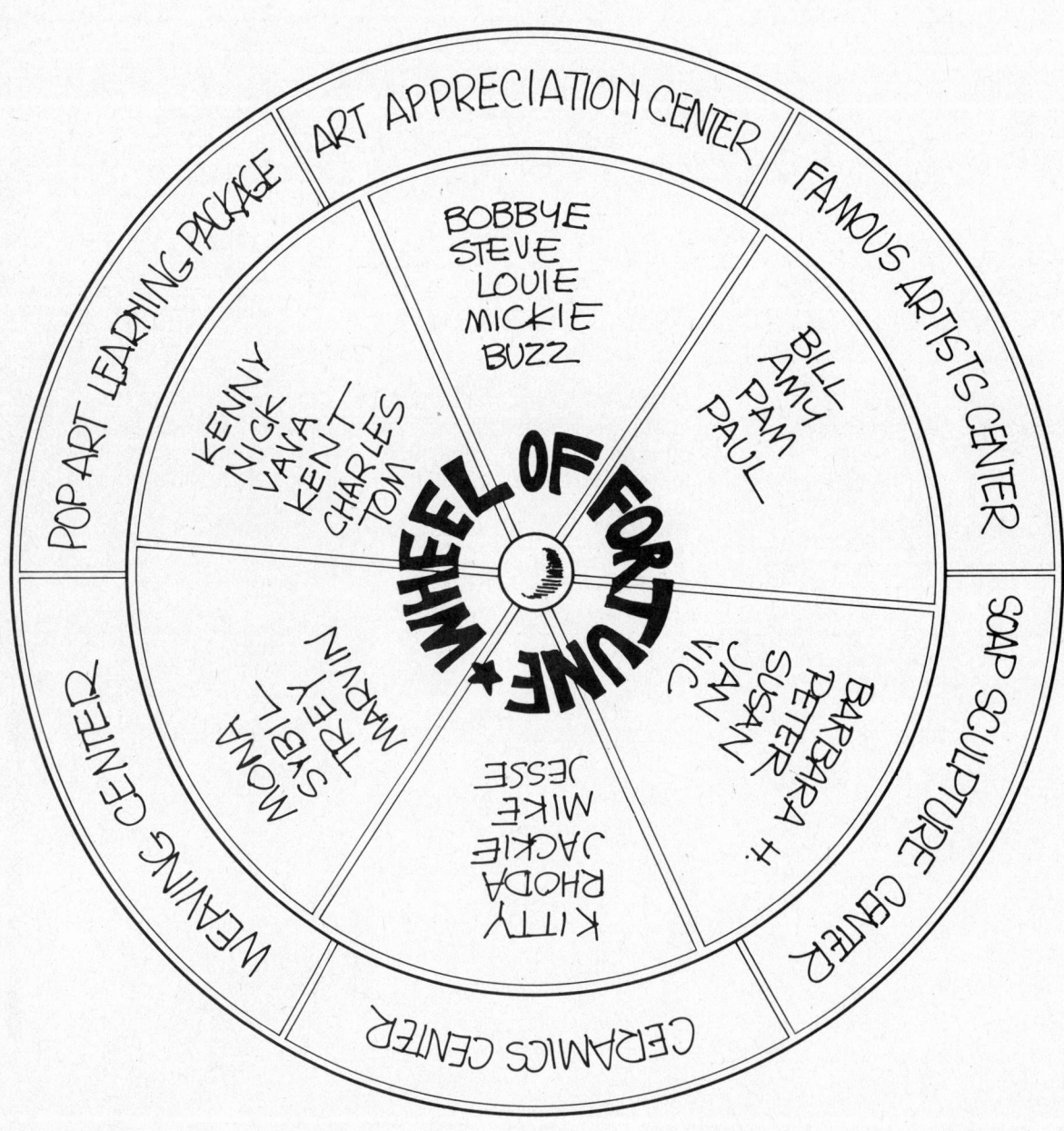

This management activity can be used effectively in a single-subject classroom. The wheel indicates which students are assigned to various individualized activities. After a few days, the wheel can be rotated to assign students to different activities.

If you need me, I have gone to...

Make a management board with names of places students can go in the school. Screw cup hooks on the board and make a tag for each student. Students place their tags on the hooks to indicate where they have gone.

LIBRARY	SCHOOL OFFICE	SCHOOL STORE	MUSIC	ART	RESTROOM
BILL				KIT	LISA
TOD					

FRED VIC SAM CORY KIM

Put Your Name on the Map

Make and post an Exploratory Center Map like the one shown below. Have students use the map to sign up for center activities on Friday. Limit places for signatures to maximum number center can accommodate.

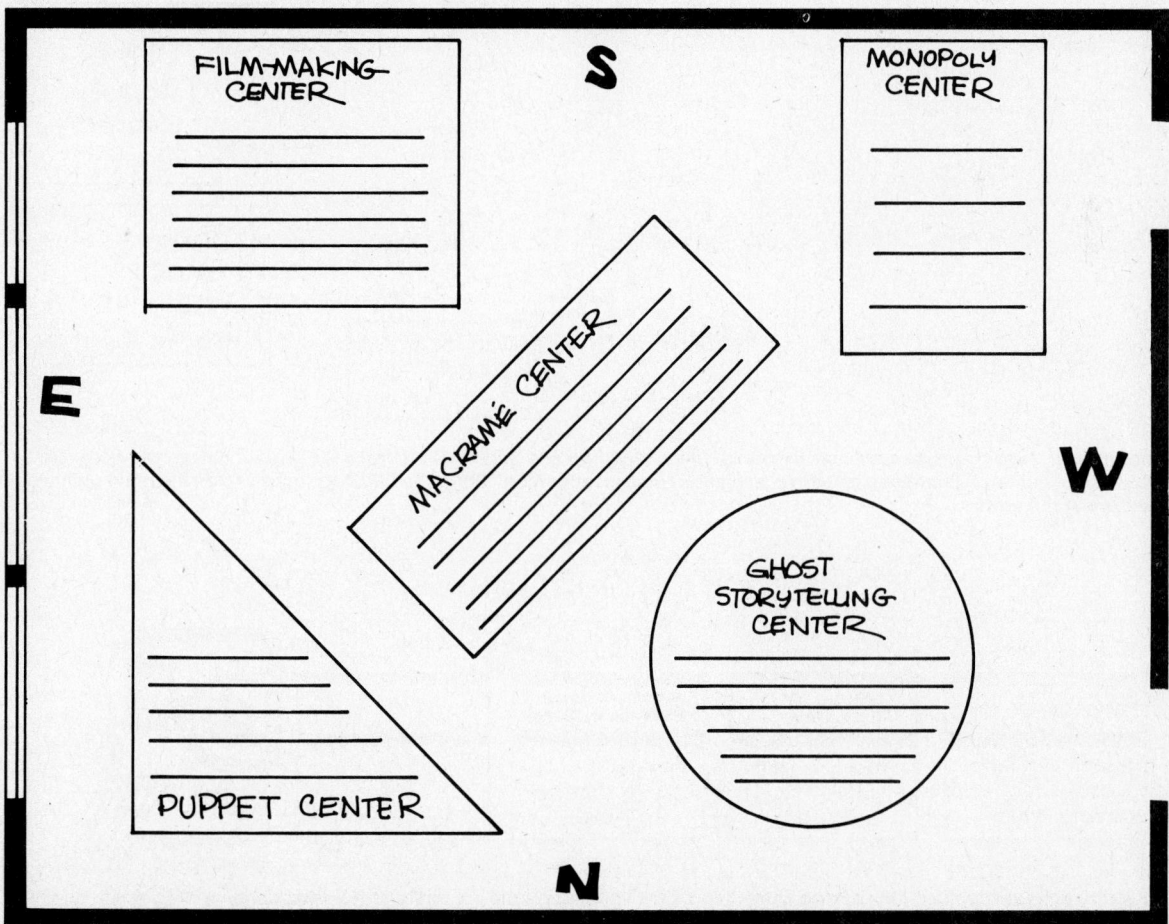

189

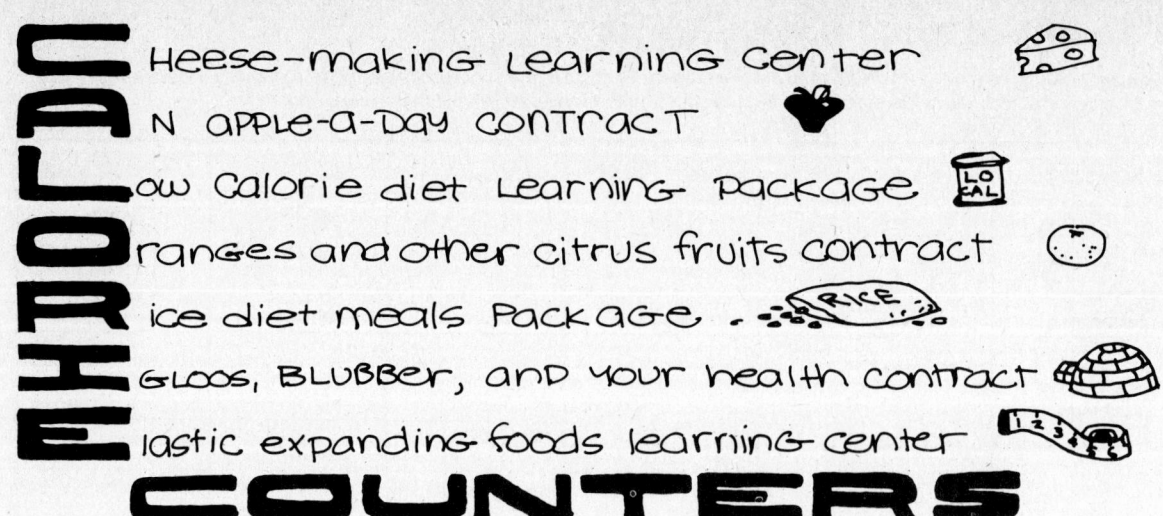

CALORIE

Cheese-making Learning Center

An apple-a-Day contract

Low calorie diet Learning Package

Oranges and other citrus fruits contract

Rice diet meals Package

Igloos, Blubber, and your health contract

Elastic expanding foods Learning center

COUNTERS

Schedule or prescribe students into these individualized activities by placing names in appropriate areas.

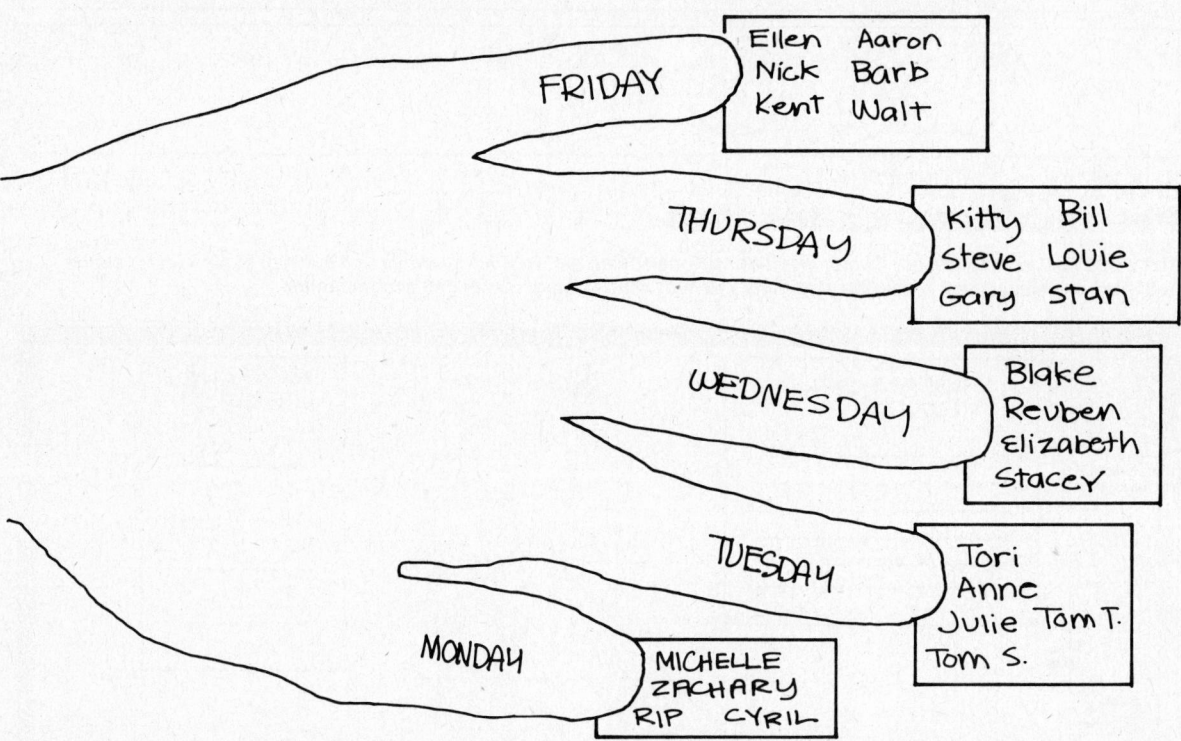

FRIDAY

Ellen	Aaron
Nick	Barb
Kent	Walt

THURSDAY

Kitty	Bill
Steve	Louie
Gary	Stan

WEDNESDAY

Blake
Reuben
Elizabeth
Stacey

TUESDAY

Tori
Anne
Julie Tom T.
Tom S.

MONDAY

MICHELLE
ZACHARY
RIP CYRIL

The Helping Hands management activity can be used to assign and schedule students for various classroom committees and responsibilities. Committee names (e.g., plants, room arrangement, library) could be substituted on the hand outline for the days of the week.

HITCH A RIDE ON OUR CENTER SPECIAL

PAPER MAKING CENTER	TOBACCO FARM CENTER	CENTER ASSIGN- MENTS FOR WEDNESDAY
Glen Alan	Andy Ike	Sonja
Larry Edie	Yuriko Tad	Cary Zeke
Carole Nan	Melanie	Susanna

CENTER SPECIAL

This schedule-assignment idea can be used to indicate which students are assigned to what centers, or indicate days or times students are assigned to centers.

INDIVIDUAL and GROUP SCHEDULE

INDIVIDUAL'S NAME: _____

or NAMES OF GROUP MEMBERS: _____

_____

_____

	MONDAY	TUESDAY	WEDNESDAY	THURSDAY	FRIDAY
8:30	Class meeting	Class meeting	School assembly	Class meeting	Trip to the Zoo
9:00	Arithmetic skills center	Arithmetic skills center		Reading Center	
9:30	Science learning package	Interest Center	Social Studies Contract	Film	

NAME _____

SUBJECT	M	T	W	T	F
art	✓				
english				✓	
math			✓		
reading					✓
science	✓				
ind. study			✓		
history				✓	

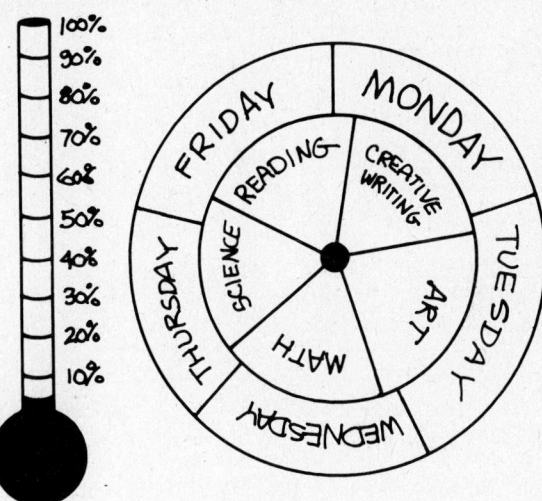

10

Individualizing Instruction Using Educational Games

The authors are indebted to Dr. Margaret Grater and Mrs. Beverly Townsley for the major work in developing and writing this chapter. Dr. Grater is a teacher trainer at the Professional Development Center in the Fresno City Unified School District, Fresno, California. Mrs. Townsley is the Inservice Training Coordinator for Teacher Corps, University of South Carolina, Columbia, South Carolina.

Some of the games in this chapter were adapted from game ideas originating in Fresno City Unified School District and the University of South Carolina's Model School Project.

An *educational game,* as the term is used in this chapter, is a learning alternative requiring manipulation of knowledge and concrete objectives to reinforce or extend a *previously taught* concept or skill. It does not mean the same as *simulations* as discussed in Chapter 8 of this book. Educational games, like any other activity used for reinforcement, should be preceded by a teacher-taught lesson.

GAME FORMATS

Although there are hundreds of games that can be used for educational activities, there are few basic game formats. Five of these are:

1. *matrix board games,* which include chess, checkers, bingo, and tic tac toe;
2. *playing board games,* using movers, dice, spinner, or cards, which include commercial games such as Monopoly and Parcheesi;
3. *card games,* such as Concentration;
4. *pieces and parts games,* which include puzzles, dominoes, and other games with movable parts;
5. *self-check games,* such as pizza wheels, string boards, or other activities where students can compete either with themselves or with another student.

By learning these formats and the advantages and disadvantages of each, the classroom teacher can easily devise manipulative activities that will not only reinforce concepts or skills taught but will also provide reinforcement through manipulation at various cognitive levels of thinking. Each format is discussed at length later in the chapter.

GENERAL CRITERIA FOR GAME CONSTRUCTION

1. *Choosing a Format.* The following questions should be considered in choosing a game format:
   a. Which format promotes the level of thinking needed for a particular goal or objective?
   b. Which format is suitable for the number of students who will play the game?
   c. Which format best suits the age of students who will use the game?
2. *Durability.* When selecting construction materials, the instructor should choose materials that will last. *The more durable the game, the less often it will have to be replaced.* For example: (a) poster board is more durable than construction paper; (b) lamination is more durable than contact paper or acetate (however, one should use contact or acetate if

laminating is not possible); (c) materials should be stapled rather than taped whenever possible. In other words, all game parts should be reinforced.

3. *Appearance.* A game that is neat and colorful will attract more students.
4. *Appropriateness.* The age and interests of the students using the game should be considered. For example, the printing of game content for primary grades is not only appropriate but usually necessary; whereas, the writing or typing of content is more appropriate for intermediate grades and necessary for junior high and high school grades. Cover designs and pictures should reflect the interests of the students and be appropriate for those who will use the game. Language used in all parts of the game should be that of the learner.
5. *Content.* The content of the game should reflect the level of thinking desired of the students. Some games can help students memorize or review, while others can help students apply or synthesize knowledge.

   Remember, a student should be able to win at a game. Losing should be due to a lack of strategy rather than to the difficulty of content. Finally, be sure to identify any prerequisite skills or knowledge necessary for students before the game is prescribed.

6. *Parts of a Game.* Each game should include:
   a. *Purpose.* Why is the student playing the game? This can also be written as an objective.
   b. *Instructions and rules.* These should be written so that each step and rule for playing

is easily understood by the students, should be written in the vocabulary of the learners, should describe the numbers of students who can play, and should specify the procedures for resolving disagreements (e.g., using answer keys).

c. *Parts and pieces.* All playing parts should be kept together. If a response sheet or marking pencil is required, these should be included.

d. *Container.* All game parts should be placed in envelopes, folders, or boxes.

e. *Answer keys.* The more often answer keys are included, the less often the teacher will have to respond to questions.

CHECKERBOARDS

Characteristics
- Games using checkerboards are limited to *two* players.
- Game boards can be designed for any age or grade level.
- Game boards can be used for various levels of thinking.

When to Use
Checkerboards may be used when you want students to
- recall ideas,
- describe parts of things,
- give examples,
- explain abstract concepts,
- make up a situation using the same learning principle.

Content—What to Use
Any subject area content can be adapted for use with checkerboards. Boards can be *permanent* or *multi-use.* Permanent boards are ones with content written permanently on them; multi-use boards have no fixed content and rely on question cards or acetate overlays to change content for different students.

How to Make
Materials
1. 2 sheets of 12″ x 18″ construction paper (select two different colors)
2. 1 sheet of heavy cardboard or heavy poster board cut to size 13″ x 16″
3. contact paper or roll of acetate (or board can be laminated)
4. scissors, cutting board, stapler, masking tape (select tape color to complement construction paper)
5. 7 sheets of 9″ x 12″ tag board or poster board (1 sheet for task cards, 2 sheets for answer key, and 4 sheets for question cards if constructing a multi-use board);
6. 2 library pockets
7. box or envelope large enough to hold game board and all parts of the game

Making the Board
1. Cut one sheet of construction paper to 12″ x 15″.
2. Measure and mark 1½″ from each edge, as illustrated in Figure 18.
3. Draw lines 1½″ apart as shown in Figure 18.
4. Cut along these lines. It is easier to use an x-acto knife or razor. Lay ruler along the line and cut.
5. Cut one sheet of construction paper into 1½″ x 12″ strips. Eight strips are needed.
6. Weave these strips into a mat (see Figure 19). Weave the first strip over and under. Work strip tight to edge of 12″ side.
7. Work second strip opposite first strip and push it tightly against the first strip.
8. Do the same for the other strips. The last strip is usually difficult to weave. It might be necessary to cut into the 1½″ edge at the end approximately ⅛″ to relieve tension on the paper.
9. Place the woven checkerboard on the 13″ x 16″ cardboard or poster board.
10. Carefully staple leaving ½″ on each side.

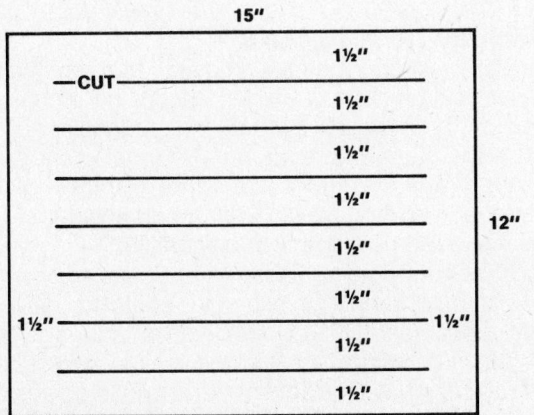

Figure 18

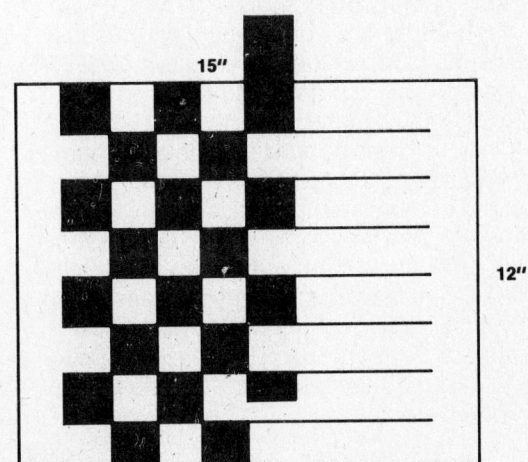

Figure 19

Adding the Content

Consider the two options available, decide which option is desired, and follow the directions for construction.

Option #1. If content is to be written permanently on the board, decide on the content and write it on the squares (Figure 20).

a. A maximum of 32 items can be used, one for each square.
b. Write the content so that both players can read it.
c. Be sure to put content on only one color of the construction paper.
d. When you complete this part, go on to "Finishing Touches."

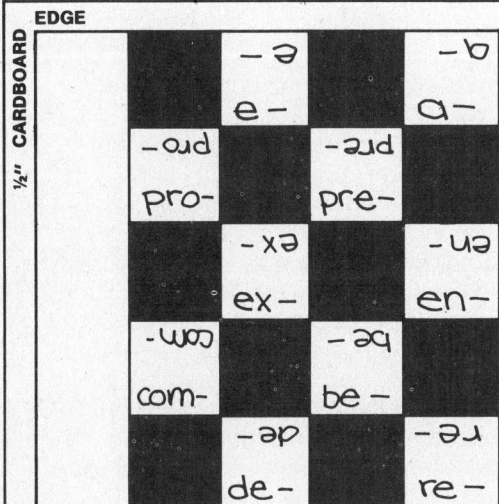

Figure 20

Option #2. A *multi-use board* or blank game board can be used to change content. There are several ways to use such a board.

a. By using acetate to cover the game board, content can be added with a grease pencil or water-based transparency pen. One advantage of this approach is that only a few boards are needed. A disadvantage is that the content might be accidentally erased or smudged while students are playing the game. If this approach is chosen, go on to "Finishing Touches."
b. The board can be left clear and cards can be used. Using this approach a student draws a card from a stack, reads it, answers it, then moves. The types of questions can be varied to promote different levels of thinking. Consider including some type of answer key with this approach, as well as with the others. If this approach is chosen, go on to "Finishing Touches." See "Making Game Task Cards."

Finishing Touches

1. *Covering the Board*
   a. Use acetate. Cut the acetate 13" x 16". Staple. Tape around the ½" edge on both sides of the board, or
   b. Laminate, or
   c. Use contact paper. Tape around edge on both sides of the board.
2. *Making Checkers*
   a. Select two different colors of construction paper or poster board.
   b. Mark 1" x 1" squares.
   c. Laminate or put contact paper on one side.
   d. Mark the same squares on the other side with any symbol of your choice to indicate the same as *crowning* in checkers.
   e. Laminate or cover with contact paper and cut.
   f. Put checkers into library pockets or envelopes marked PLAYER 1 and PLAYER 2.
3. *Making Game Task Cards*
   a. Write the purpose of the game.
   b. State what is needed to play.
      (1) 2 players
      (2) checkers and board
      (3) cards
      (4) answer key
   c. State how to play. The rules for playing are the same as for regular checkers. (Write or record these for younger children.) Other rules of the game to be written for students:
      (1) You must . . . (e.g., "answer the question," "make the word," "solve the problem") . . . in the square from which you are moving and the square to which you are going.
      (2) The winning player is the one who can remove all her opponent's checkers from the board or who can block the last checker so that the opponent cannot move without losing.
4. *Answer Key*
   Make an answer key whenever possible so that students may refer to this source.
5. *Box Up the Game*
   See "How to Make Game Containers," page 224, for ideas.

OTHER MATRIX BOARDS

How Many Squares? In making matrix boards, the number of squares to be used should be determined by the attention span of the students who will use the game (more squares = longer game); however, always make the same number of squares across and down. Doing so allows students to win across, down, or diagonally.

What Types of Content? These games can be used in any subject area (for example, chemical elements, vocabulary in any subject or language, verb tenses, telling time, multiplication tables, Dolch list) and have the advantage of providing activity for 3 students (2 players and 1 caller) or 30 to 40 students.

When to Use? These games lend themselves to reinforcing skills at Bloom's Cognitive Levels 1 (Recall-Knowledge) and 2 (Comprehension), but probably are not suitable for higher cognitive levels.

How to Start? Decide on the group of students who will play the game and the content area the students will be studying.

See-Through Solitaire

Materials
1. 1 playing board marked with nine 3'' x 2½'' rectangles; may be made on a sheet of tag board or on the folder itself
2. 1 manila folder
3. 2 library pockets
4. 1 acetate sheet, cut into nine 3'' x 2½'' rectangles
5. 3 to 4 feet of clear contact paper

Making the Board
1. Draw nine 3'' x 2½'' rectangles on tag board or on inside back cover of folder (Figure 21).
2. Type or print in each rectangle a question or statement pertaining to the subject the game is to reinforce.
3. Put a number in the lower right-hand corner of each rectangle.
4. If tag is used, glue game board to inside back cover of folder.

Finishing Touches
1. *Playing Piece Construction*
   a. Measure and cut nine 3'' x 2½'' rectangles from a piece of acetate (x-ray film or transparency film is excellent).
   b. Print with permanent transparency marker the answers to the questions or statements on game board.
   c. Put a letter in the upper right-hand corner of each playing piece. Be careful not to sequence letters with questions on game board (Figure 22).
2. *Task*
   a. Print purpose, materials, and directions on front inside cover of folder, or
   b. Type on piece of tag board, glue to front inside cover.
3. *Library Pocket Preparation*
   a. Cut front of pockets (Figure 23).
   b. Label pockets, answer key, playing pieces.
   c. Glue pockets inside front cover under directions.
   d. Label and decorate front of folder.
   e. Cover entire folder with clear contact. Slit pockets with razor blade or x-acto knife.
   f. Put playing pieces in appropriate pocket.

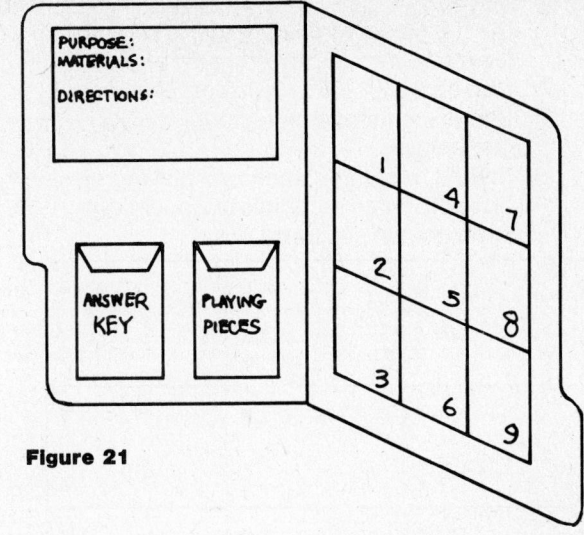

Figure 21

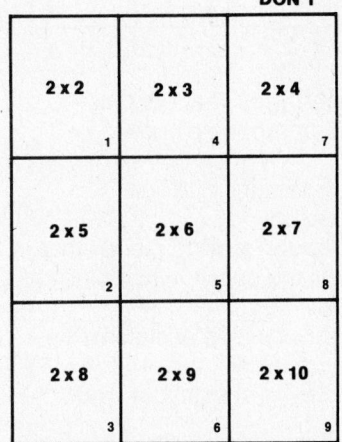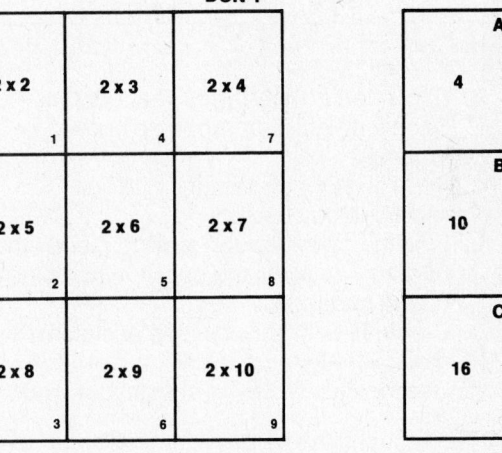

Figure 22

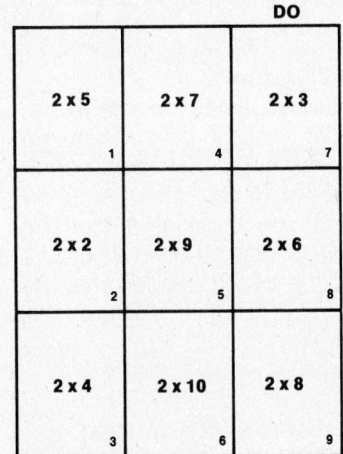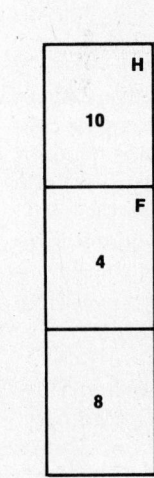

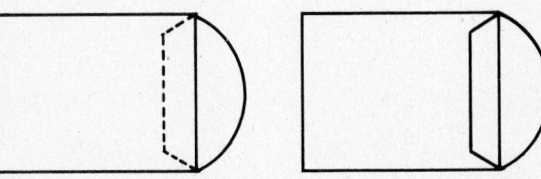

Figure 23

4. *Answer Key*
   a. Can be made from tag board or scrap of poster board.
   b. Can be a 3½″ x 3″ replica of game board.
   c. Should be numbered rectangles as on game board.
   d. Should have letter of correct playing piece on appropriate rectangle in upper right-hand corner (Figure 24).

H	L	A
1	4	7
F	B	E
2	5	8
M	C	P
3	6	9

Figure 24

   e. Should be covered with clear contact.
   f. Should be put in appropriate pocket.
5. *Directions*
   a. Read question or statement in first rectangle on board.
   b. Find the "see-through playing piece" that correctly answers the question and place it on the rectangle.
   c. Continue until all questions or statements are covered.
   d. Use the answer key to check your work.

NOTE: To make the game more challenging, make 3 to 4 extra playing pieces with incorrect answers.

Other Matrix Board Games
To make other matrix board games, choose examples from the content of a lesson or a curriculum plan. Be sure the choices represent simple challenges (e.g., one- or two-word answers, short equations, or simple math combinations). Pictures of things and/or symbols can be used also. List what will be used on the board and on the call cards.

Making the Playing Board
1. *Materials*
   a. Sheets of poster board or construction paper backed with cardboard cut to desired board size. Cut one for each student who will play the game.
   b. Contact paper, roll of acetate, or plastic for laminating.
   c. Enough poster or tag board squares cut to 1½″ x 1½″ to match content to be used.
   d. Large envelope or box, small envelopes for each player's markers.
   e. Construction paper cut into small squares for use as markers.
2. *How to Begin*
   a. Decide on the size of the board. Cut the boards. Make enough for all students who will use the game.
   b. Measure the squares and use felt tip pen or marker to outline.
   c. Add the answers
      (1) Vary the location of the answers for each card.
      (2) For more difficult games, have more answers than numbers of squares on any one board. Be sure all answers are included somewhere.

      Example: 5″ x 5″ boards allow for 25 answers. Make up 30 answers and vary their locations on the board. Do not repeat any answer on the same board. Students will not always be able to add a marker for each call.

      (3) Include a free square or include a free call card allowing students to decide their own free space.
   d. Cover with contact paper or laminate.
3. *Making Calling Cards*
   Cut poster or tag board into 1½″ x 1½″ squares. Write one desired response on each card. Cover with contact paper or laminate and cut. Be sure the cards are durable so they can be shuffled or mixed.

Examples of various matrix board games that might be made in this way are shown in Figure 25.

Finishing Touches
1. *Playing Markers.* Use beans (primary level) or cut markers from construction paper or scrap tag board. Be sure to have enough to cover all the boards. Put markers into containers or small envelopes for each player. For primary grades, cut up egg cartons and use as individual containers.
2. *Task Card.* Write, print, or type the task card information. Include: purpose of the game; instructions to the players explaining how to set the game up, how to play, and how to win; and instructions for checking answers. Laminate or cover with contact paper and put in a container for game use.
3. *Answer Key.* Laminate or cover with contact paper.
4. *Game Container.* Label all parts clearly.

MATCHING—THE SAME AS   (RECALL LEVEL)

sew	for	now	why	both
were	five	one	**was**	they
in	six	ship	two	like
some	am	to	four	three
near	from	ten	is	also

CALL CARDS

was

PLAYING BOARD

MATCHING   (COMPREHENSION LEVEL)

CALL CARDS

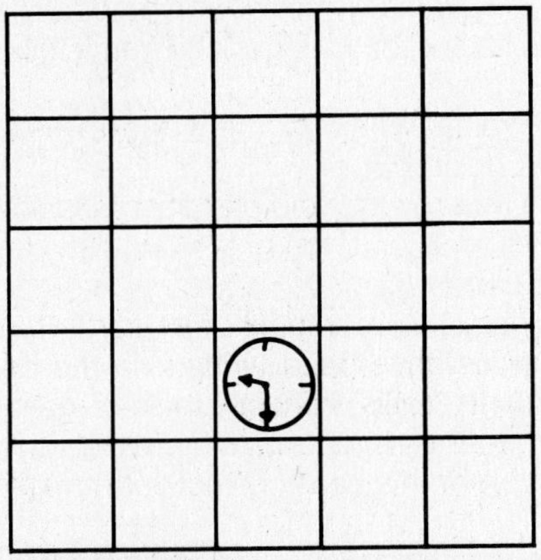

9:30

PLAYING BOARD

CALL CARDS

silver

PLAYING BOARD

Ag

CALL CARDS

with

PLAYING BOARD

avec

Figure 25. Examples of recall and comprehension level matrix board games.

How many students can sit comfortably around the game board?

used by any grade level and may be either permanent or multipurpose. For a multi-use board, cover with acetate and write the content on the acetate with a grease pencil. If a permanent board is desired, write the content directly on the board, then cover with acetate or contact paper.

Board Design

Determining Board Size
The size of the board is determined by the maximum number of students who might play the game. For example, a board 12" x 12" usually accommodates 2 students; a board 16" x 14" can easily be used by 2 to 4 students; a larger board might accommodate 5 or 6 students.

Types of Boards
A variety of boards can be made. The type of board depends upon answers to such questions as:

* Is a permanent or multi-use board needed?
* Are spinners, dice, or calling cards more appropriate?
* How many moves are needed? (A game moves faster for younger children if fewer moves are required.)
* What type of content and levels of thinking are desired?
* Are reward and penalty cards needed?

Board Ideas
Figure 26 is a multi-use board. Rewards and penalties have been written on the board. Each student draws from a stack of cards with content questions written on them. If he answers the question on his card correctly, he may move the num-

PLAYING BOARDS

Characteristics
This type of game requires students to respond to a situation before moving a token. The board itself is designed for use by 2 to 6 players, depending on the design of the game, the numbers of tokens that can be used, or the number of home bases on the board. If carefully designed, the board may be

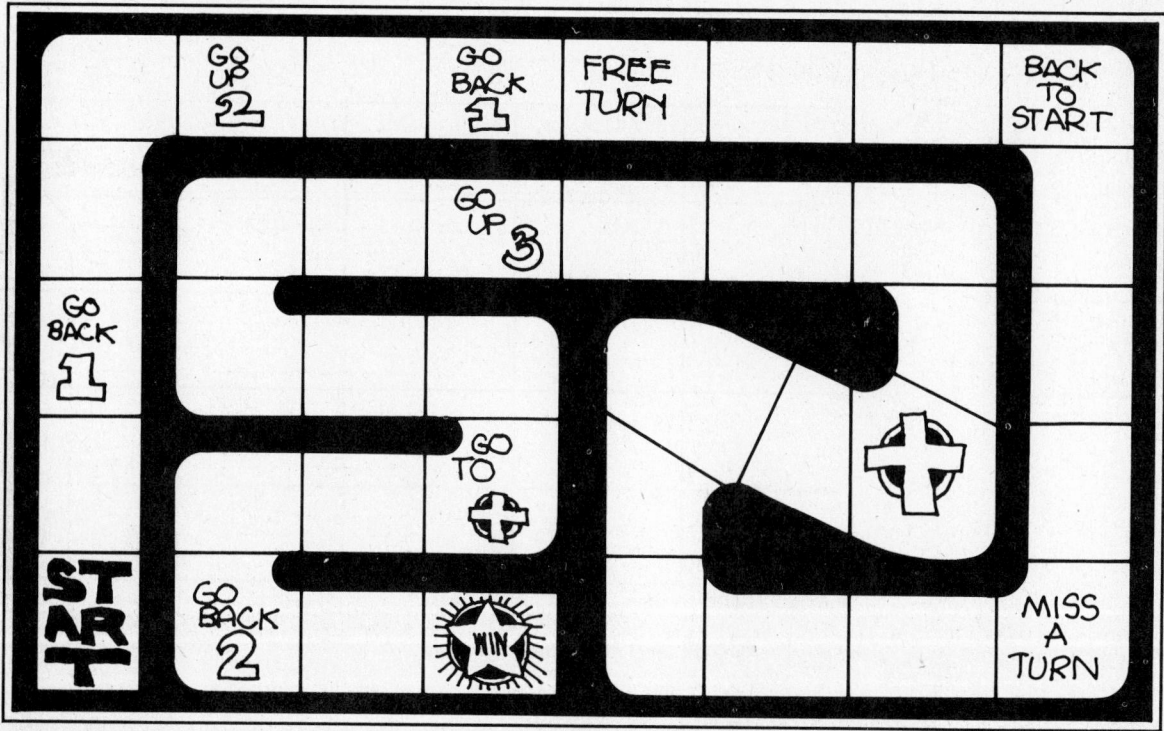

Figure 26

ber of spaces indicated on the card. Cards are "weighted" so that a correct answer to a hard question enables the player to move 3 spaces on the board, while that to an easy question earns only a 1-space move.

The board in Figure 26 might be made permanent by adding the content to the board and using a spinner or dice rather than question cards.

The boards shown in Figure 27 may be permanent or multi-use. If multi-use, the squares should be left blank. Players draw a card from the stack, answer the question on the card, and then move the indicated number of spaces. Or the card they have drawn may direct them instead to draw a REWARD or PENALTY card (Figure 27a). A REWARD card might allow the student to move ahead 5 spaces or take an extra turn. A PENALTY card might require the student to move back 5 spaces or lose a turn. If the board is to be permanent, add the content to the squares and be sure to include numerous DRAW REWARD CARD and DRAW PENALTY CARD squares.

The board in Figure 27b may be either permanent or multi-use. There are more moves but there are no REWARD OR PENALTY cards. Add these challenges to the squares.

The board in Figure 27c is designed to be permanent but can be adapted for multi-use. The small squares along the playing path are for pictures related to a story, science lesson, or other such content. This arrangement lends itself to sequencing. Tear apart a story from a book and glue pictures of events along the playing path. Comprehension questions written in the squares should relate to the sequence of pictures on the board.

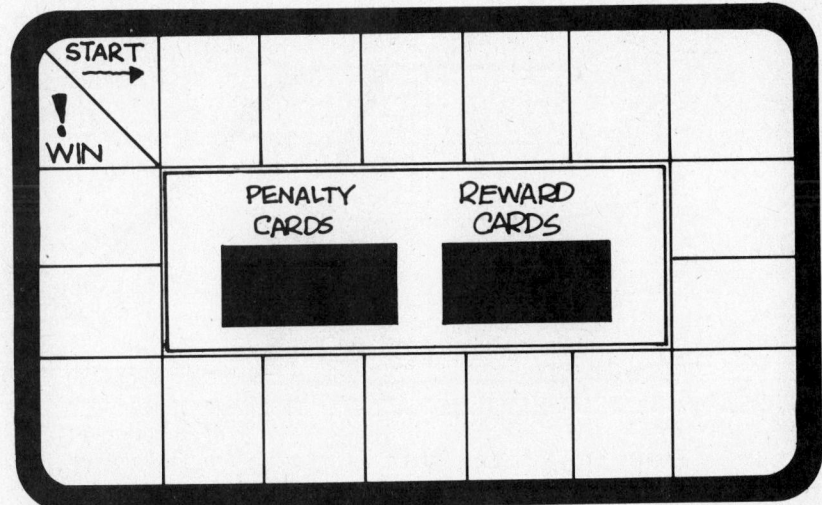

Figure 27a

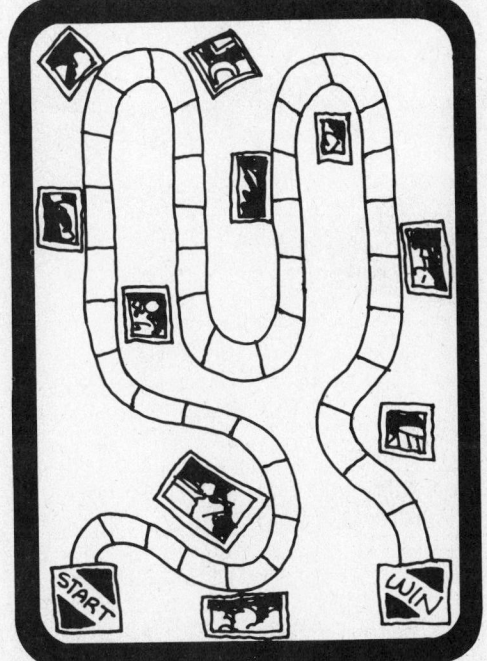

Figure 27c

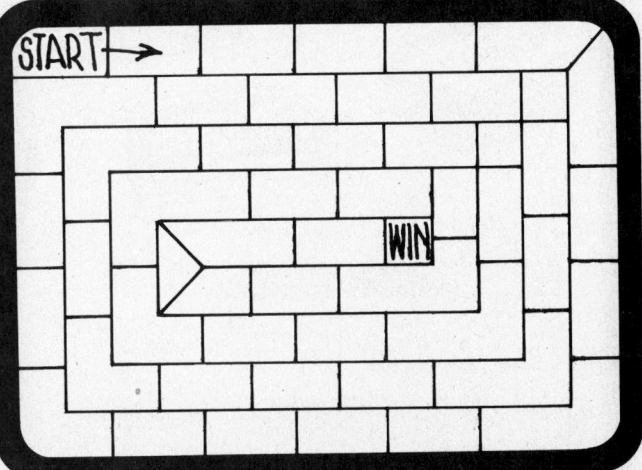

Figure 27b

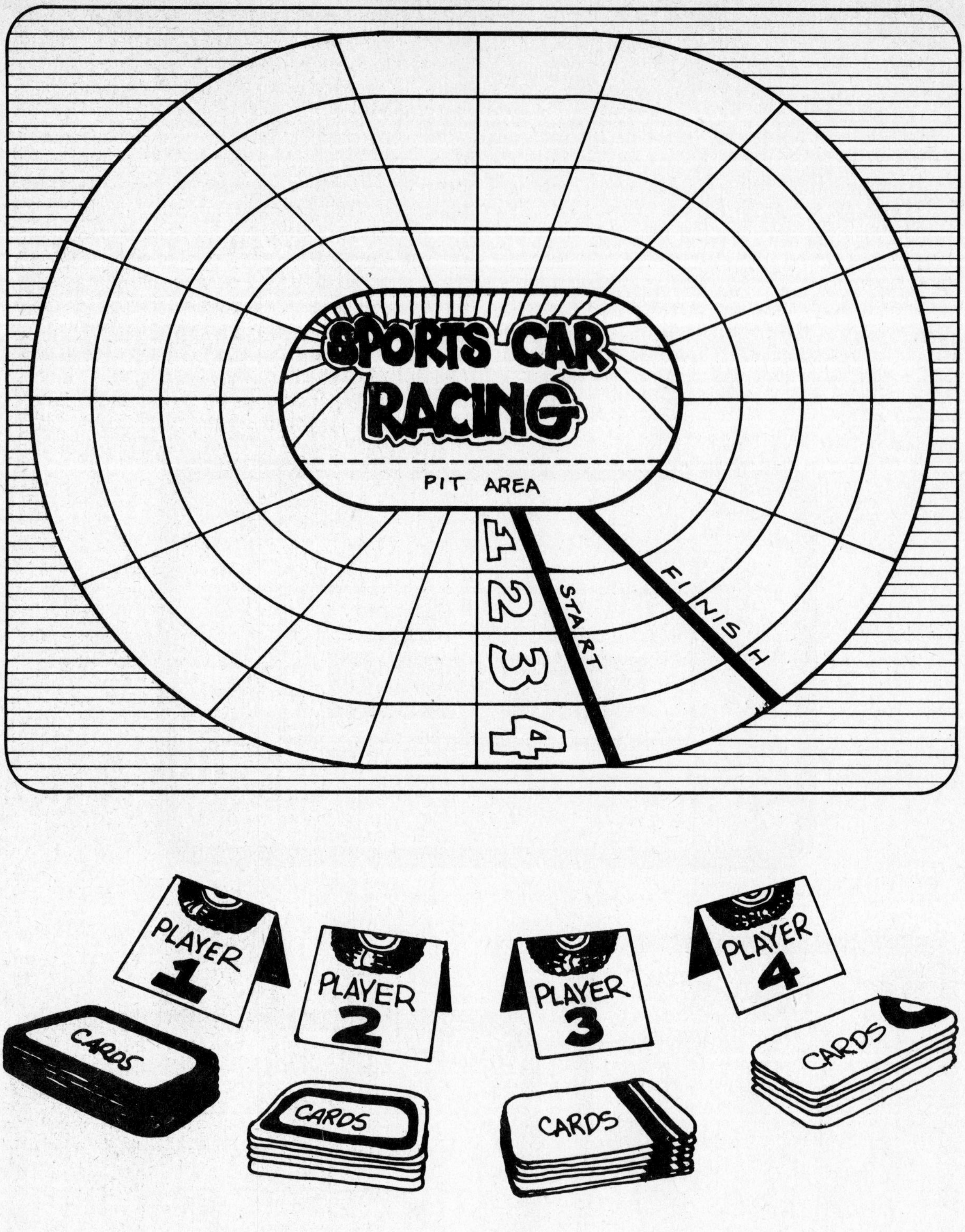

Figure 28. Sports Car Racing.

Sports Car Racing

The board shown in Figure 28 is designed to attract students interested in sports car racing and, at the same time, to reinforce content in selected subjects. An additional advantage of this board is that students may be at various levels of thinking or even be in different content areas when playing. Each player's cards are prescribed by the teacher in his area of need, and may differ from those prescribed for other players.

How to Construct the Racing Game

1. *Materials Needed*
   a. 1 large poster board
   b. 4 toy racing cars
   c. 4 sheets of tag board cut to 6″ x 8½″
   d. tag board cards cut to 2¼″ x 3½″
   e. magic markers
   f. scissors, cutting board
   g. clear contact paper and contact paper with design
   h. cardboard for task card
2. *Playing Board.* Draw the board on the poster board as illustrated in Figure 28 and use markers along lines. Outline the START and FINISH heavier than other parts. Laminate or cover with contact paper.
3. *Task Card.* Cut out, glue to cardboard, and laminate or cover with contact paper.
4. *How to Play (Instructions for Students)*
   a. You need: one deck of cards, spinner, car, and playing board.
   b. Place cards face down in front of you.
   c. Spin spinner to see who has highest number; highest spin goes first.
   d. Spin spinner. Draw card from your deck.
   e. If you can do correctly what the card asks, you move the number of spaces shown on the spinner. If you can't, put the card on the bottom of the stack. The next player has a turn after you move or put the card back. If you draw a CRASH CAR, you must go to the pit for repairs for 1 turn. On your next turn, you can return to the last square you were on.
   f. The winner is the one who reaches the FINISH first.
5. *Playing Cards*
   a. Cut tag board cards to measure 2¼″ x 2½″.
   b. Write questions on each card.
   c. Put designed contact paper on the back of the cards so that writing will not show through.
   d. Put clear contact paper on the front of the cards.
   e. Make CRASH CAR cards (Figure 29) for each stack. Use the same directions as above.
   f. Put each deck of cards in an envelope and label the content. The more cards available, the more often this game can be prescribed for different students.
   g. Fold the four tag board sheets (6″ x 8½″) in half. Write PLAYER 1, PLAYER 2, PLAYER 3, and PLAYER 4 on them. Laminate or cover with clear contact paper.
   h. Because each player may have different objectives, make one card per player or per deck of cards explaining what the purpose of the game is. Add this card to the envelope for that player or that deck of cards.
6. *Answer Key.* If possible, make an answer key for each deck of cards. Either add to the envelope or begin an answer key file for this game.

Figure 29

Ask
or
The Question Is . . .

So much of a student's time in school is spent giving answers that the skill of questioning takes a back seat. Here is a game that reverses the "question and answer" format. In this game the answers are given, and it is up to the students to give the correct questions.

The level of learning exhibited in the question the student asks will depend on the answer's degree of difficulty: answers may illicit simple recall questions or be complex enough to require analysis questions.

Materials Needed
1. Game board. Two different boards (one-panel and three-panel) are shown on the following pages.
2. 21 playing cards with answers on one side, questions on the other.
3. One subject card.
4. Score sheets.

The game board is permanent; subject and playing cards are changed depending on the concept to be reinforced.

Number of Players: 2 to 3

How to Play (Instructions for Students)
1. Check the subject pocket so you will know the area being covered.
2. Facing you, in each pocket, is a card with a word or group of words that answer a specific question. The number at the top of each panel on the game board, and in the upper right-hand corner of each card, tells you the number of points you will receive if you supply the correct question for this answer. The 5-point cards will be the easiest, while the 15-point cards will be the most difficult.
3. Before asking the question, be sure you state the pocket number and the number of points of the card you have chosen (e.g., "pocket number 3, for 5 points"). After you have stated the pocket number and points, ask the question that would have that word or group of words as its answer.

   Example: If the answer reads, "George Washington was the first," a correct question would be, "Who was the first President of the United States?"

4. Before giving yourself the points, you and your opponents are to check the back of the card to see if your question is *similar* to the one given there. It need not be *exactly* the same, but it must be in the form of a question.
5. If your question is correct, put the points on the score sheet under your name and keep the

card. If your question is incorrect, put the card in a pile in front of the game board. Do not give yourself any points.
6. When all the pockets are emptied, add up everyone's points. The player with the highest point total is the winner.
7. When finished return all cards to their pockets. The point number on each card will tell you to which panel the card should be returned. There is no specific order in which the cards need to be replaced; only the panel numbers are important.

A Variation . . . Double or Nothing
The play and rules are the same, except that the words DOUBLE OR NOTHING are printed on the bottom of a few of the cards. If a player chooses a DOUBLE OR NOTHING card and asks the question correctly, the points are *doubled* and *added* to his score. If he does not ask the correct question, the points are *doubled* and *subtracted* from his score.

GAME BOARD SHAPES

Three-Panel Board
Materials Needed
1. Three sturdy sheets of cardboard: two sheets, 17" x 11"; one sheet, 17" x 13"
2. Three yards printed contact paper
   or
3. Colored construction paper
4. Colored poster board
   or
5. Shelf paper
   or
6. Wallpaper
7. 3 yards clear contact paper if anything other than the printed contact or washable wallpaper is used
8. Four packages of 1¼" mystic tape
9. Library pockets
10. Glue
11. 2" x 3" index cards

How to Construct (see Figure 30)
1. While the cardboard sheets are separate
   a. Cover both sides of each sheet with contact paper, poster board, or construction paper.
   b. On the inside of each panel add points and library pockets (cut in half, curved, and numbered). Label and add the subject pocket.
   c. On the outside of the 5-point panel, put the name of the game and playing instructions.
   d. On the outside of the 15-point panel, add a labeled pocket for score sheet.

e. If not using printed contact or washable wallpaper, cover both sides of each panel with clear contact paper.

f. Slit all pockets with a razor blade or x-acto knife.

2. To assemble

a. Lay panels flat. Leave ¼" to ½" between panels (width depends on size of panels).

This space makes it possible to close or fold the panels for storage.

b. Use colored 1¼" mystic tape to attach, taping both inside and outside seams.

c. Bind edges with mystic tape in the same or a contrasting color.

NOTE: Most art and/or stationery stores have mystic tape.

Name of the game and directions on back of panel

Score sheets in pocket on back of panel

Figure 30. Three-panel game board.

One-Panel Board

The one-panel board (Figure 31) may be constructed to lie flat or stand up.

Self-Check Game Board (For Two Players)
Figure 32 is a self-check game board for two players. Each player's writing space is covered with acetate so he can write his response with a transparency pen or pencil. A word is printed on one side of the card, and the answer (in this case, the sound identifier word, GOOSE or BOOK) is printed on the other.

1. *Materials Needed*
   a. manila folder
   b. felt pens
   c. 24 to 30 small cards (2″ x 3″)
   d. acetate
   e. clear contact paper

2. *How to Use*
   Two students can play. Cards are mixed up and put in a stack in the center, words facing up. Players draw a card, say the word, place it under BOOK or GOOSE, and write the word. When all the cards have been used, they are turned over and checked for correct placing. Points are given for correct answers. Each student adds up the number of correct answers she has and writes her score. The student with the most points wins.

3. *Other Variations*
   a. Tell whether the *gh* or *ph* in a word is silent or makes the "f" sound.

   Examples: caught, elephant, freight

   b. Correctly form the plural of words ending in *sh, ch, s,* or *x* by adding *s* or *es.*

   Examples: stamp, dish, ostrich

Figure 31. One-panel game board.

Which Sound Is It ??

oo sounds

Score: [   ]   Score: [   ]

THEY LOOK THE SAME.....
BUT SOUND DIFFERENT

PLAYER 1
1. _____
2. _____
3. _____
4. _____
5. _____
6. _____
7. _____
8. _____
9. _____
10. _____
11. _____
12. _____
13. _____
14. _____

1. Say the word.

2. Put the word in the square for the sound in GOOSE or BOOK.

3. Write the word on the line provided for you.

4. Check your answers.

PLAYER WITH THE MOST RIGHT
ANSWERS IS THE WINNER

PLAYER 2
1. _____
2. _____
3. _____
4. _____
5. _____
6. _____
7. _____
8. _____
9. _____
10. _____
11. _____
12. _____
13. _____
14. _____

GOOSE

| Cards |

| Place word Cards here. FACE UP. |

BOOK

| Cards |

Figure 32. Self-check game board (for two players).

CARD GAMES

Characteristics

Any card game you know can be adapted to teach a concept or skill. Card games are used for matching one type of content item to another type. Examples of items that might be matched include:

- chemistry symbol to name
- words to definitions
- explorers to discoveries
- multiplication problems to answers
- English vocabulary to Spanish
- pictures to descriptions
- parts of a plant to function
- math equations to like sums

Concentration (Played Like Concentration on Television)

Materials Needed
1. Tag board
2. Manila folder
3. Library pockets
4. Contact paper (clear and designed)
5. Stapler
6. Scissors, cutting board
7. Masking tape

Concentration Cards
1. Cut 30 cards 3″ x 3″.
2. Cover back of cards with designed contact paper so that writing does not show through to other side.
3. Write words (or equations, descriptions) on 15 cards.
4. Write definitions or responses on other 15 cards.
5. Put clear contact paper on the front of each card.
6. Number the back sides of word cards from 1 to 15.
7. On the backs of the response or definition cards, number from 1 to 15. Vary the order. The number system is used for the key. Be sure the number 1 word card does not have a corresponding number 1 definition card.

Answer Key
Type the answer key to show both the number of the word cards and their corresponding response cards. For younger children the word and response should be typed out. Cover with contact paper or laminate.

Instructions
Type or write out
1. *Purpose.* This game will help you to . . .
2. *How to Play.* Shuffle the two decks of cards together and spread them out, number side showing, on a flat surface. Each player takes a turn by turning over any two cards. When a match is made, the player keeps the cards. If a match is not made, the player returns the two cards face down with number side showing. The player with the most matches wins the game.

If any player does not know the answer and questions a match, the answer key may be used.

Finishing Touches
See "How to Use Manila Folders" (page 224) for completing the game.

Card Games Played Like "Fish"

The idea of this card game is to make books of like answers. The game lends itself to synonyms, antonyms, root words, equations with like sums, and similar subject matter (see Figure 33). Be sure there are books of four cards with same or similar answers. Write out content before beginning.

Materials Needed
1. 60 tag board cards cut to 2″ x 3½″
2. Manila folder
3. Library pockets
4. Tag board for instructions and answer key
5. Clear and designed contact paper
6. Masking tape
7. Stapler, scissors, cutting board

Cards
Write the words or equations on cards. It is easier to make each book of cards together. Put designed contact paper on the backs of the cards and clear contact on the faces (or laminate).

Key
Make an answer key.

Instructions
Write the purpose and instructions.

Finishing Touches
See "How to Use Manila Folders" (page 224) for finishing the game.

Rummy Games

The rummy game format may be used to reinforce and review skills and concepts in most subject areas.

Materials
1. 76 cards cut to 3″ x 2½″. See the card "How To" section for construction hints.
2. Container, any of the following, constructed as described in the container "How To" section:
   a. box
   b. manila folder
   c. clasp envelope

3. Rules of play displayed for easy reference.
4. Answer key.

Number of Players
Two or more players are required.

Purpose
To make as many books as possible. A book consists of four (4) cards related in some specified way.

Instructions for Playing
1. Shuffle all cards.
2. Dealer deals 10 cards to each player.
3. Remaining cards are placed face down in the center of the playing surface.
4. Each player sorts the cards in his hand into books or partial books.
5. The player to the left of the dealer begins the play. If he has a book, he lays it down in front of himself and explains why it is a book. Only *one* book may be put down at any one turn.
6. If a player does not have a book, he draws a card from the stack. He may keep the card or discard it.
7. If the player keeps the card he must discard one card from his hand. Each player must discard one card after each turn. Discards are placed face up in a stack next to the original stack. During his turn, a player may pick up the *entire* discard stack, *if* he can show that he has in his hand two (2) cards from the same book as the *top* discard.
8. The game continues with each player forming books when possible, drawing cards, and discarding.
9. The game ends when all the cards in the original stack have been used. The player who has the most books is the winner. If there is any question about a player's book, the players may check the answer key.

a. Verb forms.

b. Nouns (singular, plural, singular possessive, plural possessive).

Figure 33. Cards and skill ideas.

c. States.

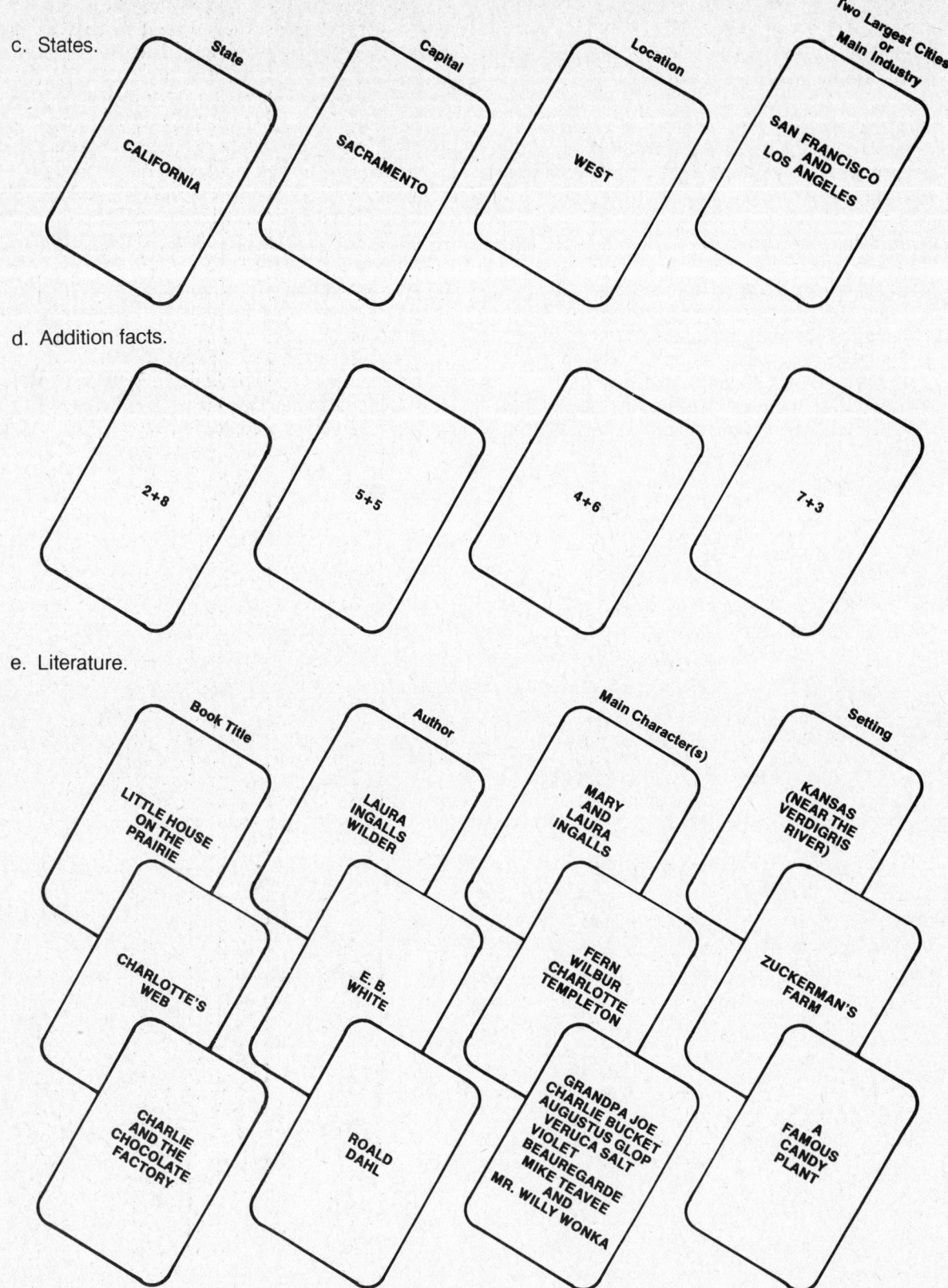

d. Addition facts.

e. Literature.

Figure 33. Cards and skill ideas (continued).

PIECES AND PARTS

Characteristics

The games in this section provide opportunities for cognitive development on several levels. The level will depend on what is desired for students and how creatively a teacher can adapt materials. (The use of commercial games like dominoes will not be discussed but would be included under this game format or category.)

Puzzles

Puzzles can be teacher-made, come from the Sunday paper, come from commercial puzzle books, or be purchased as jig-saw puzzles.

Teacher-Made
Type 1. Use a 4″ x 4″ or 5″ x 5″ matrix. Put definitions on one side of a line and words on the other side of the line, or put chemistry symbols on one side and names for symbols on the other, or use any number of other context examples. Cut the matrix apart. A student works the puzzle by matching item to response until the matrix has been completed.

The puzzle in Figure 34a may be worked by students of any age. (A math example of this game has been included at the back of this chapter.)

Type 2. A student puts the definition of a word on the word itself. When he has matched all of the words with definitions, the student turns over the pieces in place and finds a picture if all answers are correct.

To make Type 2, write definitions on a sheet of tag board measured in squares to match the sheet in Figure 34b. Find an interesting picture and glue to the back. Laminate or cover with clear contact paper. Cut apart. Be sure the definitions match the same location as the words.

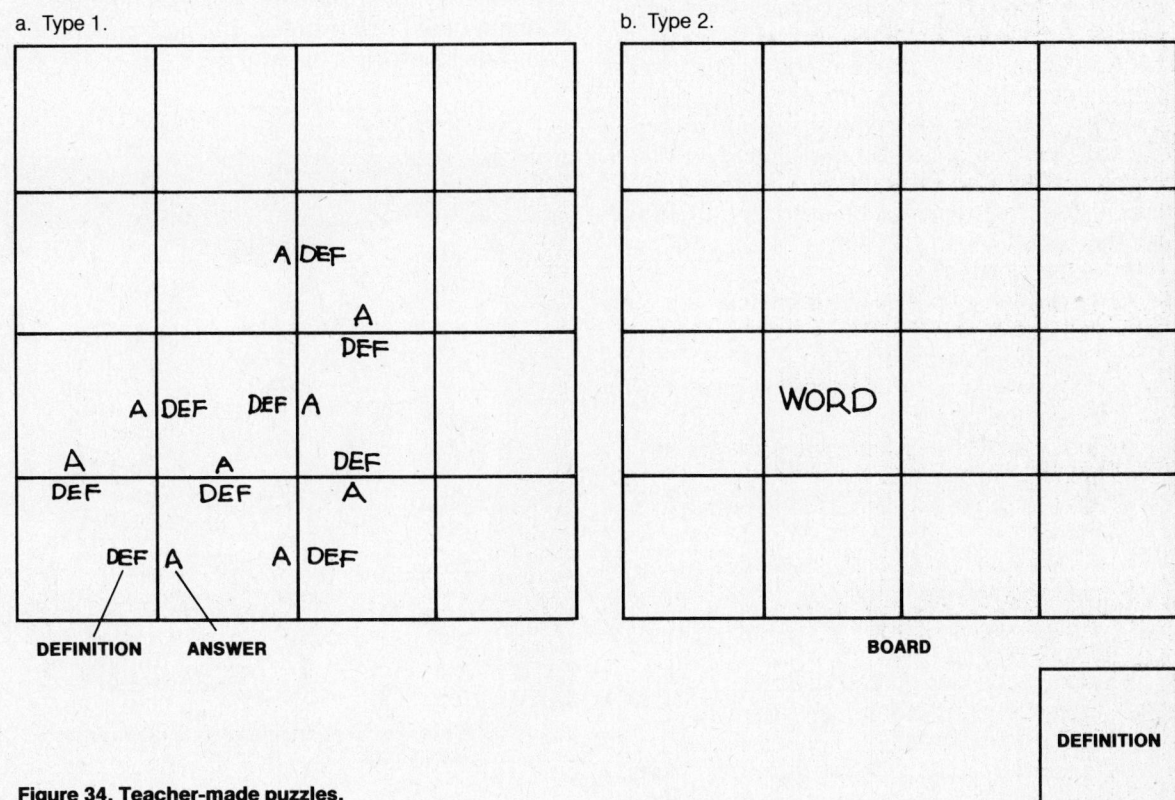

a. Type 1.

DEFINITION   ANSWER

b. Type 2.

WORD

BOARD

DEFINITION

Figure 34. Teacher-made puzzles.

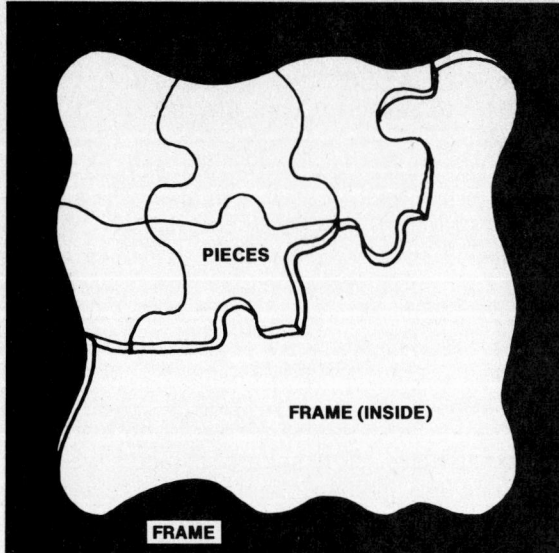

Figure 35. Be sure the puzzle rests in a frame.

Type 3. Puzzles of this type are made from commercial puzzles. When buying a puzzle to use in this way, consider the following questions: Is the puzzle interesting and the picture appropriate for students? Are there too many pieces for younger children? Will the puzzle be challenging for older students? Be sure the puzzle rests in a *frame* (Figure 35). The frame will be used for part of the activity.

1. *Materials Needed*
   a. 1 commercial puzzle in a frame
   b. Felt tip pens
   c. Clear contact paper
   d. Large envelope or construction paper the size of the puzzle
   e. Tag board for instructions and answer key
2. *Making the Puzzle*
   a. Take all of the pieces out of the puzzle frame.
   b. For younger children, outline where puzzle pieces go on the frame.
   c. Write your answers within piece outlines on the frame.
   d. Write a question on each piece to correspond to the answer written in its space on the frame.
   e. Put all the pieces back into the puzzle frame.
   f. Put contact paper on the entire puzzle.
   g. Use an x-acto knife or razor to cut the pieces apart.
   h. Make an answer key and cover with contact paper.
   i. Make a task card explaining the purpose of the puzzle and listing the instructions.

For example Take all the pieces of the puzzle out of the frame. Turn all the pieces over, picture side down. Read the verb tense on one of the pieces (Figure 36). Find the answer in the frame. When you have completed the puzzle, the picture should be correct with each piece in its proper place. Refer to the answer key if you have any questions.

Other Games for Pieces and Parts

Phonics Eggo
Players are given an egg carton and beans. In turn, each student draws a word from the word box and says the word. He tells if the vowel in the word is long or short. If he is correct, he puts a bean in the corresponding compartment of his carton (Figure 37). The winner is the student with the most beans.

Make a Square
Students who wish to play are given a copy of Figure 38. They must cut out the pieces and make a square within three minutes. The first student who completes the task is the winner.

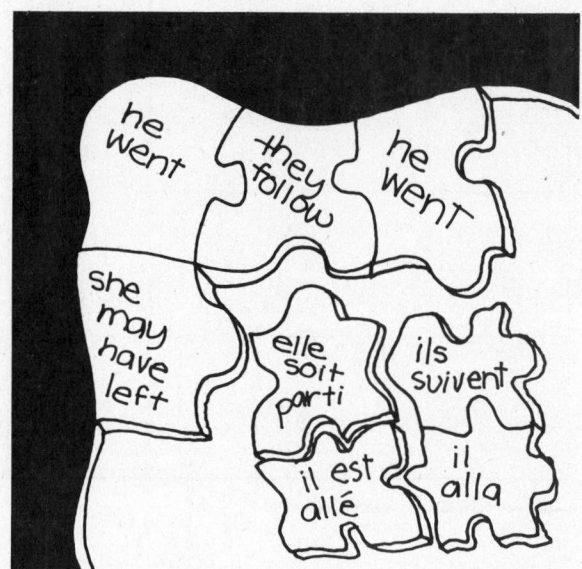

Figure 36. Commercial puzzle adapted to teach French verb forms.

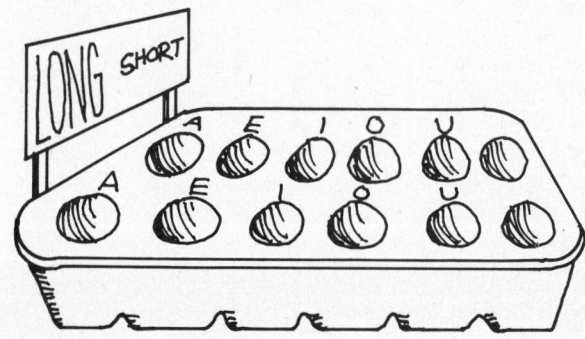

Figure 37. Phonics Eggo.

212

Figure 38. Make a Square. Use these shapes and those on page 214.

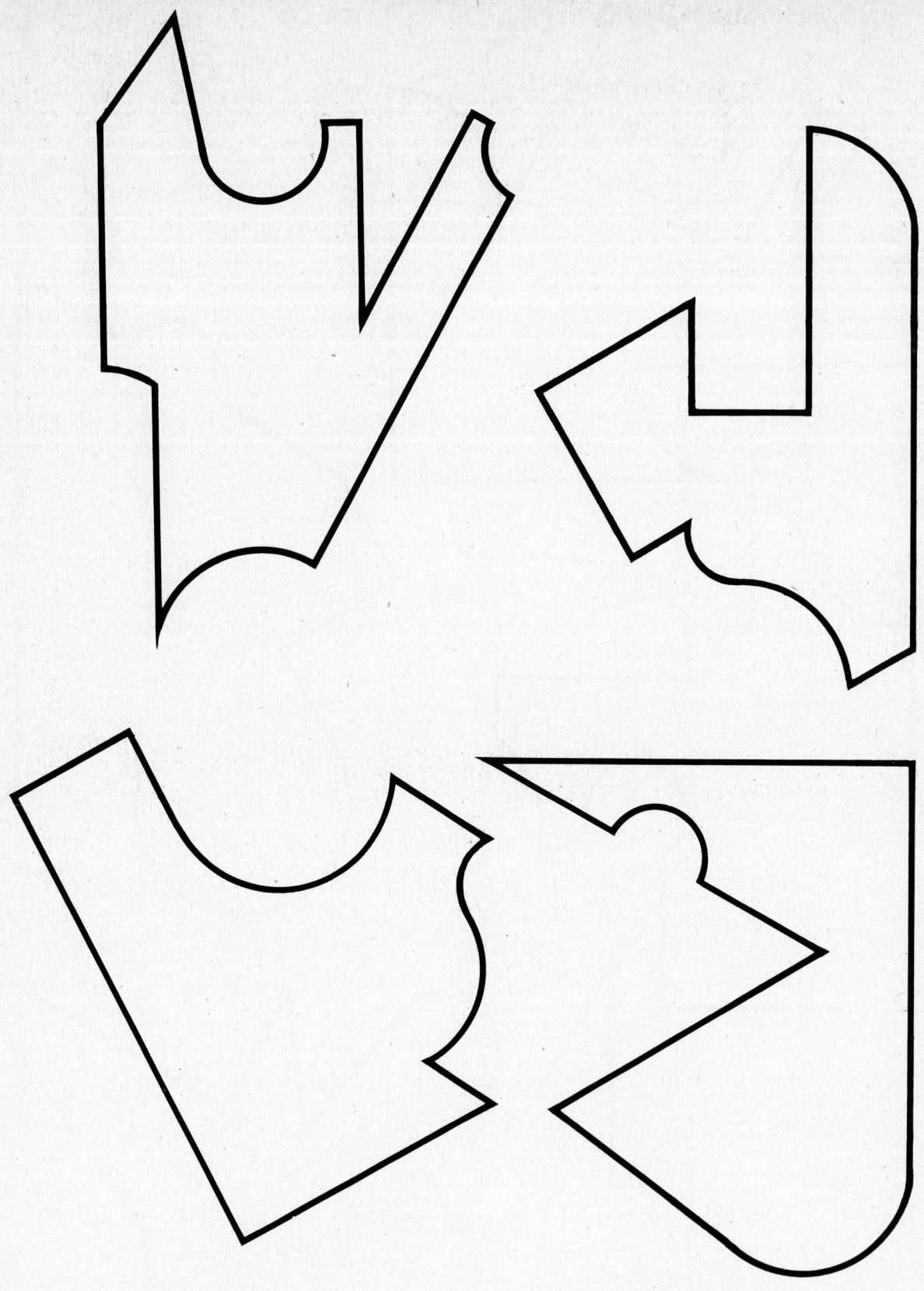

Figure 38. Make a Square (continued).

SELF-CHECK GAMES AND ACTIVITIES

Characteristics
Any game with answers may be self-checking. Self-check activities and games are usually for use by one student. The student competes against himself or a clock. These activities and games are excellent student self-tests so that the student may check his progress toward an objective or a post-test.

Content
Any subject may be used for any grade level; however, some formats within this chapter lend themselves better to the elementary grades. All of them can be *adapted* to upper grades.

Pizza Wheels
Materials Needed
1. Cardboard cut into a circle 8″ to 12″ in diameter (or visit your favorite pizza parlor and save the cardboard)
2. Clothespins
3. Magic markers
4. Box to fit the wheel
5. Contact paper or laminating plastic

Making the Pizza Board
1. Cut a circle 8″ to 12″ in diameter.
2. Draw lines as illustrated in Figure 39 until the entire circle is divided into sixteenths.
3. If light cardboard is being used, cut another circle, measure as above, and glue to back of the first circle.
4. Draw lines on the back of the wheel to correspond to the lines on the front.
5. Write the question or word on one side of the wheel. Write the answer in the corresponding area on the other side of the wheel.

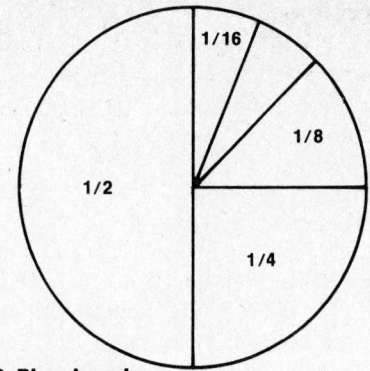

Figure 39. Pizza board.

6. Laminate or put contact paper on both sides.

Preparing the Clothespins
1. Using a permanent marking pen, write the answer on *both* sides of the clothespin.
2. Be sure there is one clothespin for each answer on the wheel.

Examples
Self-check pizza wheels may be made for homonyms (Figure 40), synonyms, parts of speech, and states and capitals, among others. For parts of speech, make pins with many examples of each part of speech. Make more than one wheel. Number the wheels as to their difficulty. Place all parts-of-speech wheels in the same storage box. Write instructions and put into box. When a student completes a game, he turns over the wheel and checks his answers against the answers on the clothespins.

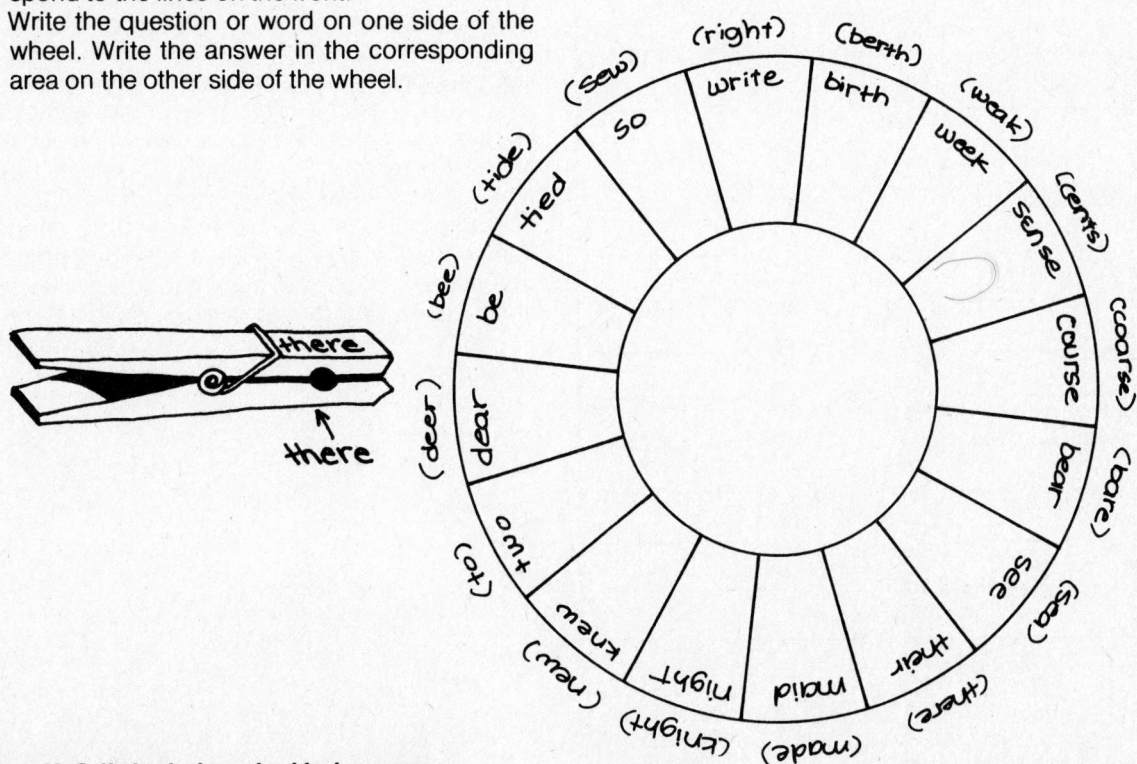

Figure 40. Self-check pizza wheel for homonyms.

String Boards

String boards are usually used in the primary grades. Any content that can be developed into a *matching test* can be used for a string board.

Materials Needed
1. 12" x 15" cardboard
2. Hole punch
3. Yarn
4. Contact paper, clear.
5. Gummed or self-sticking reinforcements
6. Masking tape
7. Scissors and marking pens

Making the Board
1. Measure lines for stem question and match with lines for response.
2. Measure and mark holes.
3. Reinforce holes with reinforcements.
4. Cover front of board with contact paper.
5. Cut one 15-inch length of yarn for each hole.
6. Put yarn through hole on right side and tape back side.
7. Tape ends of yarn tightly (Figure 41). Make a sharp point.
8. Draw answer key on the back of the board.
9. Write purpose and instructions on task card or on the back of the board.
10. Cover back of board with contact paper.
11. Punch or cut out marked holes.
12. Make a container for the board. If there are several boards, put them into a string board activity box.

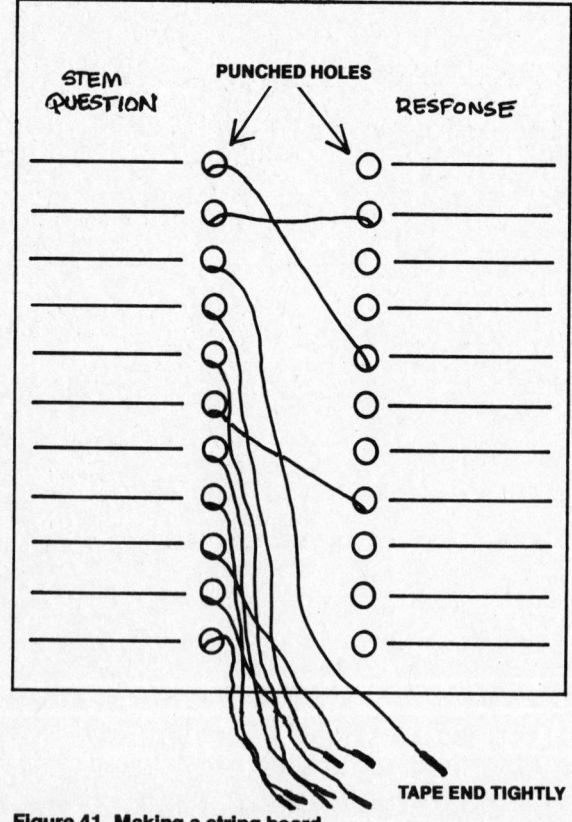

Figure 41. Making a string board.

THE USE OF GAMES IN LEARNING CENTERS

A promising way to use a game in a learning center is with a corresponding prescription sheet or contract. One plan for setting up a center using games is to arrange centers by activity, for example, a center where the primary activity is playing reinforcement, manipulative games.

A *game center* is a learning center designed around many concepts and skills. Generally there are two ways such a center can be organized.

1. *Add-to Center.* Add games to the center as they are needed. Students usually work with games in prescribed areas but can return to games dealing with concepts they learned earlier. Consider the "add-to" approach if there is (a) sufficient space to store games at the center, and (b) if students demonstrate they can do prescribed activities first.
2. *Add-delete Center.* Include games in math, reading, and other skills being taught or practiced in class. Delete a game when the lowest student group has mastered that concept or skill. This approach is good for classrooms where students have had too many games in the past and the teacher wants to regulate their use. For example, in programs originally developed around using games to reinforce a skill, some students misuse the games. Under these circumstances, the teacher may wish to withdraw all games and to introduce games one at a time when students express a desire to return to that form of learning. This problem may be prevalent among students who have spent several years using learning centers of all types.

If there is not sufficient space within a room to set up a permanent game center, games may be placed in vegetable bins, boxes, and other containers. Several games, or even an entire bin, may then be prescribed for a group of students to use at a table or while sitting at their desks.

Game centers may be arranged by concept rather than by activity. A concept center contains all games, worksheets, audiovisual and other materials pertaining to one concept or skill.

The use of games in a game or concept center is illustrated in Figures 42, 43, 44, and 45.

Figure 42. Game center arranged by type of game. Students would play games at their desks, on the floor, in the hall.

Figure 43. Game center in which games are arranged by subject.

Figure 44. Shelves may be used as a game center.

MAKING WORDS CENTER · FIRST, MIDDLE, LAST

At this center I can:
1. Learn 3 word Parts
2. Read
3. Watch and listen
4. Play word games
5. Use practice wheels
6. Make 10 new words

Figure 45. Games may be used as one activity within a center arranged by concept or skill.

TIPS FOR MAKING AND USING GAMES

- Play the game and become thoroughly familiar with it.
- *Students* can make games. Although student-made games may not always meet appearance criteria, if students have a stake in the production, they are less likely to destroy the materials.
- *Games should be prescribed.* A game might be one of several activities prescribed in order to give students choices, but it should be presented as an alternative only when it is consistent with particular goals and objectives. After students have played the game, they might be allowed to return to it at later times without a specific prescription.
- Orient students to a game before prescribing it. Include in the orientation how to play the game, rules for the game, and reasons for playing. Stress the necessity for playing the game as intended and do not allow students to play without using the content of the game (often a problem with matrix and playing boards).
- Use some type of student accountability system requiring feedback. You might wish to use the prescription sheet as a record-keeping system and ask students to sign or check after completing a game. Or you could include content from the game in your teacher conference.
- If critics insist that games are of no educational value, (a) invite them into your classroom to observe children playing games, or (b) have them play the game. The THIMK game at the end of this chapter is especially appropriate.
- For young children, include free exploration of a game or game pieces to promote creativity. Students might be allowed to make up their own rules.

HOW TO

How to Make a Spinner

What You Need: 1 cardboard, 1 spinner, 1 paper clip, 1 brad

1. Bend the paper clip (Figure 46a).

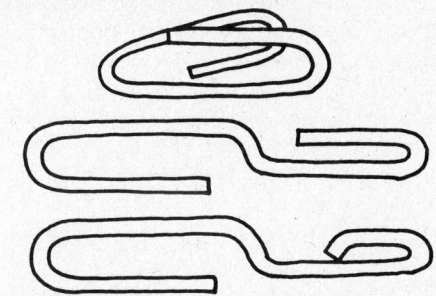

Figure 46a

2. Put the looped end of the paper clip over the hole in the spinner board (Figure 46b).

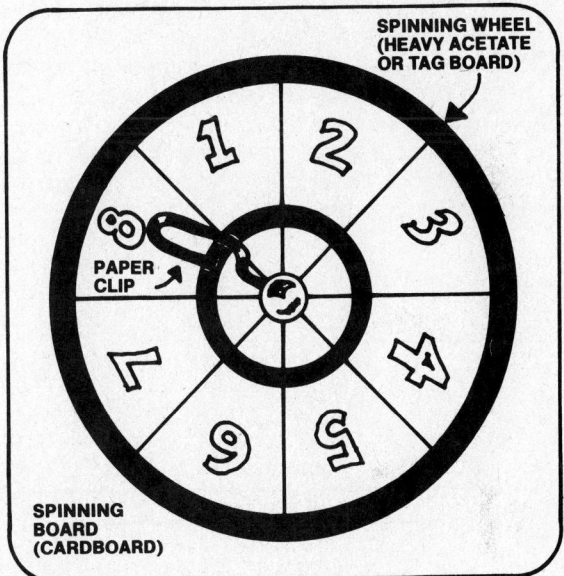

Figure 46b

3. Insert the brad in the hole and bend back (Figure 46c).

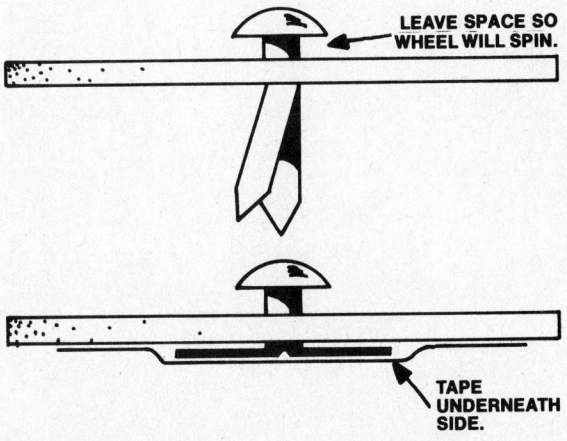

Figure 46c

How to Use Contact Paper

The application of clear contact paper can preserve hours of labor for an indefinite period of time. The following steps are recommended for its use:

1. Find a clean, uncluttered surface to work on. A formica surface is ideal.
2. If covering pictures from magazines or newspapers, back them with tag board, poster board, or cardboard.
3. Measure the article to be covered.
4. Measure and cut the contact, allowing ½" to ¼" overlap on all sides.
5. Place article to be covered face up on the clean surface.
6. Using your thumbnail, pry apart the contact from the backing at one corner.
7. *Slowly* pull backing away and down about 1" to 1½".
8. Fold backing down so that 1" to 1½" of contact is free of the backing.
9. *Carefully* place the contact over the article to be covered, making certain the overlap is relatively even on all sides.
10. Press into place, smoothing contact with both hands from the center toward the edges.
11. Take one hand and *slowly* pull backing toward you, using the other hand to smooth the contact as you pull. Continue until article is completely covered.

12. Overlap may be folded and pressed down on the back of the article.

or

If covering both sides, trim the overlapping edges and repeat steps 4 through 11.

13. After all articles have been covered, it might be desirable to:
    a. Place work on an ironing board under plain newsprint, butcher paper, or a paper bag.
    b. Set iron at its lowest setting and carefully iron entire article, paying particular attention to the edges.

This procedure will cause contact paper to adhere to the article in much the same way a laminating machine does, and is especially useful on articles where both sides have been covered and the edges trimmed.

Even in the best laid contact paper, trouble spots will appear. Some steps that might help are:

1. Try to smooth out the trouble spot with your hand, working toward the edges.

or

2. Use a round object, such as a scissors handle, spoon, or tongue depressor, to smooth the trouble spot.

How to Make Game Cards

1. Decide on the size card you want. Consider amount of content on cards, size required for playing board if applicable, and size easiest to handle for the students who will play the game.
2. Cut the cards. Use the heaviest, flexible material available.
3. Make.

a. Card Face

(1) Write content.
(2) Laminate or cover with contact paper.

b. Card Back

(1) Glue on construction paper and cover with contact paper or laminate.

or

(2) Cover with designed or dark-colored contact paper.

How to Make Game Task Cards

1. Cut tag board.
2. Write out your rough draft.
3. Read aloud. Check vocabulary level and clarity.
4. Try out instructions with a student.
5. Write task card (see Figure 47).
6. Cover with contact paper or laminate.
7. Decorate back or use designed contact paper.
8. Add to game folder or put in envelope and label.

GAME TITLE   (game number)

NUMBER OF PLAYERS

PURPOSE (or objective)

   This game will help you learn...

HOW TO PLAY

What you need (e.g., playing board, dice, tokens.)
To play

   1. How to select the first player.
   2. Rules of the game.
   3. Winner is the player who...

ANSWER KEY with instructions on when to use

RECORD-KEEPING INSTRUCTIONS (e.g., check on

   your prescription sheet.)

Figure 47

How to Make Game Containers—Boxes

TAPE EDGES OF TAG ENVELOPES.

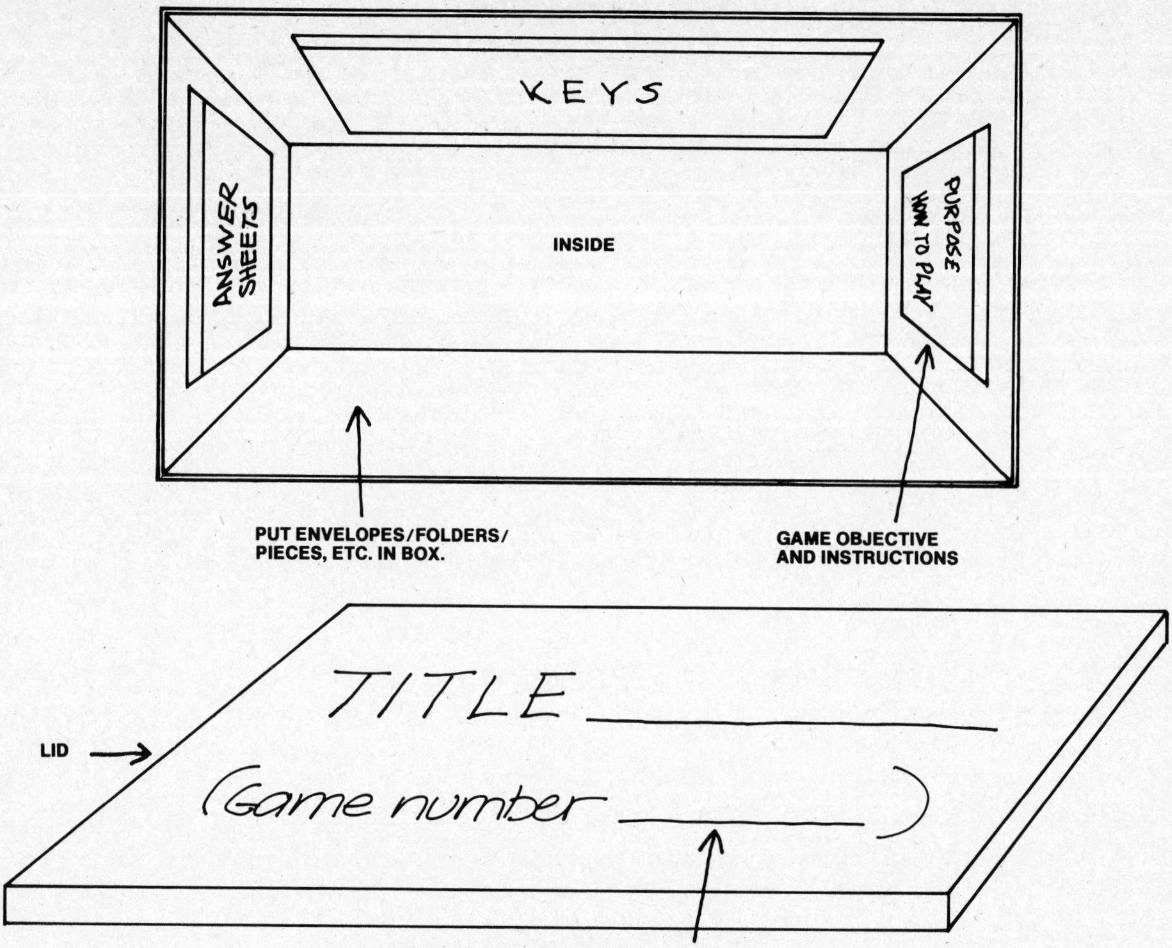

KEYS

ANSWER SHEETS

INSIDE

PURPOSE HOW TO PLAY

PUT ENVELOPES/FOLDERS/
PIECES, ETC. IN BOX.

GAME OBJECTIVE
AND INSTRUCTIONS

TITLE _____

(Game number _____)

LID →

FROM YOUR SEQUENCE OR PRESCRIPTION

How to Use Manila File Folders

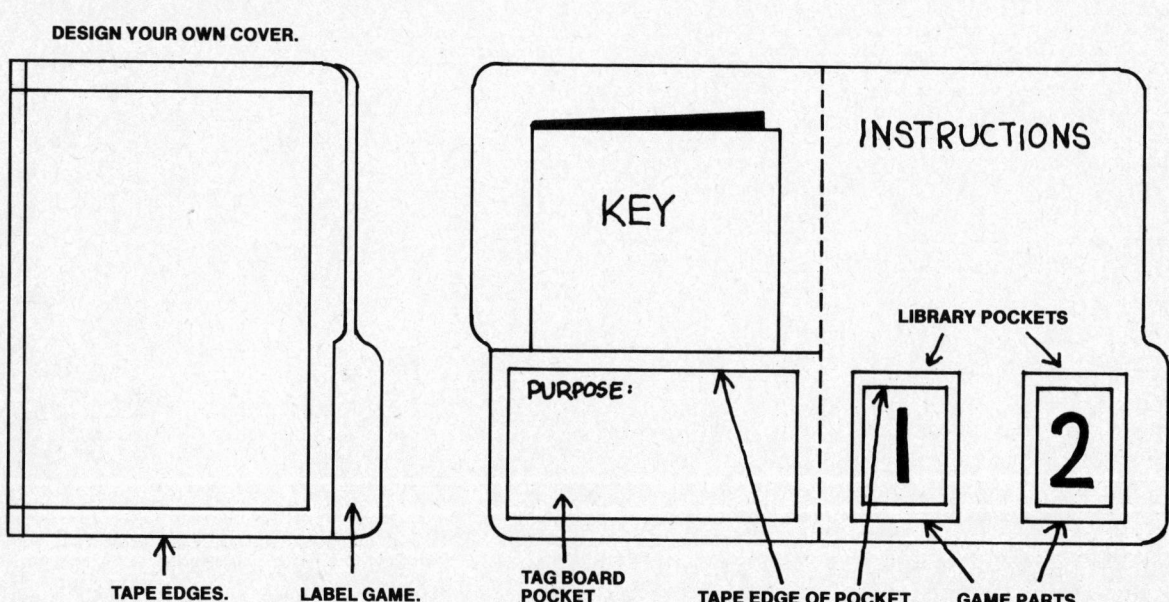

DESIGN YOUR OWN COVER.

KEY

INSTRUCTIONS

PURPOSE:

LIBRARY POCKETS

1

2

TAPE EDGES.

LABEL GAME.

TAG BOARD
POCKET

TAPE EDGE OF POCKET.

GAME PARTS

How to Use Clasp Envelopes (9″ x 12″)

Front Treatments

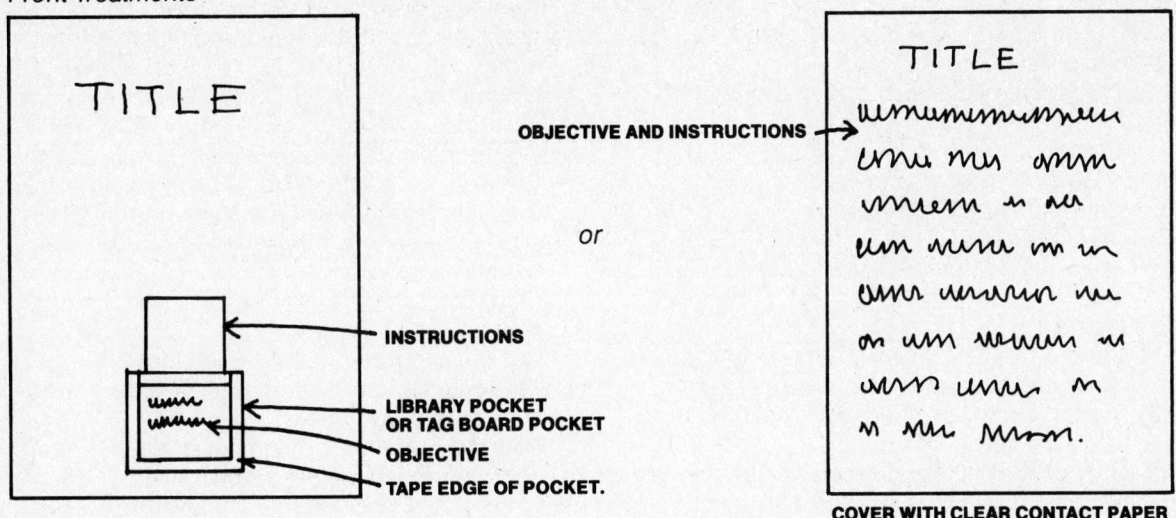

INSTRUCTIONS

LIBRARY POCKET
OR TAG BOARD POCKET

OBJECTIVE

TAPE EDGE OF POCKET.

OBJECTIVE AND INSTRUCTIONS

or

COVER WITH CLEAR CONTACT PAPER

Back Treatments

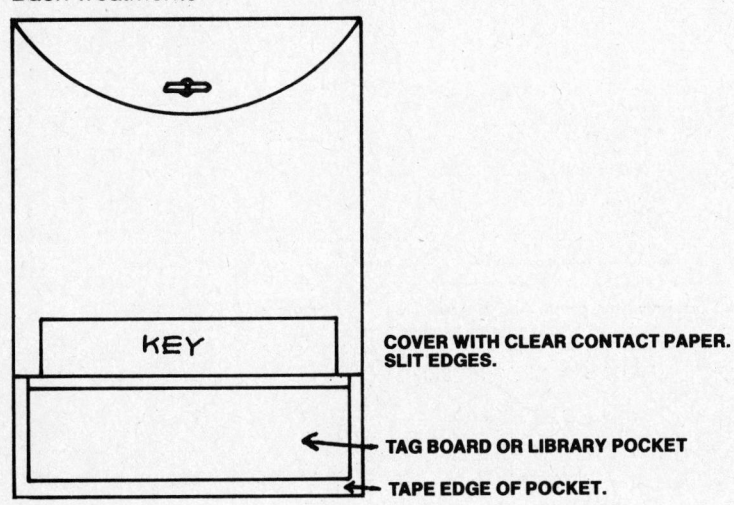

COVER WITH CLEAR CONTACT PAPER.
SLIT EDGES.

TAG BOARD OR LIBRARY POCKET

TAPE EDGE OF POCKET.

Or, Reverse Sides . . .

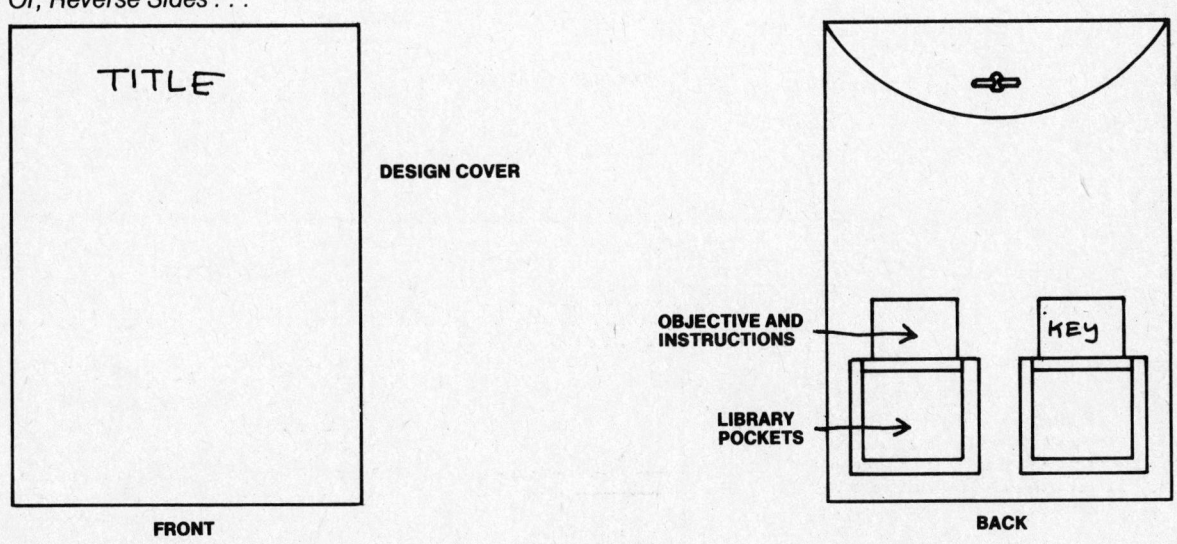

DESIGN COVER

FRONT

OBJECTIVE AND
INSTRUCTIONS

LIBRARY
POCKETS

BACK

How to Make Practice Wheels

Self-check wheels may be used in any activity where there is a question or a statement and a response.

Materials Needed

1. 2 cardboard circles cut to 7″ in diameter
2. Glue
3. 2 brads
4. 2 sheets of tag board cut to 7″
5. Magic marker and felt tip pen
6. Contact paper
7. 1 sheet tag board cut into two strips 8½″ x 2″

To Assemble

1. Cut out page 227. Using a thermofax copier, make a ditto master of the page.
2. Run off copies as needed for patterns or actual assembly.
3. Cut out one of these patterns and use to make two tag board circles and two cardboard circles.
4. Using the sample strip provided, make two strips.
5. On Circle 1 write a stem question, a statement, or a word (see Figure 48).
6. On Circle 2 write the responses, but vary the order.
7. On the back of Circle 1 write the same as on the front.
8. On the back of Circle 2 write the same as on Circle 1. The student should be able to match one side and check the answer on the other side. If she selects the wrong answer, the stem will show up wrong.
9. Cover each circle front and back with contact paper.
10. Cut out the view boxes on the strips.
11. Put together the wheels so that they correspond front and back.
12. Add the brads to the centers of each wheel and the centers of the strips.
13. Write a task card and laminate it or cover it with contact paper.
14. Make a container for the practice wheels.

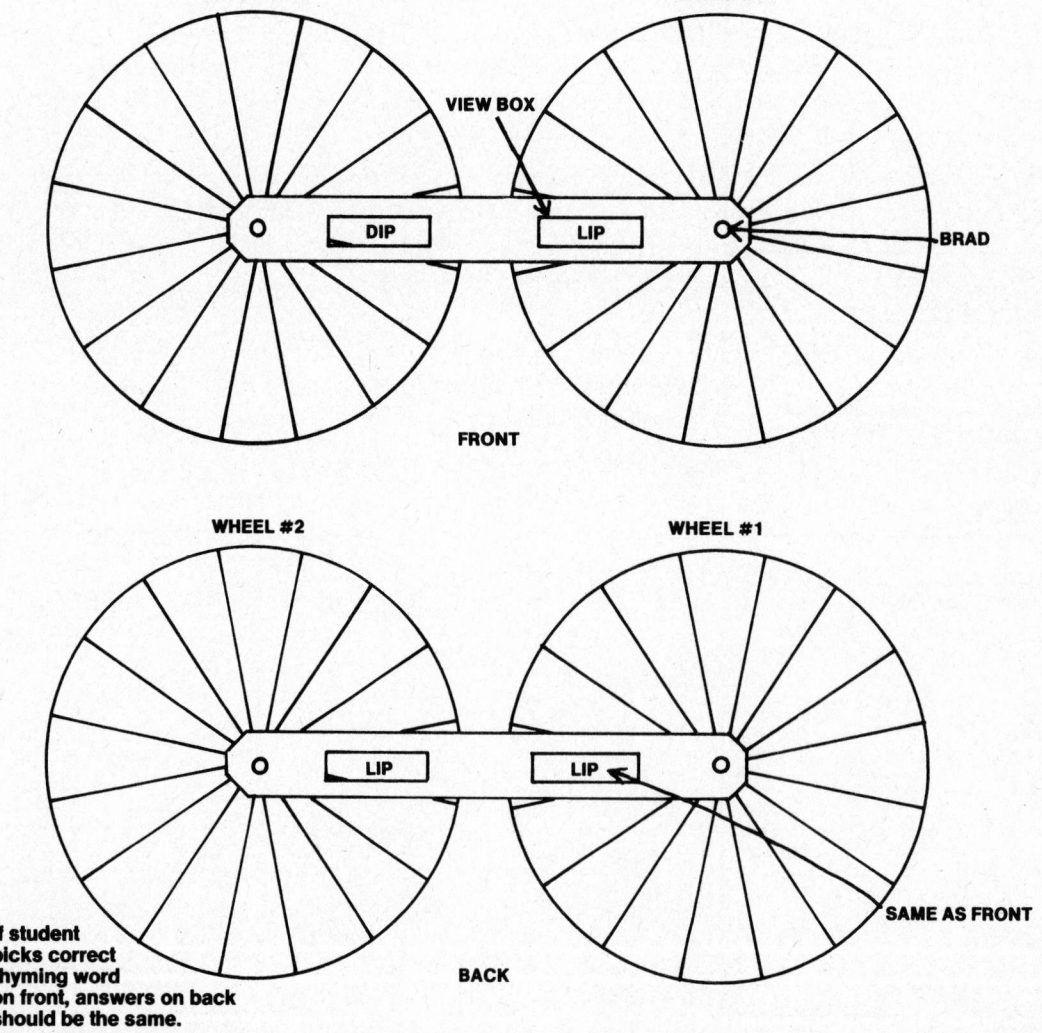

Figure 48. Rhyming words practice wheel.

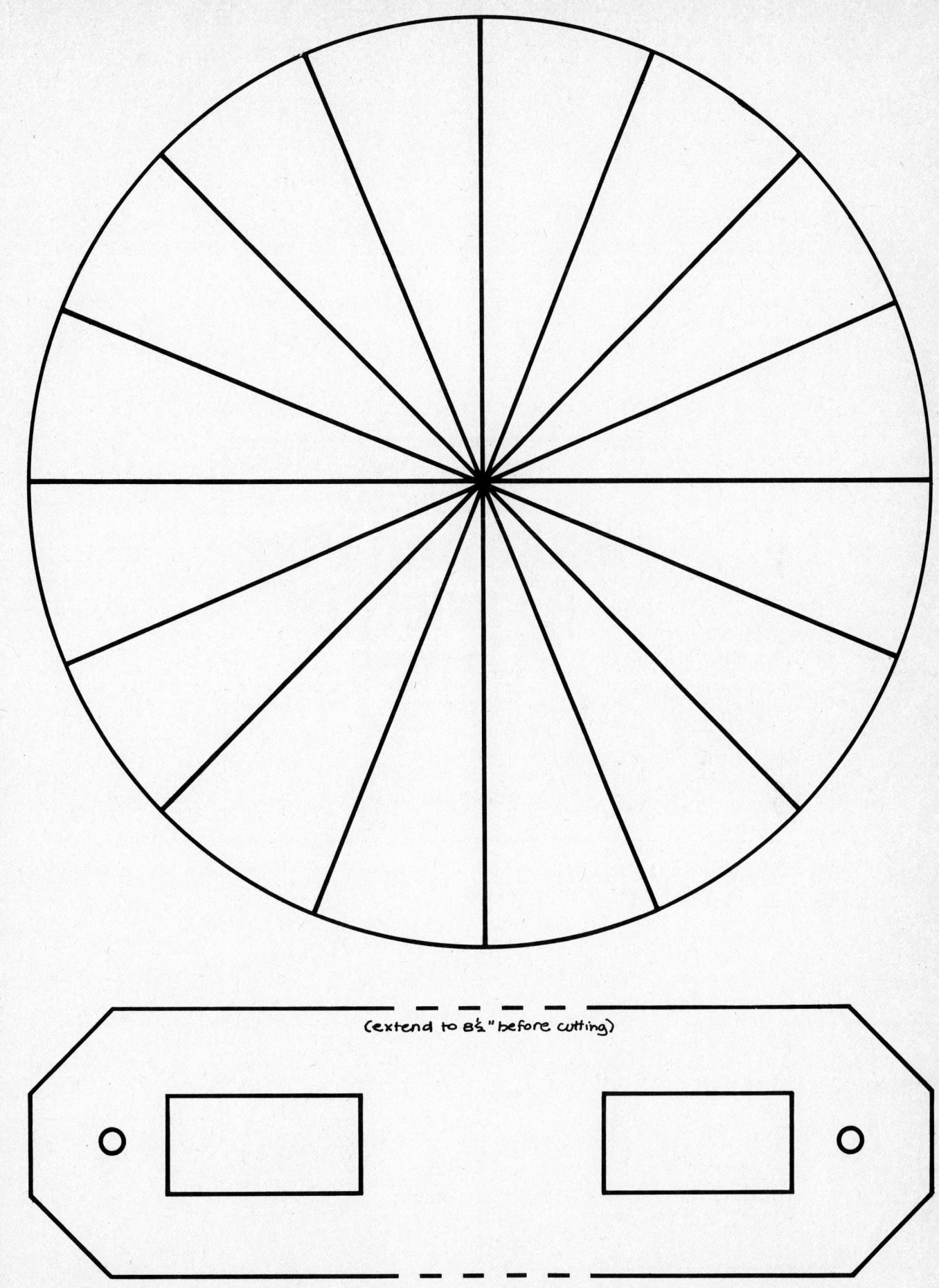

(extend to 8½" before cutting)

How To Make And Play A Variety Of Games

Math Match

81 9×9 24	6×4 49	7×7	
30	5×5	56	32
5×6	25	7×8	4×8
14 2×7 18	3×6 77	7×11	
56	9×5	30	63
8×7	45	3×10	9×7
24 8×3 24	2×12 48	6×8	
7×5	8×5	3×5	4×4
35	40	15	16
12 3×4 42	7×6 18	2×9	

Cut out this page. Using a thermofax copier, make a ditto master of it. Run off as many copies as needed. Glue each copy to tag board or poster board. Laminate or cover with clear contact paper. Cut apart to make a puzzle. See "Pieces and Parts" section for additional information. Make instructions and put into game envelope with purpose written on the envelope.

THIMK

1. Cut out pages 231 and 232.
2. Using a thermofax copier, make ditto masters of these pages
3. Run off as many copies as are needed.
4. Color
    all circles one color.
    all squares a second color.
    all triangles a third color.
    all hexagons a fourth color.
5. Cut out all the shapes and the game board.
6. Cut out the instructions.
7. Make a manila folder game container.
8. Glue parts (instructions and game board) and cover with contact paper.
9. Decorate cover of folder.

Answer Key
There are many ways to arrange the shapes, but one way is

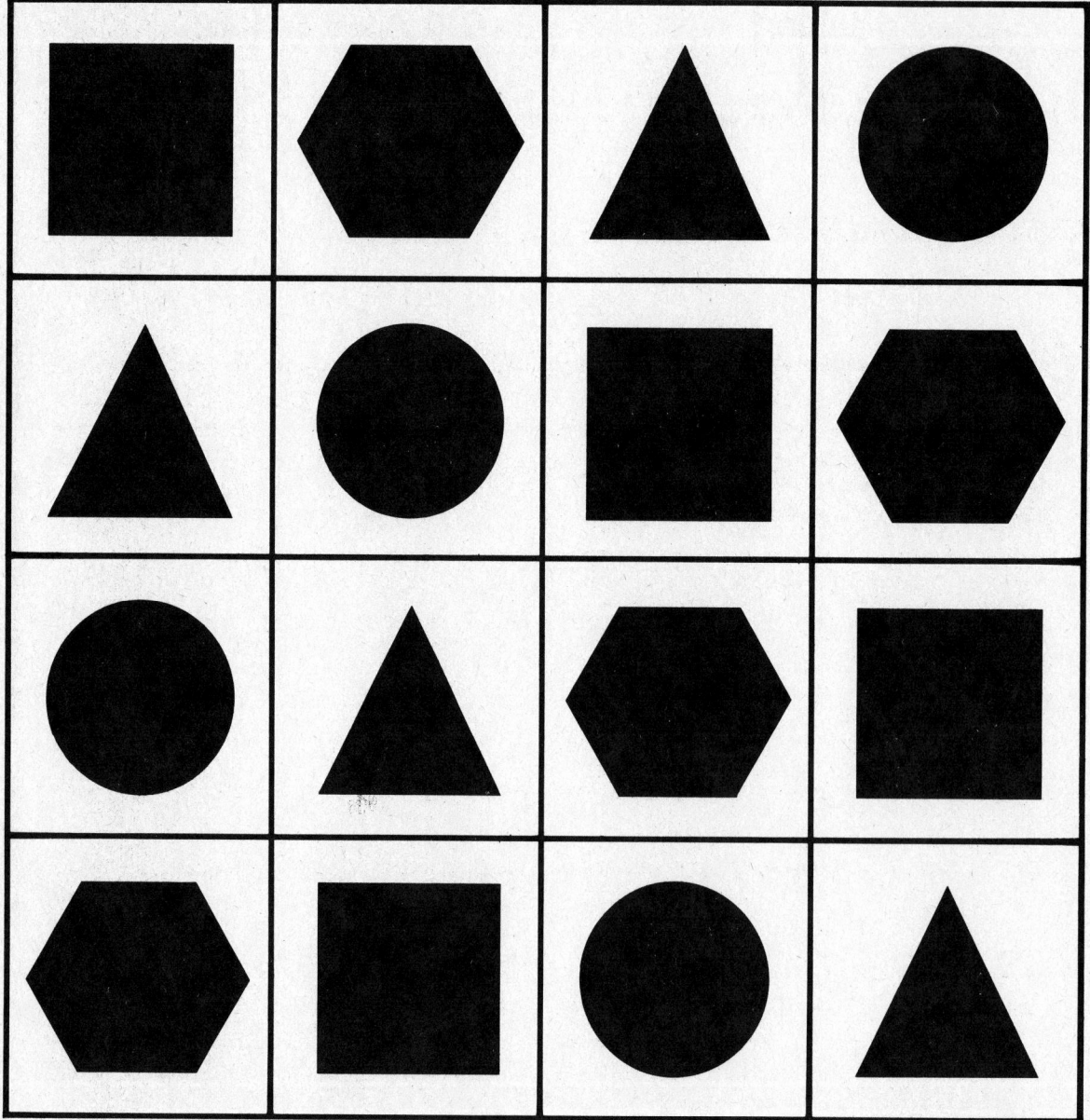

Directions for THIMK

This is a game of logic. It will teach you to think carefully and learn to consider "strategy." To play, place one of *each* color and shape in *each* row, column, and diagonal. You should have one color and shape in each ✕ , each ⟷ , and each ↕ .

Shapes for THIMK

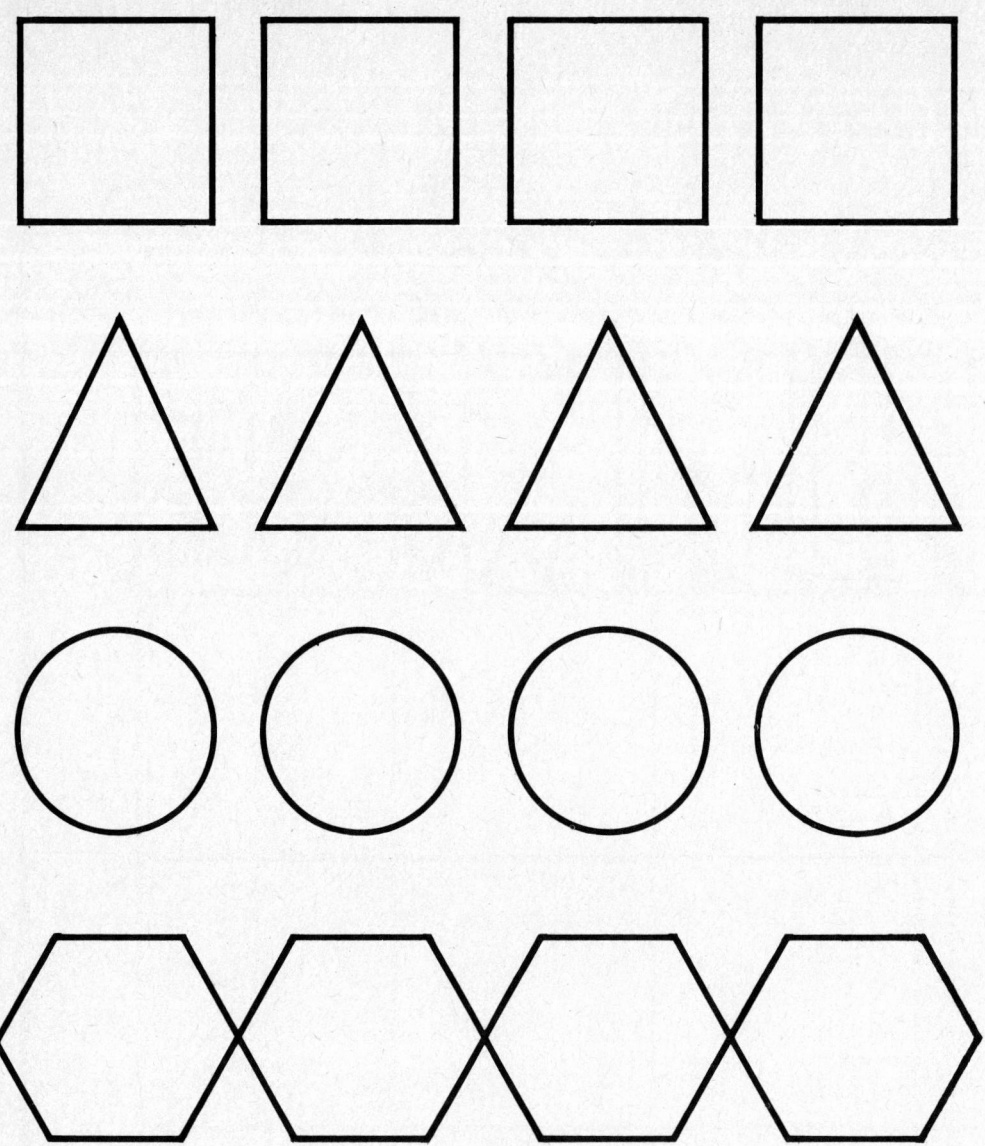

5 x 5 Matrix

5 x 5 Matrix

Game Board 1

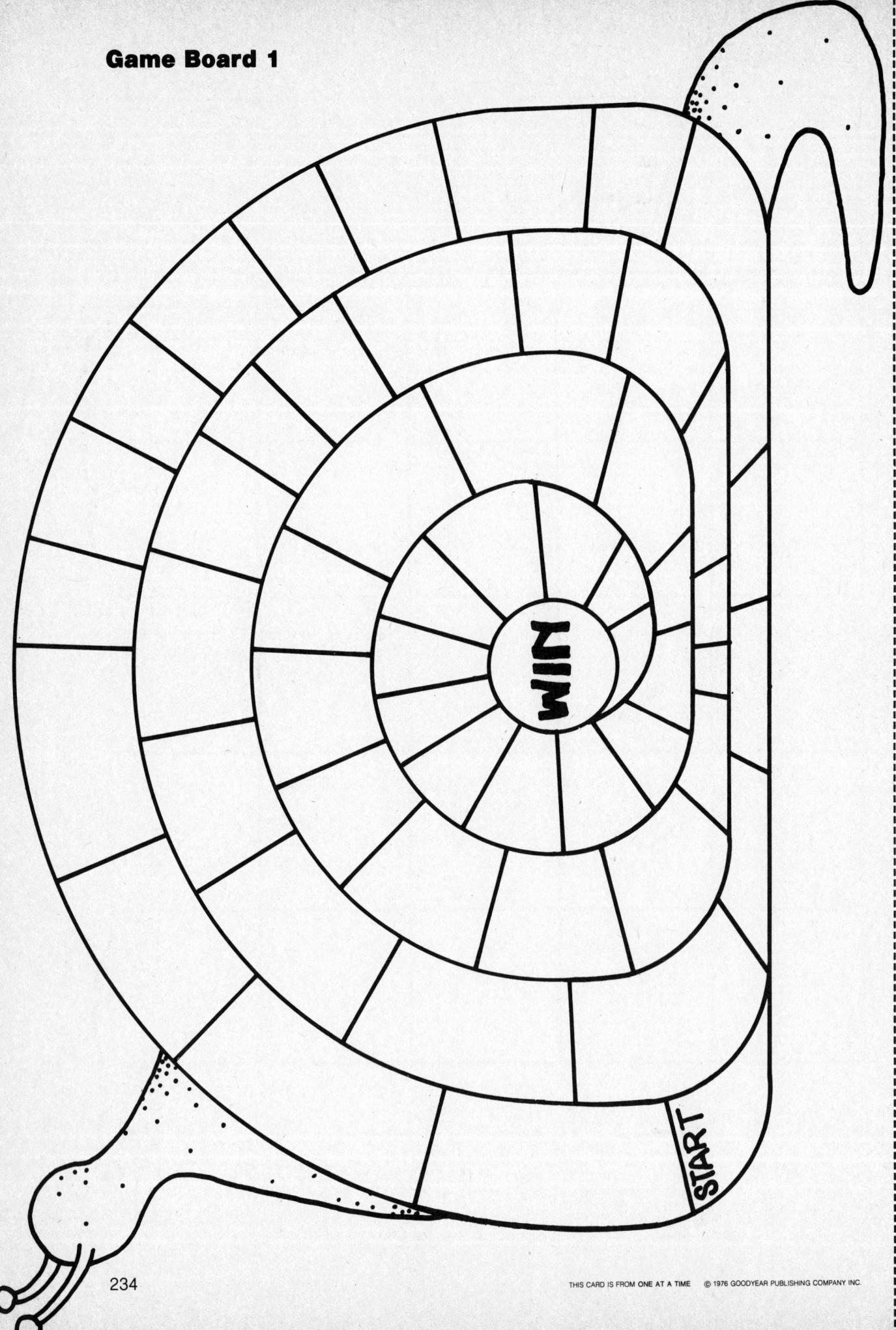

WIN

START

Game Board 2

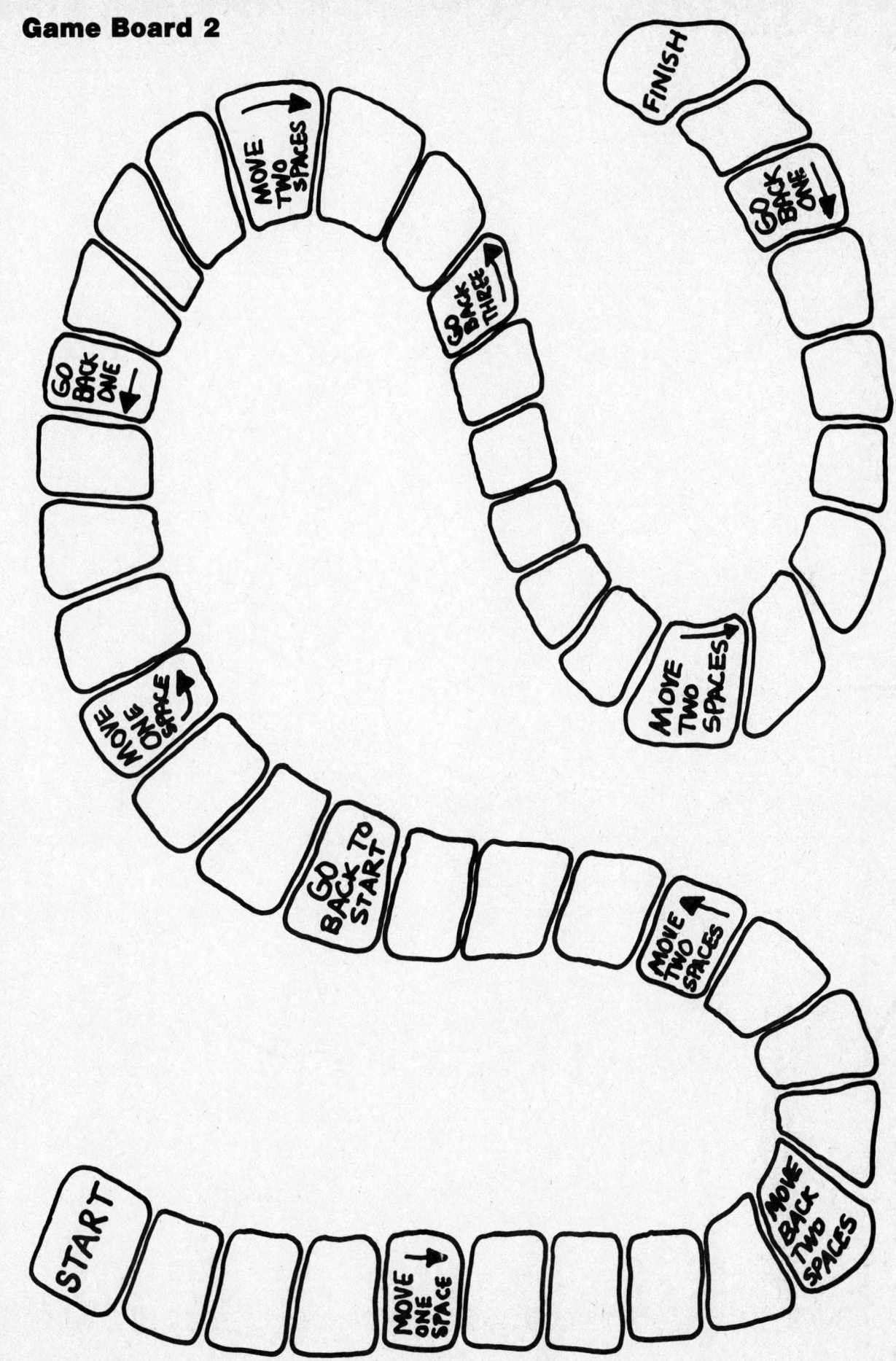

FINISH

GO BACK ONE

MOVE TWO SPACES

GO BACK THREE

MOVE TWO SPACES

GO BACK ONE

MOVE ONE SPACE

GO BACK TO START

MOVE TWO SPACES

START

MOVE ONE SPACE

MOVE BACK TWO SPACES

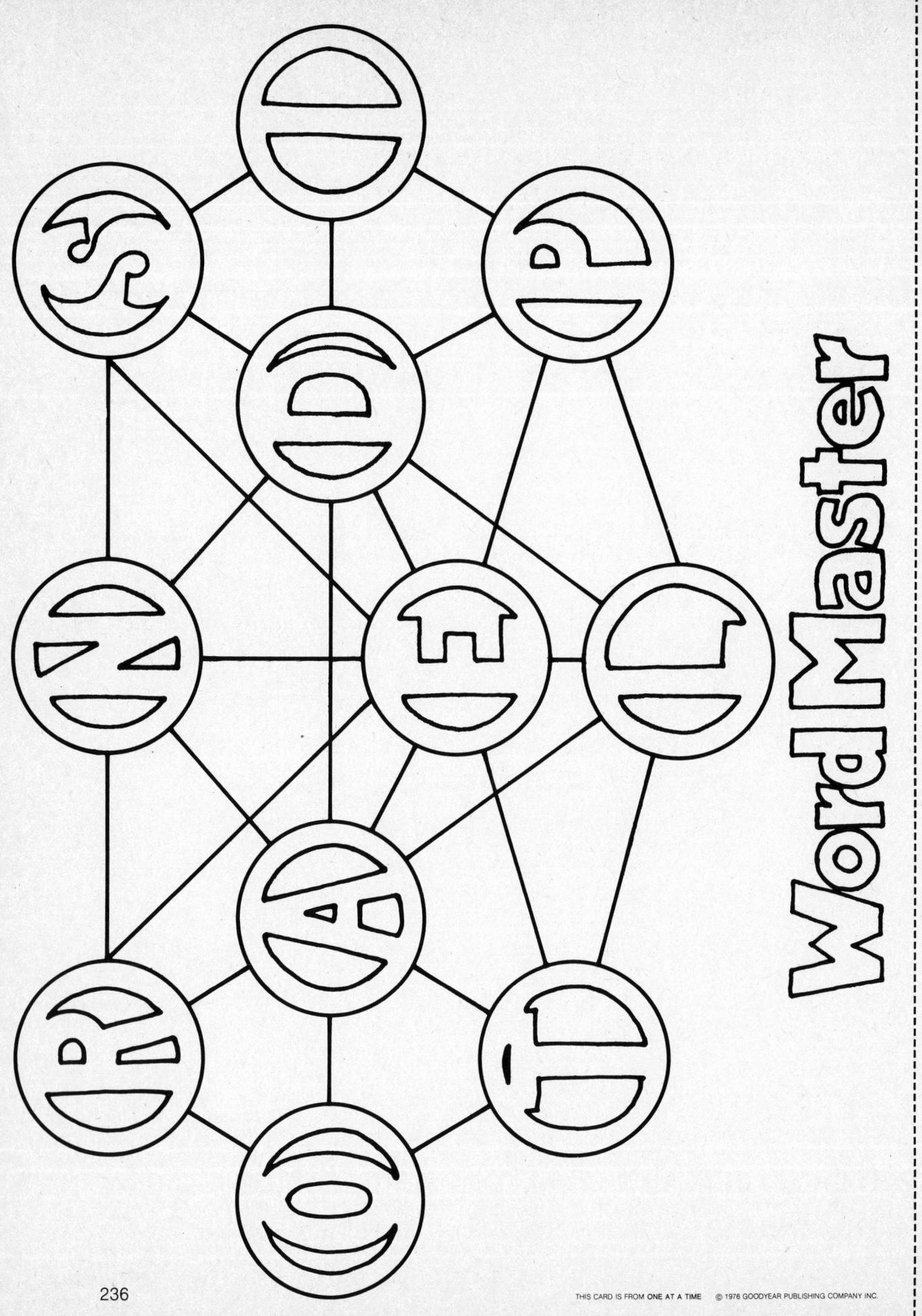

WordMaster

Word Master

Directions

(2 or more players)

This game is used to help you make new words. Use only the lines given you.

Trace your finger over the lines and make words.

    No skips.

    No plurals.

    No proper nouns.

    No abbreviations.

Scoring:

    3 letter word = 1 point

    4 letter word = 3 points

    5 letter word = 5 points

    6 letter word = 10 points

    7 letter word = 20 points

Keep track of your own score. Winner is player with the most points.

    Questions about a word? Check your dictionary.

Answer Key

Here are *some* of the words that can be made: ale, and, darn, dead, dear, den, dip, earn, earned, end, ended, lane, late, led, lend, near, neat, oat, oral, pear, pen, pend, plan, plane, plea, plead, ran, rat, rate, roar, sear, send, set, side, sip, tale, tan, tar, tear, ten, toad, torn

FRACTION TIC-TAC-TOE

To Make

1. Cut out pages 239, 240, and 241.
2. Using a thermofax copier, make a ditto master of these pages.
3. Run off as many copies as are needed.
4. Cut apart boards and back with cardboard.
5. Cover with clear contact paper or laminate.
6. Cut out spinner and finish as directed. Or, if you do not want a spinner, make call cards.
7. Cut out small squares from tag board for use as markers. (You will need at least 40.)
8. Cut out task card and complete as directed.
9. Make game container.

For more advanced students,

1. Make a spinner using a different shape for each fraction.
2. Make a larger game using fractions like 2/3, 4/7, 3/5, etc. You may need to make a deck of call cards instead of using a spinner.

Directions

(2 to 4 players; 5 if using call cards)

Purpose

This game will help you learn fractions.

What You Need

Tic-tac-toe board, markers, spinner.

How to Play

- Spin the spinner to see who has the LARGEST Fraction.
- Player with the largest fraction spins the spinner and calls the fraction.
- All players may put a marker on their cards for that fraction.
- Next player spins the spinner, etc.
- Winner is the player who has markers in a row, column, or diagonal.
- There is no key with this game.

Variation on Instructions

Player cannot put a marker on a fraction unless he spins it.

238

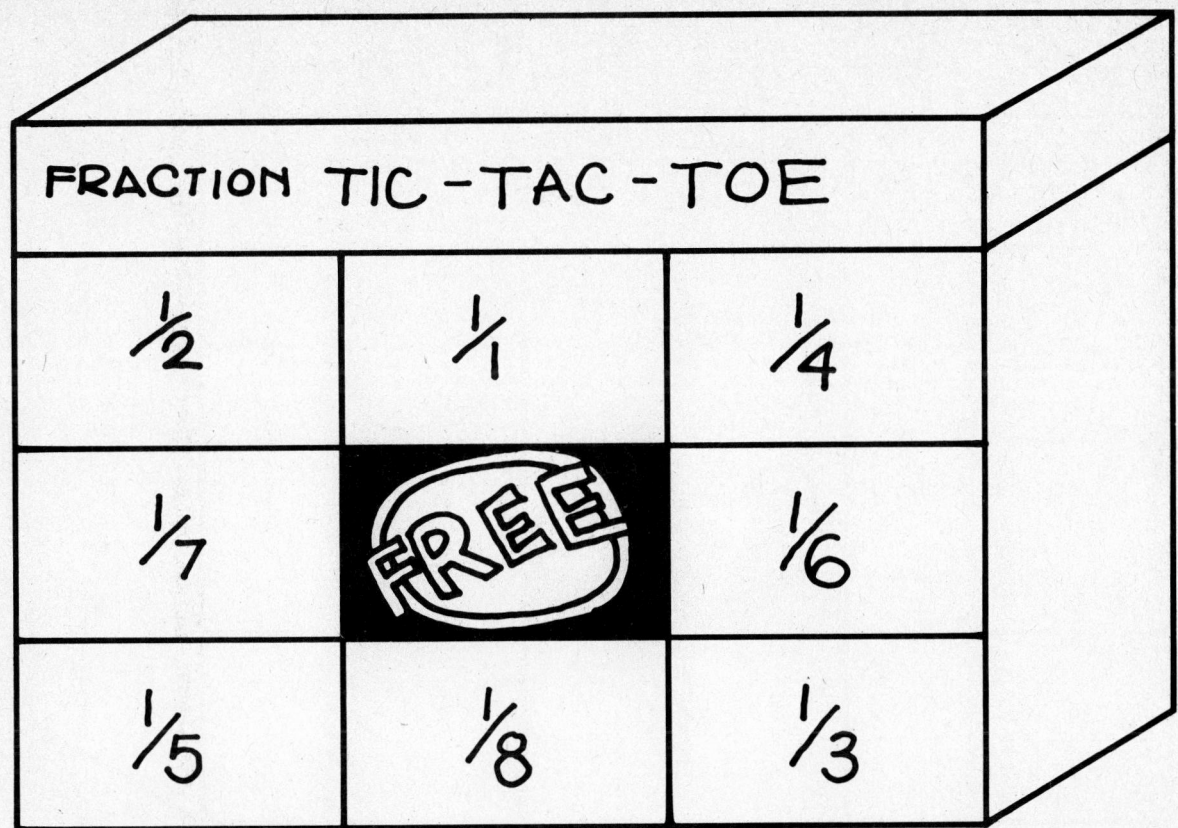

FRACTION TIC-TAC-TOE

½	1/1	¼
1/7	**FREE**	1/6
1/5	1/8	1/3

FRACTION TIC-TAC-TOE

1/7	½	1/1
1/3	**FREE**	1/6
1/8	¼	1/5

FRACTION TIC-TAC-TOE

$\frac{1}{1}$	$\frac{1}{4}$	$\frac{1}{7}$
$\frac{1}{3}$	free	$\frac{1}{2}$
$\frac{1}{6}$	$\frac{1}{8}$	$\frac{1}{5}$

FRACTION TIC-TAC-TOE

$\frac{1}{8}$	$\frac{1}{5}$	$\frac{1}{6}$
$\frac{1}{4}$	free	$\frac{1}{3}$
$\frac{1}{1}$	$\frac{1}{2}$	$\frac{1}{7}$

Fraction Tic-Tac-Toe Spinner

1. Cut this page out of the book.
2. Using a thermofax copier, make a ditto master of it.
3. Run off as many copies as are needed.
4. Cut out spinners.
5. Glue to cardboard backing.
6. Laminate or cover with contact paper.
7. Add brad and paper clip
   (see "How to Make a Spinner," page 221).

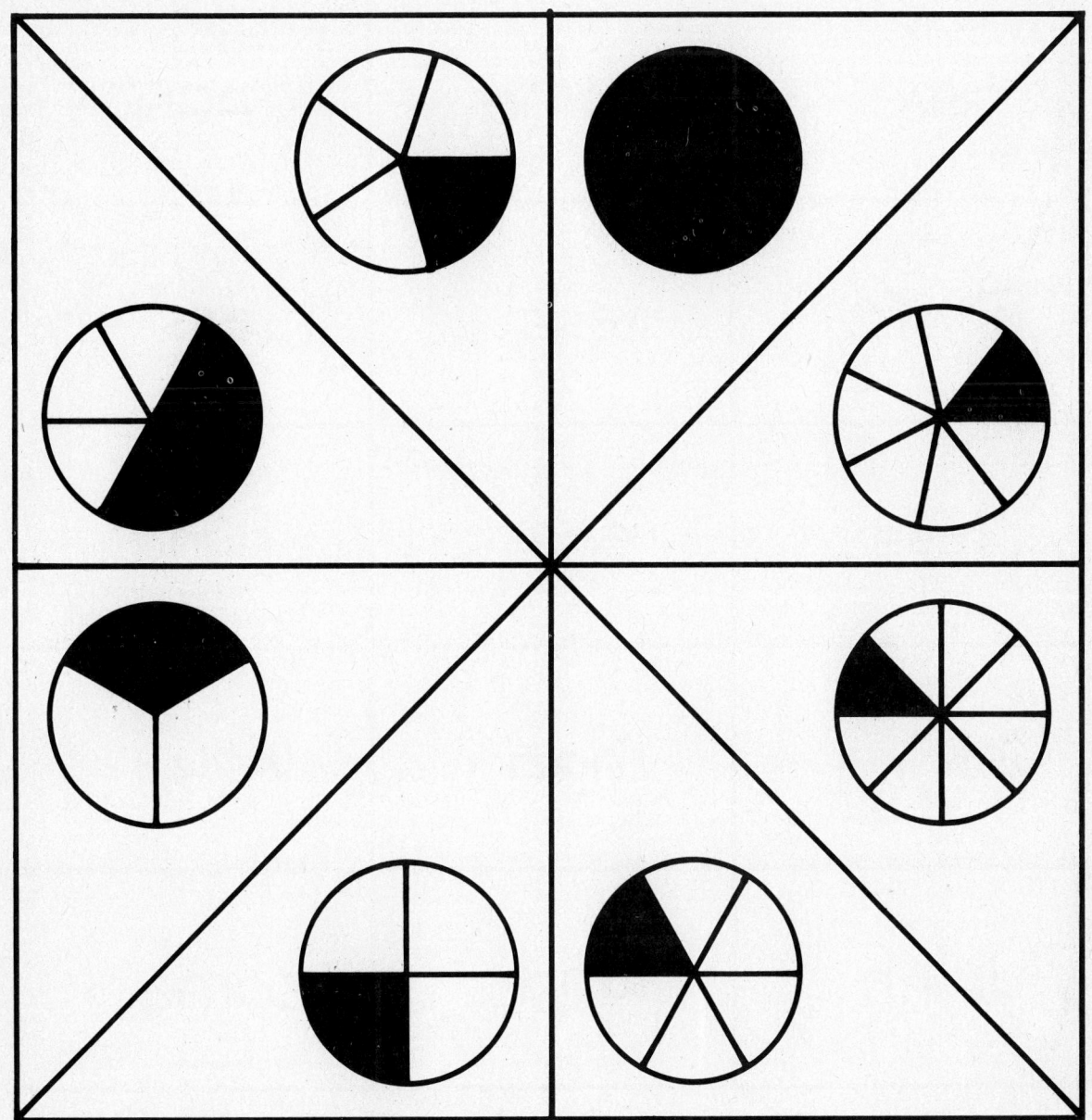

Compound Word Game

form	selves	thing
time	some	man
knife	less	less
less	self	hand
string	man	way
down	land	some

COMPOUND WORD GAME
To Make
1. Cut pages 242, 244, and 245 out of this book.
2. Using a thermofax copier, make a ditto master of these pages.
3. Run off as many copies as are needed on ditto paper or on tag or poster board.
4. Do *not* cut words apart yet. If run on ditto paper, glue entire sheet of words to tag board.
5. Put designed contact paper on back.
6. Put clear contact paper on front or face of word cards.
7. Cut apart word cards.
8. Cut out instructions and answer key. Back with poster board. Cover with clear contact paper.
9. Make game container and decorate.

Directions
(2 to 4 players)
Purpose
This game will help you learn to make compound words.
What You Need
Deck of cards.

How to Play
1. Shuffle the cards.
2. Each player takes two cards.
3. Put the rest of the deck face down.
4. Player draws a card. If he can make a word, he puts it down and draws again. If he can't use the card he drew, he puts it on the discard pile.
5. The next player draws either from the stack or the discard pile.
6. Players take turns drawing until all the words are gone. (The discard pile may be turned over and reused.)
7. Player with the most compound words in front of him wins.

Some word combinations are listed in the answer key. Check your dictionary for others.

Answer Key
ourselves	harmless	monkeyless
yourselves	highjack	noontime
yourself	stringless	handsome
herself	postman	someway
shoestring	highway	lordless
shoeshine	herdless	landlord
timeless	touchdown	handless
sometime	handkerchief	landless
knifeless	formless	selfless
jackknife	something	sundown

Compound Word Game

our	touch	time
lord	way	knife
high	post	less
harm	kerchief	thing
monkey	sun	your
noon	down	form

Compound Word Game

string	land	shoe
hand	man	her
selves	some	boy
jack	shine	self
self	herd	less
less	less	down

Wordless Wonder

Directions: Put a single numeral in each empty space. Each number sentence should be correct when worked from top to bottom and from left to right.

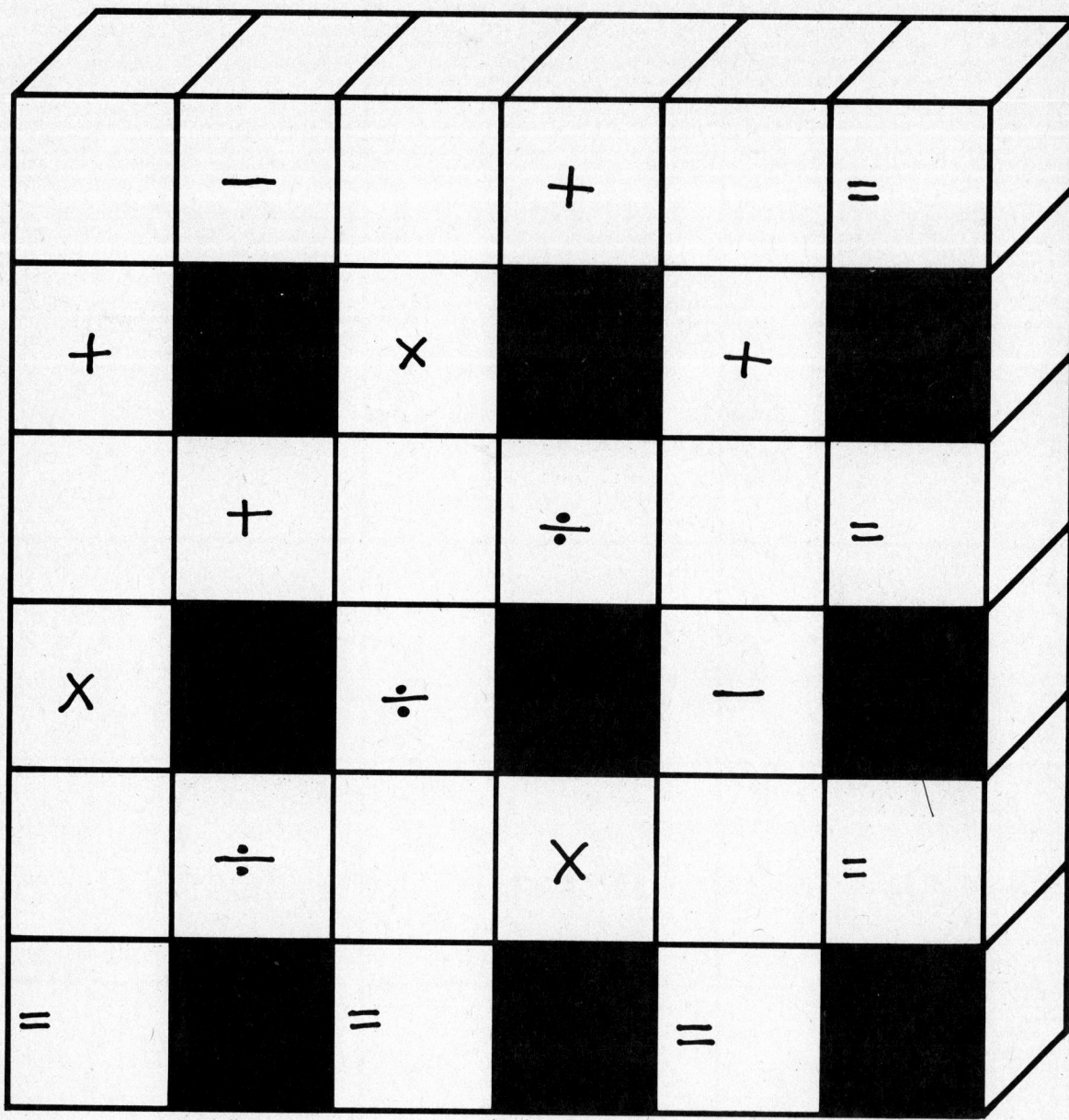

Cut out. Glue or staple to poster board. Use acetate to cover the puzzle. Tape edges of acetate. Put in game center or add to a puzzle box. Student will need a grease pencil to fill in numerals.

THIS CARD IS FROM **ONE AT A TIME** © 1976 GOODYEAR PUBLISHING COMPANY INC.

YELLOW PAGES
Of Selected
Resources For
Individualizing
Curriculum
And
Instruction

There are a variety of publications, materials, and other sources available to assist classroom teachers and other education personnel in developing and carrying on individualized programs. The information contained in these Yellow Pages is only a small sampling of the many fine, diverse, and practical materials available. We have attempted to select references representative of the categories presented in the Yellow Pages.

Persons engaged in developing, implementing, and evaluating individualized programs are encouraged to solicit further information from professional organizations, local schools and school districts, and commercial publishing companies. Each of these agencies can be extremely helpful in supplying information regarding specific programs and materials related to individualization.

RESEARCH, MATERIALS DEVELOPMENT, AND DISSEMINATION SOURCES

Association for Educational Communication and Technology (AECT)
1201 Sixteenth Street, N.W.
Washington, D.C. 20036
AECT is a professional organization concerned with the improvement of instruction through technology. The association has some pertinent publications available for individualized program development. Two resources of impact from the association are listed and described below:

Individualized Instruction Kit
Consists of 6 filmstrips and audio tapes, 6 script books, 46 case study brochures, and an administrator's manual. These materials are based upon actual programs centered throughout the United States. The kit materials can be used for inservice education for school personnel and for community education.

Individualized Instruction Filmstrips
The 6 filmstrips available in the kit described above can also be purchased separately. The filmstrips are in color and are accompanied by an audio tape and a script book.

Center for Individualized Instructional Systems
P.O. Box 11343
Durham, North Carolina
The center is an affiliate of the National Laboratory for Higher Education, formerly known as the Regional Educational Laboratory for the Carolinas and Virginia. The center's best-known work in individualized programs is the Individualized Mathematics System (IMS). IMS is a tightly sequenced math curriculum containing ten topics (e.g., numeration, addition, fractions), nine levels of difficulty within each topic, and 376 skills. A student is diagnosed and then placed in an appropriate skill folder for individual work.

Education Development Center, Inc. (EDC)
55 Chapel Street
Newton, Massachusetts 02160
The Education Development Center is a nonprofit, publicly supported corporation. EDC provides many sources related to individualization including bibliographies, curriculum materials, and films. Curriculum materials are primarily available in science, mathematics, and social sciences.

Research for Better Schools, Inc.
1700 Market Street
Philadelphia, Pennsylvania 19103
Research for Better Schools has developed and disseminated some of the best-known materials and programs for individualization. The center's publication on *Research and Development in Motion* lists the individualized programs and materials developed by the center and provides information regarding availability of the materials. Sample titles of center-developed materials are: Individualized Science (IS), Systematic Progress in Reading and Literature (SPIRAL), IPI Mathematics, Individualized Middle Mathematics (IMM), IPI Reading, IPI Spelling.

Westinghouse Learning Corporation
770 Lucerne Drive
Sunnyvale, California 94806
Westinghouse is representative of a growing number of publishing companies that produce widely known individualized materials. Four products from Westinghouse pertinent to an individualized program are:
1. *Behavioral Objectives* (4 volumes of objectives covering the areas of language arts, social studies, mathematics, and science);
2. *Learning Directory* (8 volumes of educational materials related to various subjects for different educational levels);
3. *Developing Individualized Instructional Material* (tool for developing learning packages);
4. *PLAN* (A Program for Learning in Accordance with Needs). The American Institutes for Research, Westinghouse, and teachers from 13 school districts developed the basis for PLAN. These individualized materials are available for language arts, social studies, science, mathematics, and home economics. Each PLAN individualized course contains performance objectives, learning alternatives, optional resources, criterion-referenced tests, and classroom management materials.

**The Wisconsin Research and Development Center
for Cognitive Learning
The University of Wisconsin
1025 West Johnson Street
Madison, Wisconsin 53706**

This center focuses upon research related to cognitive learning and instructional processes and on materials that facilitate learning. The center provides curriculum materials and curriculum and school organization designs for individualizing curriculum and instruction. Representative products of the center are IGE (Individually Guided Education) and the Wisconsin Design for Reading Skill Development. IGE centers upon school and staff organization and processes for implementing an individualized program. IGE curriculum materials for reading, motivation, prereading, mathematics, and environmental education are being developed.

LEARNING PACKAGE AND INSTRUCTIONAL OBJECTIVES SOURCES AND BANKS

Fort Lincoln New Town Objectives (FLINT)
General Learning Corporation
5454 Wisconsin Ave., N.W.
Washington, D.C. 20015

I/D/E/A—The Unipac Bank (Unipacs available for grades K-12)
University of California
Suite 950
1100 Glenden Ave.
Los Angeles, California 90024

Individualized Learning Systems
(learning packages primarily for career and vocational education)
Continuing Education Publications
1633 S.W. Park Avenue
P.O. Box 1491
Portland, Oregon 97207

Instructional Objectives Exchange
P.O. Box 24095
Los Angeles, California 90024

Learning Objectives for Individualized Instruction
Westinghouse Learning Press
770 Lucerne Drive
Sunnyvale, California 94086

Nova Schools (elementary and secondary school learning packages)
Department of Dissemination
3600 S.W. College Avenue
Ft. Lauderdale, Florida 33314

Teacher Unipac Bank
(An exchange bank, where teachers who put in acceptable packages are able to withdraw and use other packages.)
Tulare County Department of Education
County Courthouse
Visalia, California
Contact: Dr. Rudy Weyland

EXEMPLARY SCHOOL PROGRAMS

Duluth, Minnesota (The Duluth Plan)
Duluth Public Schools have developed individualized programs at the elementary and secondary levels. Emphasis is on involving students in the learning process, both in terms of prescribing work for themselves and in evaluating their work. Contracts are used as the primary means of prescription.

Miami Springs, Florida
Miami Springs High calls its program "Personalized Learning—Freedom of Choice." The program offers regular high school courses but uses a schedule that allows a student to decide what classes he/she wants to take, when to attend school, and how much work will be covered in a given amount of time. Classes run continuously from 7:00 A.M. to 5 P.M., with evening classes twice a week. Learning packages, mostly teacher-developed, form the bases for individualized instruction.

Greenville, South Carolina, Experimental Schools Project (NIE)
The Greenville project is a K-12 design that focuses on learner and community involvement in developing an individualized program in all subject areas. Strong emphasis is placed on affective as well as cognitive development. Teachers are retrained to diagnose and prescribe for students on an individual basis.

Hackensack, New Jersey, Public Schools— Project LEM
Learning Experience Module is a school organization and instructional program designed for open space schools. It involves multiaged grouping, team-teaching/differentiated staffing, and shared responsibility. LEM utilizes large group, small group, and personalized instruction. Contracts, projects, and peer teaching or tutorials are used for individualizing. For further information write:
  Eleanor Russo
  Hillers Elementary School
  Longview Avenue
  Hackensack, New Jersey 07601

Source:
  Project LEM Organization and Curriculum
  Hackensack Public Schools

Kahala Elementary School, Honolulu, Hawaii
Kahala operates an independent study program in grades 2-6; the program is not only for bright, highly motivated students, but also is designed to help motivate underachievers and students with learning problems. The teacher, the independent study coordinator, and the librarian form a team to help a student plan and complete an independent study project. Students learn standard library procedures and use various media to gain information. They often use media in presenting their learnings to teachers and other students.

Meadowbrook Junior High School, Newton, Massachusetts
Meadowbrook Junior High School in Newton, Massachusetts, is organized around units of 225 students, across age, interest, and ability levels. Staff prescribe for individual students on different levels within the units.

Nova Schools, Fort Lauderdale, Florida
Nova Schools constitute an educational park for students in all grades, kindergarten through college, and of all ages, including adults. They were among the first to employ Learning Activity Packages (LAPs) widely. Packages are written and prescribed for each part of the instructional sequence; students have some choice in order of packages, rate of progress, and media and activities to be used. Packages are distributed on a low-cost basis.

Pacoima Elementary School, Los Angeles, California
Pacoima Elementary School uses student tutors across grade levels to achieve individualization in "the Tutorial Community."

Temple City, California

Temple City uses the concept of differentiated staffing (and pay: a teacher has received a higher salary than the superintendent) to foster individualizing. It has used some of the major "think tanks" in the country in totally reexamining instructional content and processes.

Woodlake Union High School, Woodlake, California

Part of the National Model School Project (NASSP), the Woodlake program includes demand flexible scheduling, differentiated staffing, variable credit, team teaching, resource rooms, and use of the teacher-counselor concept.

In addition to the above examples of exemplary programs, the following sources are suggested for additional information about schools with successful individualized programs.

IGE: Individually Guided Education and the Multi-Unit School, a publication of the National School Public Relations Association, 1801 N. Moore Street, Arlington, Virginia, 22209. Contains lists of IGE schools affiliated both with I/D/E/A and with the Wisconsin Research and Development Center.

IGE: Focus on the Multiunit School, a publication of the Wisconsin Research and Development Center, 1025 West Johnson Street, Madison, Wisconsin, 53706. Describes the IGE school and lists regional centers and implementation materials available.

Individualized Instruction Kit. Contains 46 case studies of individualized programs throughout the United States. This is a publication of the Association for Educational Communication and Technology (ASCT), 1201 Sixteenth Street, N.W., Washington, D.C., 20036.

NATIONAL AND REGIONAL INFORMATION AND MATERIALS SOURCES

Education Products Information Exchange (EPIE)
386 Park Avenue South
New York, New York 10016

A private, nonprofit organization designed to evaluate teaching and learning materials, equipment, and systems. EPIE gathers data from users of materials and equipment, from individuals and agencies commissioned to evaluate the content, objectives, and procedures of various materials and equipment, and from descriptive information provided by producers. Subscription memberships.

Educational Resources Information Center (ERIC)
National Institute of Education
Code 401
Washington, D.C. 20202

ERIC is a decentralized, nationwide information system designed and supported by the United States Office of Education. It is designed to aid in the development of educational programs by disseminating research results, research-related materials, and other information of interest to educators. Publishes *Research in Education (RIE),* a monthly journal that abstracts ERIC report literature, and *Current Index to Journals in Education (CIJE),* a monthly journal that indexes and abstracts periodical literature.

ERIC computer searches can be conducted on a wide variety of educational topics at minimal cost because of government financing.

National Information Center for Educational Media (NICEM)
University of Southern California
University Park
Los Angeles, Calif. 90007

An independent information center and clearinghouse designed to collect, catalog, and disseminate information about all audiovisual materials distributed in this country. Provides printed indexes of various types of media and materials such as films, audio tapes, video tapes, transparencies, filmstrips, and records.

San Mateo County Educational Resources Center
333 Main Street
Redwood City, Calif. 94063

Designed as a "one-stop" center for teacher-developed materials and research information. Disseminates Learning Center Activity Packages and UNIPACS (single-concept learning packages). Operates yearly contracts between the center and other countries, special projects, or regional agencies eligible for SMERC services.

GUIDES AND RESOURCE BOOKS FOR MATERIALS RELATED TO INDIVIDUALIZATION

Henrie, Samuel N., senior ed., *A Sourcebook of Elementary Curricula Programs and Projects* (San Francisco, Calif.: Far West Laboratory for Educational Research and Development, 1972).
A 493 page source book which includes references to several recent curricula and programs for individualization. Arranged by chapters devoted primarily to curriculum/subject matter areas. Extensive information is given for each entry.
Order from:
    Superintendent of Documents
    U.S. Government Printing Office
    Washington, D.C. 20402
    Stock No. 1780-1072

Salisbury, Gordon, *Catalogue of Free Teaching Materials* (Riverside, Calif.: Rubidoux, (1973-76 revision).
Over 300 pages of categorized materials, with specific directions and addresses for ordering. Includes books, government reports, maps, posters, leaflets.
Order from:
    P.O. Box 1075
    Ventura, California 93001
    ($3.00)

Wittich, W. A., ed., *Educators Guide to Free Tapes, Scripts, and Transcriptions* (Randolph, Wis.: Educators Progress Service, Inc., 1970).
A guide to *selected* tapes, scripts, and transcripts free (no rental service or sales cost) to schools and libraries.
Contact:
    Dr. Walter A. Wittich
    30 Wailupe Circle
    Honolulu, Hawaii 96816

ANNOTATED BIBLIOGRAPHY OF READINGS IN INDIVIDUALIZED INSTRUCTION

Adams, Dennis M., *Simulation Games: An Approach to Learning* (Worthington, Ohio: Charles A. Jones, 1973).
For teachers and administrators, this book serves as a concise, practical guide to the understanding, design, construction, and use of simulations, games, and related experiences for learning. In addition, there is a bibliography.

Beggs, David W., and Edward G. Buffie, *Independent Study* (Bloomington: Indiana University Press, 1965).
A collection of readings concerned with independent study practices that have stood the test of time, this book deals primarily with the nature and goals of independent study, and ways schools can organize for implementing an independent study program.

Biddle, Bruce, and Edwin Thomas, *Role Theory: Concepts and Research* (New York: Wiley, 1966).
Scholars, researchers, students, and instructors may find this book a useful one. It offers a penetrating analysis of the many aspects of role theory.

Brown, Dr. B. Frank, *Education by Appointment* (West Nyack, N.Y.: Parker, 1968).
This book describes a number of strategies for implementing an independent study program in any type of school situation. It includes a brief but complete history of independent study, an analysis of the need for such programs, and an impressive argument for them. Especially interesting is the final chapter which consists of a series of vignettes written by high school students about their experiences in and evaluations of independent study programs.

College and University Self-Study Institute, *The Individual and the System,* edited by John Minter (Boulder, Colo.: Western Interstate Commission for Higher Education, 1967).
A collection of papers presented at the Ninth Annual College and University Self-Study Institute. The talks are varied but all show concern that the large number of students involved in higher education will mean that it loses its humaneness, the very value for which it stands. In a most interesting paper, "A Conservative Approach to Radical Reform," Warren Bryan Martin describes the architectural environment of most campuses as representing outdated values such as departmentalization of disciplines and *in loco parentis*. He makes the point that the large libraries built in this electronic age "may turn out to be monuments of antiquity, high-rise hitching posts for a world that has moved on," and presents alternatives for the colleges of the future.

Day, Barbara, *Open Learning in Early Childhood* (Riverside, N.J.: Macmillan, 1975).
Discusses issues and practices related to individualization, such as, physical organization of learning centers, use of contract teaching, self-corrective materials, and multiage grouping. Ten learning center ideas are presented in detail. Also presents suggestions on record keeping and evaluation.

Drumheller, Sidney J., *Handbook of Curriculum Design for Individualized Instruction: A Systems Approach* (Englewood Cliffs, N.J.: Educational Technology Publications, 1971).
Proposes a modified taxonomy of educational objectives based closely on Bloom et al., and presents a design for curriculum construction based on the objectives determined through the use of a modified taxonomy. This guide book for curriculum designers is constructed as a workbook.

Duane, James E., *Individualized Instruction: Programs and Materials* (Englewood Cliffs, N.J.: Educational Technology Publications, 1973).
A collection of readings presenting practical approaches to particular areas of individualization, this book is organized into four parts: (1) The Transition from Group to Individualized Instruction; (2) Established Individualized Instruction Formats; (3) Media in Individualized Approaches; and (4) The Evaluation for Individualized Instruction. The three appendices, annotated bibliographies of textbooks and media on individualized instruction and sample individualized instruction packages, are valuable.

Dunn, Rita, and Kenneth Dunn, *Practical Approaches to Indiviudalizing Instruction: Contracts and Other Effective Teaching Strategies* (West Nyack, N.Y.: Parker, 1972).
As the title suggests, this book offers a variety of ways, "tried and proven," to vary and improve teaching techniques, with the ultimate goal being effective learning for all students. The emphasis is on the development and utilization of learning contracts. In addition, role playing, team teaching and learning, circles of knowledge, simulations, brainstorming, and case studies are discussed with practical guidelines and samples provided by the authors.

Esbensen, Thorwald, *Working with Individualized Instruction: The Duluth Experience* (Belmont, Calif.: Fearon, 1968).
Robert Mager proclaims in his Foreword that this book is about individualized instruction in action. The book consists of four parts. The first part is a detailed description of what individualized instruction is and is not, practical suggestions for initiating it, and a discussion of performance objectives. The other three parts of the book describe three projects in Duluth, Minnesota, which involved elementary schools of varied populations and which used individualized instruction.

Gale, Fred L., *Determining the Requirements for the Design of Learner Based Instruction* (Columbus, Ohio: Merrill, 1975).
Designed to help the teacher provide for learner differences. Discusses requirements for instructional design, instructional strategies, role of media in learner-based instruction, development of a media program, and program evaluation. Several practical examples of instructional designs are included.

Gibbons, Maurice, *Individualized Instruction, A Descriptive Analysis* (New York: Teachers College Press, 1971).
Gibbons begins by pointing to the humanistic appeal of the term individualized instruction and the factors that have led to a growing number of programs claiming to individualize instruction during the past few years. He gives a description of the various types of programs beginning with tutoring, the original individualized instruction, and ending with a catchall category of trivial, vague methods. The author offers systems for classifying individualized instruction programs and a profiling system for different types of programs in existence, and concludes that the use of these will permit individualized instructional programs to be both coherent and consistent.

Gross, Ronald, and Judith Murphy, *Educational Change and Architectural Consequences: A Report on Facilities for Individualized Instruction* (New York: Educational Facilities Laboratories, 1968).
This book examines just what the title indicates. It was designed as an aid to the laymen, members of school boards and building committees, who make many of the crucial decisions in school planning. Part I examines the spirit of the recent changes in education and makes the point that the idea is no longer one teacher–thirty children, but one child–one program which will take place at different times in groups of various sizes. Part II describes the types of instruction in today's schools, and Part III gives sample plans for pre-primary, primary, middle, and secondary schools.

Kapfer, Philip G., and Glen F. Ovard, *Preparing and Using Individualized Learning Packages for Ungraded Continuous Progress Education* (Englewood Cliffs, N.J.: Educational Technology Publications, 1971).
Individualized learning packages emerged during the past few years as a way of individualizing instruction. This book "practices what it preaches" in that it is written in ILPs. Lessons are built around the concept that a continuous progress curriculum provides for individual differences. For this concept, specific learning objectives, alternate learning activities, a method of evaluating the learning, and examples of a quest for breadth and depth are given.

Kaplan, Sandra, et al., *Change for Children* (Pacific Palisades, Calif.: Goodyear, 1973).
A book of practical ideas for teachers to use in an individualized elementary classroom. Includes drawings of and directions for learning centers, games, and classroom management techniques. Many of the pages are perforated so that they may be torn out and duplicated.

Kaplan, Sandra, et al., *A Young Child Experiences* (Pacific Palisades, Calif.: Goodyear, 1975).
A sequel to *Change for Children,* but designed for early childhood programs.

Kibler, Robert J., et al., *Objectives for Instruction and Evaluation* (Boston: Allyn and Bacon, 1974).
The authors present a four-part closed-loop instructional model which helps classify the relationship between objectives and the teaching/learning process. Contains a programmed appendix for teaching how to use instructional objectives.

Langdon, Danny, *Interactive Instructional Designs for Individualized Learning* (Englewood Cliffs, N.J.: Educational Technology Publications, 1973).
This book's stated intention is "to provide a series of practical instructional designs that the reader may choose to replicate." Langdon begins by defining an instructional design as a format which prescribes student learning requirements and events, and describes an effective instructional design as one that facilitates learning for students to the fullest possible extent. He lists three basic requirements in achieving an effective instructional design: behavioral objectives, interactive instruction, and validation.

Mager, Robert F., *Preparing Instructional Objectives* (San Francisco, Calif.: Fearon, 1962).
A highly readable book on the development and use of behavioral objectives. One of the earliest and most popular books on the subject.

Manlove, Donald C., and David W. Beggs III, *Flexible Scheduling* (Bloomington: Indiana University Press, 1968).
One of the *Bold New Venture* series, this text is designed primarily for teachers and administrators who are serious about getting down to the practical aspects of teaching. The flexible scheduling concept described is the Indiana Flexible Schedule, a model that can be used as presented, modified, or expanded. The Indiana Flexible Schedule presents detailed, specified ways to change the rate of instruction; to allow teachers to teach what they teach best; to make alterations in class size; and to make changes in the time allotments for various subjects.

Murray, Evelyn, and Jane Wilhour, *The Flexible Elementary School* (West Nyack, N.Y.: Parker, 1971).
This book focuses primarily on the implementation of flexible, nongraded programs in the elementary classroom, including essential guidelines for setting up such a program in a school, and offers many practical instructional suggestions for the classroom teacher. Various aspects of nongradedness,

including flexible grouping, team teaching, independent study, and tutorial work, are discussed in clear, easy-to-read language.

Musgrove, G. Ray, *Individualized Instruction: Teaching Strategies Focusing on the Learner* (Boston : Allyn and Bacon, 1975).
This book rejects an emphasis on facilities or organizational designs as ways of promoting individualized instruction to focus instead on various in-class grouping patterns and independent study as ways of allowing students to work at their own pace. In addition, there are chapters dealing with accountability through evaluation and the development and implementation of programs that focus on the learner.

McNamara, Helen, Margaret Carroll, and Marvin Powell, *Individual Progression* (Indianapolis: Bobbs-Merrill, 1970).
This book begins with a theoretical framework for individual progression: a curriculum based on the worth of each student and his potential at a given moment. It relates the story of Helen McNamara, one of the authors and a teacher in a traditional classroom for twenty-five years, who made the change to an individualized approach. Included are the background and reasons for her change, as well as a list of her beliefs about children and learning. Other parts of the book concern creating the environment for such instruction, descriptions of machines that might be used, practical suggestions for teachers making such a change, and a diary observation of Miss McNamara's class "in action."

National School Public Relations Association, *Individualization in Schools: The Challenges and the Options* (Washington, D.C.: Education, U.S.A., 1971).
Although people have talked many years about the unique nature of each human being and the need to attune the educational system to that, little has been done about it until the past few years. This booklet describes eight approaches to individualization employing major systems available for implementation in the schools in 1971. These are: the Program for Learning in Accordance with Needs (PLAN); Individually Prescribed Instruction (IPI); Individually Guided Education (IGE); Individualized Mathematics System (IMS); Programmed Logic for Automated Teaching Operations (PLATO); the Duluth Plan for Individualization; Miami Springs' "Personalized Learning"; and Hawaii's Independent Study Program. This publication also presents a classification system with four general types of individualized instruction based on whether the school or the individual determines the objectives, materials, and pace.

Noar, Gertrude, *Individualized Instruction: Every Child a Winner* (New York: Wiley, 1972).
"How do you teach individual children in a class of thirty or more who are far below grade level while others are far above? What do you do when they can't read? How do you turn them on?" The author presents concrete examples of manageable ways that individual needs can be met in the classroom. A valuable book for teachers trying to individualize instruction.

Noble, Judith, *Games Children Play and Learn From* (Dubuque, Iowa: Kendall-Hunt, 1973).
This collection of games and other related learning activities could be an aid to many primary teachers' search for an informal approach to dealing with individual differences. Though most of the activities described are designed for use in developing readiness for reading and mathematical skills, most could be adapted to higher levels. Each game has a specified purpose, a list of materials needed, and directions for construction and playing.

Peter, Laurence J., *Individual Instruction* (McGraw-Hill, 1972).
The first in a series of four books written to be used primarily as texts for the instruction of teachers in the individualization process. Approaches individualization through what is termed the Prescriptive Teaching System. Progress through the system helps prepare the student teacher for teaching one

pupil individually, and in turn to generalize or transfer this knowledge of individualized instruction to the regular classroom.

Research for Better Schools, Inc., *A Progress Report: Individually Prescribed Instruction* (Philadelphia: Research for Better Schools, 1969).
Describes the chief progress and findings concerning Individually Prescribed Instruction through August 1969, gives abstracts of fifty studies on IPI, and contains an annotated bibliography of studies on IPI. The results of these studies were interesting but inconclusive.

Sarason, Irwin, and Barbara Sarason, *Constructive Classroom Behavior* (New York: Behavioral Publications, 1974).
Using specific situations in which modeling and role playing might be employed either to eliminate or to achieve specific behavior, this book provides an understanding of both.

Sartain, Harry W., *Individualized Reading* (Newark, Del.: International Reading Association, 1970).
This annotated bibliography purports to select from the six hundred plus articles on individualized reading that have been published during the last fifteen years those that will give the reader various points of view on the subject. The bibliography itself is divided into four sections: Varied Views of Individualized Reading; Experimentation and Research; Classroom Practices; and Materials of Instruction.

Smith, Helen K., *Meeting Individual Needs in Reading* (Newark, Del.: International Reading Association, 1971).
Contains some of the papers given at the Fifteenth Annual Convention of the International Reading Association on the theme, "Reading and the Individual." The papers are about the effect reading has on a person's self-concept and the methods used in teaching reading which recognize the peculiar needs, interests, desires, abilities, and backgrounds of those being taught. The first part of the book deals with individual differences found in pupils, ways of identifying and meeting these differences in reading programs, and supportive patterns of classroom organization. Part II deals with individualizing programs for particular groups of children, such as retarded, nonacademic, and black.

Stahl, Dona K., and Patricia M. Anzalone, *Individualized Teaching in Elementary Schools* (West Nyack, N.Y.: Parker, 1970).
The authors state that the purpose of this book is "to provide some specific, concrete suggestions for putting theory about individual instruction into realistic, workable, effective practice." They do so by first giving a rationale for individualizing instruction, then presenting strategies for individualizing, including different grouping patterns and independent study. They discuss ways media and games might be used, and the ways to develop oral communication, inquiry methods, and listening skills.

Strang, Ruth, *Group Work in Education* (New York: Harper, 1958).
Written primarily to assist in group organization and evaluation, this text offers many suggestions for using group work of all types, from civic to social, and explores the dynamics of group work. The author is thorough in her perception of human needs and how these can be met within the group.

Taylor, John C., and Rex Walford, *Simulations in the Classroom* (Baltimore, Md.: Penguin Books, 1972).
Six games using simulations are described in detail to amplify the introduction and explanation (including history, advantages, and disadvantages) of what simulations are all about. The simulations and games described are most suitable for secondary classrooms.

Thomas, George I., and Joseph Crescinbeni, *Individualizing Instruction in the Elementary School* (New York: Random House, 1967).
This book is an encyclopedia of information and might best be used as a reference work. Part I includes a history of the individualized instruction movement, summary of the evolution of learning theory, and discussions of behavior theory and statistics. Part II deals with ways to individualize instruction and is divided into subject areas. The sections on developing more effective work-study skill patterns and meeting individual and group needs in reading contain ideas that could and should be used in all fields.

Voight, Ralph Claude, *Invitation to Learning: The Learning Center Handbook* (Washington, D.C.: Acropolis Books, 1971).
Designed as a handbook for teachers, *Invitation to Learning* has a brief introduction to classroom learning centers, specific steps for designing and implementing centers, and many examples of centers. The last section presents a series of questions or problems teachers might encounter in using learning centers and proposes answers and/or solutions. A very practical book.

Wiley, W. Deane, and Lloyd K. Bishop, *The Flexibly Scheduled High School* (West Nyack, N.Y.: Parker, 1968).
Identifies the need for and problems found with flexible scheduling in secondary schools and goes one step further by providing a "how-to-do-it-way" of solving the problems and implementing a sound program. Reports step-by-step the work done by the authors at Claremont (California) High School, as they attempted to set up a flexible/modular class schedule.

Weisgerber, R. A., ed., *Developmental Efforts in Individualized Learning* (Itasca, Ill.: Peacock, 1971).
Describes some of the major developmental programs related to individualized instruction going on around the country, for example, PLAN, IPI, and the I/D/E/A Unipac Bank.